D1605556

ROMNEY

ROMNEY

∞∞∞

And Other New Works About Philadelphia

Owen Wister

EDITED BY JAMES A. BUTLER

The Pennsylvania State University Press
University Park, Pennsylvania

LIBRARY OF CONGRESS CATALOGING-IN-PUBLICATION DATA

Wister, Owen, 1860–1938.
Romney : and other new works about Philadelphia / Owen
Wister ; edited by James A. Butler.
p.   cm.
Wister's unfinished and previously unpublished novel about
Philadelphia.
Includes bibliographical references and index.
ISBN 0-271-02121-7 (acid-free paper)
1. Philadelphia (Pa.)—Fiction. 2. Philadelphia (Pa.) I. Butler,
James, 1945– II. Title.
PS3345 .R66 2001
813'.52—dc21
00-140089

Preface and Acknowledgments, Abbreviations,
Chronology, Introduction, Note on the Text,
Afterword, and Notes and Commentary copyright
© 2001 The Pennsylvania State University
All rights reserved
Printed in the United States of America
Published by
The Pennsylvania State University Press,
University Park, PA 16802-1003

It is the policy of The Pennsylvania State University
Press to use acid-free paper for the first printing of all
clothbound books. Publications on uncoated stock
satisfy the minimum requirements of American
National Standard for Information Sciences—
Permanence of Paper for Printed Library Materials,
ANSI Z39.48–1992.

∞∞∞∞

Time present and time past
Are both perhaps present in time future,
And time future contained in time past.

—T. S. ELIOT

CONTENTS

ILLUSTRATIONS

Philadelphian Owen Wister's *The Virginian: A Horseman of the Plains* (1902) created the American "Western novel" and the myth of the heroic cowboy, sold phenomenally well for decade after decade, inspired five film treatments and a long-running television series, and is still in print in many editions. In 1951 the Grolier Club, the oldest, largest, and perhaps most prestigious society in America for bibliophiles, selected *The Virginian* as one of the hundred outstanding books published in English during the first half of the twentieth century.

Despite his success as a Western novelist, Wister's failure to write about Philadelphia has been lamented by many for the loss of a literary "might-have-been." If only, sighed Wister's contemporary Elizabeth Robins Pennell in 1914, the novelist could understand that Philadelphia was as good a subject as the Wild West *(Our Philadelphia,* 363). According to John L. Cobbs in his *Owen Wister* (1984), the author "knew the city better than any other writer, and he might have given American literature a fictional Philadelphia to rival Wharton's New York or Marquand's Boston" (31). E. Digby Baltzell, the University of Pennsylvania sociologist who coined the term "WASP" as an acronym for White Anglo-Saxon Protestants, grieves that Wister, "born and bred at the very heart of intellectual Philadelphia," "would not, or could not, write of his native city" in his projected Philadelphia novel *(Puritan Boston and Quaker Philadelphia,* 299). That Wister novel about Philadelphia simply "never materialized" agrees John J. Burke in *The Writer in Philadelphia, 1682–1982* (47). For the last several decades, those who write on Wister recount the same sad tale: his Philadelphia book was called *Monopolis* and unhappily came to nothing, petering out after just four chapters. They are wrong.

The mistake in giving the name of Wister's Philadelphia novel as *Monopolis* is so pervasive that it is hard to trace the error to its source. Perhaps it all comes from the somewhat ambiguous phrasing of Nathaniel Burt in his 1963 book *The Perennial Philadelphians:* "The projected novel about a Philadelphia which [Wister] called 'Monopolis' never progressed" (385). Owen Wister in his Philadelphia novel did refer to his native city as "Monopolis," but the book itself he titled at first *Dividends in Democracy* and then *Romney.* Indeed, two years after Wister's death, the *Bulletin of the Philadelphia Museum of Art* published in May 1940 a small section (1,800 words) of the novel, giving its title as *Romney.*

Whether or not it was Nathaniel Burt who unintentionally caused *Romney* to be known as *Monopolis,* this mix-up has had serious consequences: it has directed researchers to just one folder of the 26,000-item Wister archive at the Library of Congress, one labeled "Unfinished Novel about Philadelphia, ca. 1912." What is in that folder in itself belies the myth of the "four-chapter" novel that "never progressed," because nearly seven chapters are there present. But those who are looking for material on a Philadelphia novel called *Monopolis* do not look in folders called "Romney" where much more of the 48,000-word fragment survives. For example, even Darwin Payne's perceptive and painstaking 1985 biography of Wister ignores those "Romney folders" and dismisses the Philadelphia novel in just a dozen sentences (*Owen Wister: Chronicler of the West, Gentleman of the East,* 281–85; 359 n. 42). After composing *The Virginian* (1902) and *Lady Baltimore* (1906), a novel of the old South meeting new tides, Wister in *Romney* (1912–14) undertook what would have been his longest work of fiction. Together with those two published novels, *Romney* was to form a trilogy, portraying the American West, South, and East as the nation looked back on its past but remade itself at the start of the twentieth century.

Those who write about Wister's work may be incorrect about the name and extent of his Philadelphia novel, but they are certainly astute about what would be such a novel's literary and cul-

PREFACE AND ACKNOWLEDGMENTS XIII

tural significance. Even in its incomplete—but considerable—state, Wister's *Romney* indeed does for Philadelphia what Edith Wharton and John Marquand have done for New York and Boston. Furthermore, Wister's acute analysis in *Romney* of what differentiates the Philadelphia and Boston upper classes anticipates by more than half a century the classic study by E. Digby Baltzell in *Puritan Boston and Quaker Philadelphia: Two Protestant Ethics and the Spirit of Class Authority and Leadership* (1979). Like Baltzell, Wister analyzes the urban aristocracy of Boston and Philadelphia, finding in Boston a Puritan drive for achievement and civic service but in Philadelphia a Quaker preference for toleration and moderation, all too often leading to acquiescence and stagnation. Wister's appraisal of Philadelphia, in a novel that both his contemporaries and his modern critics have mourned for Wister's supposed inability to write it, can at long last be read in the sizable and significant portion that he did complete.

ooooo

My work on *Romney* is particularly indebted to the Wister family. The late Frances Kemble Wister Stokes arranged for her father's manuscripts to go to the Library of Congress, thus making possible this edition. Her son, John Stokes, shared important information about the family in response to my many inquiries. From Owen Wister's last surviving child, William Rotch Wister II, I heard stories nowhere else available; when I interviewed him shortly before his death in 1993, I spoke to perhaps the last living person whom Theodore Roosevelt had tossed in the air at the White House. My friend, the late Malcolm ("Mike") Lloyd Wister, told me about his great-grandfather's first cousin Owen Wister.

My colleagues at La Salle University rose to the challenge of providing me with arcane information from many fields, and I am pleased to recognize these knowledgeable and generous people: Joseph Brogan, Brother Gabriel Fagan, F.S.C., Kevin Harty, Stuart Leibiger, Francine Lottier, Paul McNabb, Linda Merians, Georgina Murphy, John Rossi, and Stephen Smith. La Salle's best manuscript editors, John Keenan and Robert Fallon, read my typescript with sharp eyes and busy pencils; the book is immeasurably better because of their labors. Early stages of my research were supported by a travel grant awarded by the La Salle University Leaves and Grants Committee.

Mark Reed, of the University of North Carolina at Chapel Hill, has for thirty years answered my questions about William Wordsworth; he has now made an effortless transition to provide advice on Owen Wister. Mary Kelly Persyn of the University of Virginia's College at Wise explained the intricacies of the Haitian Revolution to me. The Internet has put expert assistance just a mouse click away, and I marvel at the helpfulness of people whom I have never met (but would certainly like to know): Stephen Joseph Agostini, Pennsylvania Railroad Historical and Technical Society; Christopher Baer, Hagley Museum and Library; Jane Davidson, University of Nevada at Reno; Richard Keiser, Carleton College; Linda Milano and Victoria Kalemaris, Theodore Roosevelt Association at Oyster Bay, New York; Byron Miller, South Carolina Ports Authority; Bryan Richards, Harvard Public Services Network.

Without libraries and librarians, little of value could be accomplished. John Baky, Director of the La Salle University Connelly Library, has smoothed the way for my research for many years; every member of the Connelly Library staff deserves my thanks. At the Germantown Historical Society (an underappreciated Philadelphia treasure), I am particularly indebted to Judith Callard, Mary Dabney, David Moore, and Nicholas Thaete. Gerald Francis, Director of the Lower Merion Historical Society, has gone very far out of his way to support my project. I also thank the unfailingly helpful people at the Friends Historical Library of Swarthmore College, the Historical Society of Pennsylvania, the Houghton Library of Harvard University, the Library Company of Philadelphia, and the Library of Congress.

On the day the prospectus for *Romney* arrived on his desk, Peter Potter, Editor-in-Chief of Penn State University Press, telephoned me with the first of his many and much-appreciated expressions of support and advice; he has been the perfect editor. Cherene Holland, Managing Editor of the Press, brought to this project not only her professional expertise but also knowledge of Philadelphia's "Main Line" suburbs, where she grew up. Two masters of Philadelphia's rich history and literature (David Contosta, Professor of History at Chestnut Hill College, and Daniel Traister, Curator for Research Services at the Walter H. and Leonore Annenberg Rare Book and Manuscript Library of the University of Pennsylvania) significantly improved my presentations, discreetly pointed out my errors, and —best of all—enthusiastically applauded Wister's new novel.

Láura Haines Belman no words can adequately thank. Her generosity to the Wister Family Special Collection at La Salle University puts all present and future scholars of Wister in her debt. As a great-niece of Owen and Mary Channing Wister, an active member of several Philadelphia historic groups, and an enthusiastic and perceptive student of United States history and of Philadelphia society, Laura is an endlessly fascinating conversationalist and correspondent. We discussed nearly every sentence in my introduction and notes to *Romney,* and she made insightful suggestions. My work on *Romney* was a pleasurable task, but the real joy was working on it with Laura, to whom I dedicate this volume.

James A. Butler
Philadelphia

ABBREVIATIONS

Baltzell   E. Digby Baltzell, *Puritan Boston and*
Puritan Boston   *Quaker Philadelphia: Two Protestant*
Ethics and the Spirit of Class Authority
and Leadership (New York: Free Press,
1979)

Baltzell   E. Digby Baltzell, *Philadelphia*
Philadelphia Gentlemen   *Gentlemen: The Making of a National*
Upper Class (Glencoe, Illinois: Free
Press, 1958)

Burt   Nathaniel Burt, *The Perennial*
Philadelphians: The Anatomy of an
American Aristocracy (Boston and
Toronto: Little, Brown, 1963)

Chippendales   Robert Grant, *The Chippendales* (New
York: Charles Scribner's Sons, 1909)

Cobbs   John L. Cobbs, *Owen Wister* (Boston:
Twayne, 1984)

Kehl   James A. Kehl, *Boss Rule in the Gilded*
Age: Matt Quay of Pennsylvania
(Pittsburgh: University of Pittsburgh
Press, 1981)

Lady Baltimore   Owen Wister, *Lady Baltimore* (New
York: Macmillan, 1906)

Lukacs   John Lukacs, *Philadelphia: Patricians*
and Philistines, 1900–1950 (New York:
Farrar, Straus, Giroux, 1981)

OWW   *Owen Wister Out West: His Journals and*
Letters, ed. Fanny Kemble Wister
(Chicago: University of Chicago Press,
1958)

OWP   Owen Wister Papers, in the Library of
Congress, Manuscript Division,
Washington, D.C.

Payne   Darwin Payne, *Owen Wister:
Chronicler of the West, Gentleman of the
East* (Dallas: Southern Methodist
University Press, 1985)

Roosevelt   Owen Wister, *Roosevelt: The Story of a
Friendship, 1880–1919* (New York:
Macmillan, 1930)

Virginian   Owen Wister, *The Virginian: A
Horseman of the Plains* (New York:
Macmillan, 1902)

Weigley   *Philadelphia: A 300-Year History,* ed.
Russell F. Weigley (New York and
London: W. W. Norton, 1982)

OWEN WISTER: A CHRONOLOGY
(With Emphasis on the Composition of ROMNEY*)*

14 JULY 1860   Born in Germantown section of Philadelphia.

1878–82   Studies at Harvard, concentrating on philosophy and music; meets fellow-student Theodore Roosevelt.

JULY 1885   Makes first trip to Wyoming; nine additional trips to the West by 1895.

1885–88   Studies at Harvard Law School.

1892   Publishes in *Harper's Monthly* "Hank's Woman" (written 1891), his first Western story to appear in print.

21 APRIL 1898   Marries Mary (Molly) Channing Wister of Germantown, daughter of his second cousin William Rotch Wister.

APRIL 1902   Publishes novel *The Virginian: A Horseman of the Plains,* dedicated to Theodore Roosevelt.

APRIL 1906   Publishes novel *Lady Baltimore;* receives letter from Theodore Roosevelt arguing that the novel hinders the process of social reform.

OCTOBER 1907   Publishes "The Keystone Crime: Pennsylvania's Graft-Cankered

Capitol" in *Everybody's Magazine* (see Appendix II).

FEBRUARY 1908 Runs, unsuccessfully, for Philadelphia's Select Council as Seventh Ward candidate of the reformist City Party.

SEPTEMBER 1911 Begins planning a new novel and drafts "Designs" for the never-written "The Star Gazers" (see Appendix I).

LATE 1911 Campaigns, along with his wife, for the progressive Keystone Party candidate for mayor, Rudolph Blankenberg, who wins the election.

APRIL 1912– AUGUST 1913 Wister's wife, Mary Channing Wister, serves as president of the influential Civic Club of Philadelphia, a municipal improvement women's organization that she had co-founded in 1894.

AUTUMN 1912 Asks Theodore Roosevelt which of three planned novels he should write. Roosevelt says Wister "must begin" with *Dividends in Democracy,* eventually retitled *Romney.*

AUTUMN 1912– JULY 1913 Writes Chapters I–X of *Romney.*

JANUARY 1913 Delivers "Address Read at the Memorial Meeting of Horace Howard Furness" at the College of Physicians, Philadelphia—a talk about the civic importance of the scholar (see Appendix II).

24 AUGUST 1913   Suffers loss of his wife Mary Channing Wister, in childbirth.

JANUARY–APRIL 1914   Revises opening seven chapters of *Romney.*

12 FEBRUARY 1914   Delivers address about James Logan (William Penn's secretary) and civic responsibility to the Logan Improvement League, Philadelphia (see Appendix II).

10 APRIL–C. LATE JUNE 1914   Writes—first in Philadelphia and then in Europe, for which he departs on 2 May—Chapters XI–XIII of *Romney,* the last surviving sections.

27 APRIL 1914   Sends revised Chapters I–VII of *Romney* (100 pages of typescript), to George Brett, his editor at Macmillan.

LATE 1915   Writes two drafts revising the opening of *Romney;* those drafts are apparently the last surviving work on the novel (see Appendix I).

LATE 1924–1938   Has principal residence at "Long House," ten miles from Philadelphia in suburban Bryn Mawr, the "Main Line" community he called "Ap Thomas" in *Romney.*

1928 Publishes *The Writings of Owen Wister* in eleven volumes.

1930 Publishes *Roosevelt: The Story of a Friendship, 1880–1919.*

21 JULY 1938 Dies of a cerebral hemorrhage at Saunderstown, Rhode Island.

It may seem strange that Owen Wister, originator of the literary "Western," in his spectacularly popular *The Virginian: A Horseman of the Plains* (1902), should have moved from writing about Wyoming cowpunchers to depicting the rarified upper reaches of nineteenth-century Philadelphia society. In fact, the writing of *The Virginian* is what requires an explanation, for Wister was not a Western cowboy but an aristocratic Philadelphian, a man who "can lay claim to being the best born and bred of all modern American writers" (Cobbs, 1). No work by a Philadelphia writer has been more read than Wister's *The Virginian,* with the possible exception of either *Poor Richard's Almanack* or the *Autobiography* by that refugee from Boston, Benjamin Franklin (see Burt, 384). Indeed, some have contended that Wister's story about elemental good and evil resolved in the classic showdown gunfight was read by more Americans in the first half of this century than any other novel.[1] And *The Virginian*, the source of the hit television series of the 1960s and of five film treatments, one starring Gary Cooper in 1929 in his first "talkie," still sells well today in multiple paperback editions. *Lady Baltimore,* Wister's first novel after *The Virginian,* was a best-seller book in 1906 and is still in print more than nine decades later. His third and last novel, the Philadelphia one, entitled *Romney*, survives as a substantial 48,000-word fragment written between 1912 and 1915. The full text of *Romney* first appears in this volume.[2]

---

1. D onald E. Houghton, "Two Heroes in One: Reflections upon the Popularity of *The Virginian," Journal of Popular Culture* 4 (1970), 497; see also Payne, xii.

2. A small section (1,800 words) of *Romney* appeared in the *Bulletin of the Philadelphia Museum of Art* 35 (May 1940), 3–5.

Owen Wister is one of those rare native Philadelphians who, after achieving national and international renown, stayed on in the city of his birth. His feelings for Philadelphia were mixed, however, especially in his condemnation of character traits that also pervade *Romney:* a cautious and deadening "Moderation" that produced stuffiness, and a conformity that stifled initiative. As a young man, Wister in his letters and diaries describes the city as "a stupid hole,"[3] and "not the place I should choose either for my friends or myself if I could help it" (*OWW,* 130). As Wister's early Western short stories began to win applause, he confided to his diary that "the only people who, as a class, find fault with what I write are my acquaintances who live in the same town" (*OWW,* 202). He even began to publish his anti-Philadelphia sentiments: "We of Philadelphia seem to steer wide of this amiable and hasty encouragement. We seem to distrust our own power to do anything out of the common; and when a young man tries to, our minds close against him with a civic instinct of disparagement. A Boston failure in art surprises Boston; it is success that surprises Philadelphia."[4] Criticisms of Philadelphia even more barbed appear in *Romney* and in the various related pieces included below in the appendixes. Wister could see the all-encompassing political corruption that muckraking journalist Lincoln Steffens thundered made Philadelphia the most dishonest place in the country, a city "Corrupt but Contented."[5] But as he grew older Wister's censures, strongly worded as they sometimes are, sound more like those of a disappointed lover hoping for reformation and reconciliation. This "Philadelphian

---

3. Fanny Kemble Wister [Stokes], "Letters of Owen Wister, Author of *The Virginian,*" *Pennsylvania Magazine of History and Biography* 83 (1959), 3.

4. Thomas Wharton, *"Bobbo" and Other Fancies,* intro. by Owen Wister (New York: Harper & Bros., 1897), xiv.

5. Lincoln Steffens, "Philadelphia: Corrupt But Contented," *McClure's Magazine* 21 (July 1903), 249–63; this article was reprinted in Steffens's *The Shame of the Cities* (New York: McClure and Phillips, 1904).

of Philadelphians"[6] was too deeply enmeshed in the city's social web ever to abandon the City of Brotherly Love. To give just a few examples: he received an honorary degree from the University of Pennsylvania, served as president of the Library Company of Philadelphia and of the Philadelphia Club, became a life member of the Historical Society of Pennsylvania, and was a member of the Philadelphia bar for four decades. As "Philadelphia's last distinguished gentleman of letters,"[7] Wister was a Philadelphian to the core, and in *Romney* he has left us an indelible portrait of his city in the nineteenth century.

Wister sites are strewn throughout the Philadelphia area (especially in the Germantown section), and they tell the story of his privileged life. He was born on 14 July 1860 at 5203/5 Germantown Avenue, near his paternal ancestors' eighteenth-century mansions of "Vernon" and "Grumblethorpe" (the latter dwelling eminent enough to have had British General Thomas Agnew bleed to death on its floor during the Battle of Germantown). The Pennsylvania heritage of Wister's paternal ancestors precedes William Penn's arrival by two months, dating back to Dr. Edward Jones's coming ashore at Upland (now Chester) on the Delaware on 13 August 1682.[8] On the maternal side, Wister's lineage is equally distinguished. He was a descendant of Pierce Butler, a South Carolina delegate to the Constitutional Convention, whose namesake and grandson married Fanny Kemble, one of the most famous

---

6. Cornelius Weygandt, *Philadelphia Folks: Ways and Institutions In and About the Quaker City* (New York: Appleton-Century, 1938), 7.

7. Baltzell, *Philadelphia Gentlemen,* 155.

8. This descent runs Dr. Edward Jones (1645–1727), Jonathan Jones (1680–1768), Owen Jones (1711–1793), Lowry Jones (b. 1742), Charles Jones Wister (1782–1865), Dr. Owen Jones Wister (1825–1896), Owen Wister (1860–1938). On Edward Jones's and John ap Thomas's purchase of part of the "Welsh Tract" (now called the "Main Line"), see Charles H. Brownrigg, *Welsh Settlement of Pennsylvania* (Baltimore: Genealogical Publishing Co., 1967), 45–78. Owen Wister set part of *Romney* on the "Main Line," calling the community there "Ap Thomas" after one of the co-purchasers of this land from William Penn.

Fanny Kemble

Likeness from a painting by Sir Thomas Lawrence

FIG I

Owen Wister's grandmother, Fanny Kemble. E. Digby Baltzell called Kemble, a writer and actress, "the most fascinating and creative woman who ever lived in Philadelphia."

actresses of the nineteenth century. Wister's grandmother Fanny has been called "the most fascinating and creative woman who ever lived in Philadelphia."[9] At the maternal mansion of Butler Place (now gone, but once standing three miles northeast of Germantown), portraits of family members by Thomas Sully, Sir Thomas Lawrence, and Sir Joshua Reynolds, as well as a framed letter from George Washington to an ancestor, hung on the walls. Visitors to this house and its three hundred acres included such writers as Henry James, Matthew Arnold, and William Dean Howells; Owen Wister's mother, the quirky Sarah, inspired characters in Henry James's fiction (see Payne, 16–17).

Young Owen's education was appropriate to his social class, including boarding school (fashionable St. Paul's in Concord, New Hampshire) and then as one of two Philadelphians in his Harvard class of 1882. Fanny Kemble's connections opened the doors of Bostonian society to Wister, where he observed the subtle differences between that city's most prominent citizens and those of his native Philadelphia. He also made a friend in Theodore Roosevelt (Harvard, Class of 1880). Throughout his life, Roosevelt wrote frequent and warm letters to "Dan" Wister, who visited Roosevelt both at the White House and at Sagamore Hill, Oyster Bay, New York.[10]

A Phi Beta Kappa graduate in 1882 with first honors in music, Wister hoped for a musical career. Wister's physician father, however, wanted a more practical profession for his son. For two years the new Harvard graduate worked at the Boston Union Safe Deposit Vaults, where perched on a high stool below stairs he performed one of his principal duties: calculating, over and over, interest at two-and-a-half percent. Eventually Wister escaped the

---

9. Baltzell, *Puritan Boston,* 299.

10. Wister's father wanted his son to be christened Daniel, but the mother's choice of Owen (with no middle name) won out. "Dan," however, became Owen Wister's nickname.

Vaults, giving in to his father's insistence that he pursue a profession more "respectable" than music: Wister wrote his father
that he would work for most of 1885 at the Philadelphia law
office of Francis Rawle and then in the Fall enroll at Harvard
Law School (see *Roosevelt,* 27–28). "He hated law," wrote Wister's cousin Alice, Lady Butler: "His father forced him into it."[11]
Another blow to his artistic aspirations came in May 1885. Wister then wrote to William Dean Howells to ask his opinion
about a manuscript novel, co-authored with Wister's cousin
Langdon Mitchell. These two hundred thousand words—about
a young man who wanted to be a painter but was forced into
business by his father—showed talent, Howells answered, but
should "be never shown to a publisher" (*Roosevelt,* 23).

In June 1885, Owen Wister suffered a mental and physical
collapse. No doubt his capitulation to his father's demands and
his disappointment with Howells's assessment of his novel both
played some part. Whatever the precise cause of Wister's illness,
his neurasthenia was a common ailment of his social class. Such
nineteenth-century writers as physician George M. Beard contended that nervous illness was an understandable reaction of
the most sensitive and refined in America, especially those of
Anglo-Saxon stock, to the pressures of modern life. As cultural
historian Tom Lutz observes, "Beard expresses some typical
late-Victorian fear of the possible degeneration of the handful of
people who are the caretakers of a fragile civilization and argues
that while those affected by the disease constitute a very small
part of the culture as a whole, the rest of the population was as
unrefined as it was healthy."[12] Besides Beard, the other main
contemporary theoretician of neurasthenia was Wister's cousin,

---

11. As told to N. Orwin Rush; see his *The Diversions of a Westerner* (Amarillo,
Texas: South Pass Press, 1979), 61.

12. *American Nervousness, 1903: An Anecdotal History* (Ithaca: Cornell University Press, 1991), 7–8.

the physician and novelist S. Weir Mitchell. Mitchell's frequent prescription was an enforced rest cure, a treatment horrifyingly documented by his patient Charlotte Perkins Gilman in her story "The Yellow Wall-paper." But some men who consulted Mitchell received advice about a temporary change to a more vigorous lifestyle. For Wister, his cousin prescribed a trip West for his health. Mitchell told the patrician Wister, "There are lots of humble folks in the fields you'd be the better for knowing."[13] The rest is history—or the history of the "Western," that most ubiquitous of American cultural constructs.

Wister made extended trips to the West ten times between 1885 and 1895, at first to escape the boredom of those distasteful law studies at Harvard from 1885 to 1888. Within a week of his arrival at Medicine Bow, Wyoming, in 1885, he could write, "I'm beginning to be able to feel I'm something of an animal and not a stinking brain alone" (*OWW*, 32). "Fresh from Wyoming and its wild glories," in the autumn of 1891, Owen Wister and Walter Furness, son of the great Shakespearean scholar Horace Howard Furness, sat in the exquisitely paneled dining room at the exclusive Philadelphia Club and discussed the primitive West: "Why wasn't some Kipling saving the sage-brush for American literature?" After the oysters and the coffee and while drinking the excellent claret, Wister told his friend, "Walter, I'm going to try it myself! I'm going to start this minute." And so he did, going to the club's library and that night writing much of his first published Western story, "Hank's Woman."[14] Many of

---

13. OWP, Box 1, "Miscellaneous Items: At the Hot Springs," as quoted in Payne, 76.

14. This tale is here presented as Wister recounted it in his *Roosevelt* (29), published in the author's seventieth year. However, a few months before that Philadelphia Club meeting, on 20 June 1891, Wister wrote in his journal that he wanted to write of the West and in fact was then composing a story, "Chalkeye." What was finished of "Chalkeye" was posthumously published in *American West*, 21 (January–February 1984), 37–52.

FIG 2
Owen Wister in the early 1890s, during a period when he made several extended trips to the West.

the Western short stories that he wrote over the next decade were integrated with some new material and published in April 1902 as *The Virginian*; the book was dedicated to his friend Theodore Roosevelt (then serving as President). Almost immediately Wister became a famous man—and steadily more famous as *The Virginian* went through forty printings from April 1902 to October 1911.

No doubt to his publisher's dismay, Wister—desiring, he said, "to turn to other themes for a while, even if the box-office receipts should fall away"—followed up on one of the nation's all-time best-selling novels by writing a far different one about high-society manners in Charleston, South Carolina (*Roosevelt*, 245–46). Wister had, as he had discussed with Walter Furness at the Philadelphia Club, "saved the sage-brush for American literature," but he knew the actual old West was gone for good. As he wrote his mother, "The frontier has yielded to a merely commonplace society. . . . When I heard that Apache squaws now give their babies condensed milk, my sympathy for them chilled" (*OWW*, 210). He wrote other Western stories after *The Virginian*, but they increasingly eulogized what had been.

Thus Wister turned to the South, setting his narrative at the dawn of the twentieth century. A wedding cake (made from the "Lady Baltimore" recipe) is ordered for a Charleston wedding that never happens. John Mayrant, the bridegroom-to-be, is a wholly admirable representative of southern refinement. The supposed bride, Hortense Rieppe, is also a southerner, but she has allied herself with decadent, materialistic, unfeeling *nouveaux riches* of the North; those people are "the Replacers" of all that was once civilized and valuable in America. John Mayrant and Hortense Rieppe eventually find more appropriate spouses. Mayrant weds a woman combining modern sensibilities with Charleston gentility; Rieppe marries a reprehensible leader of "the yellow rich," surrounded by a bridal party "composed

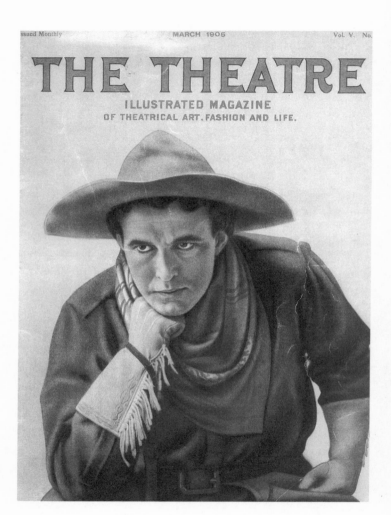

ssued Monthly   MARCH 1905   Vol. V. No.

THE THEATRE

ILLUSTRATED MAGAZINE
OF THEATRICAL ART, FASHION AND LIFE.

FIG 3

Dustin Farnum as "The Virginian" on the cover of a 1905 theater magazine. Farnum played the role on Broadway for four months in 1904, on the road for several years, and in the first film version (1914), directed by Cecil B. De Mille.

exclusively of Oil, Sugar, Beef, Steel, and Union Pacific" (*Lady Baltimore,* 385).

In Charleston, Wister experienced a society—fragile, threatened, but at least for the moment hanging on—that reminded him of what Philadelphia and Boston and New York used to be in a world less driven by capitalist greed and political corruption, and less subject to recent waves of non-Anglo-Saxon immigration:

> I had found in Charleston, and wherever I had gone in the South, many more people, whether urban or rustic, who were the sort of people I was, with feelings and thoughts and general philosophy and humor and faith and attitudes toward life like my own: *Americans;* with whom I felt just as direct a national kinship as I felt with the Western cowpunchers, and which I feel less and less in places like New York, Boston, and Philadelphia, that are affected by too many people of differing traditions. So I wrote *Lady Baltimore,* not as a tragedy but as a comedy: calling Charleston Kings Port, owing to the suggestion made by Henry James that I invent some slight disguise for the real name; it would help me to move more freely. (*Roosevelt,* 247)

Anyone who recoils from Wister's attitudes toward immigrants of "differing traditions" (or, for that matter, from his later serving as vice-president of the Immigration Restriction League or writing the essay "Shall We Let the Cookoos Crowd Us From Our Nest")[15] would be repelled by the racial attitudes of Wister's narrator Augustus in *Lady Baltimore.* Such viewpoints, and others, provoked Theodore Roosevelt to send, immediately after publication of the book in 1906, a five-thousand-word letter of protest to the author. To his credit, Wister prefaced *Lady Baltimore* in his *Collected Works* (1928) by printing Roosevelt's

---

15. *The American Magazine* 91 (March 1921), 47.

reproving letter in full and revising some of the most painful passages in the novel. In particular, Wister came to accept the objections that Roosevelt had outlined in the postscript to his 1906 letter. For Roosevelt, *Lady Baltimore* in its comparison of North and South presents a partial and thus inaccurate picture, especially in its depiction of those Northerners with "new money" as crass, immoral, and essentially irredeemable. In such getting of "the picture completely out of perspective," continued the President, *Lady Baltimore* resembles the anonymously published and acidic novel *Democracy.* (Roosevelt apparently did not know—but Wister was fairly certain—that historian Henry Adams authored *Democracy.*)[16] Hence, Wister's work "hinders instead of helping the effort to secure something like a moral regeneration." True, writes Roosevelt, "there is very much which needs merciless attack both in our politics and in our industrial and social life." But he concludes with words that must have badly stung Wister coming from his hero and friend, the President, writing to him on official White House stationery: *Lady Baltimore* makes one feel "that there is no use of trying to reform anything because everything is so rotten that the whole social structure should either be let alone or destroyed" (*Roosevelt,* 247–57).

The charge that *Lady Baltimore* hindered the reform movement would have particularly dismayed Wister, because the author thought of himself as "Progressive" in politics. Wister once went to Capitol Hill to shake the hand of Progressive leader Robert ("Fightin' Bob") La Follette, telling the Wisconsin

---

16. Wister said Roosevelt disapproved of *Democracy* because "he disliked pessimistic *generalizations*" (see *Roosevelt,* 257, 150–51). A text of *Democracy* (originally published in 1880 and reprinted more than a dozen times in the next four decades) is conveniently available in The Library of America edition of Henry Adams's *Novels, Mont Saint Michel* and *Chartres,* and *The Education of Henry Adams* (1983); see 1217 for Adams's secret authorship of the book.

senator that even though Wister was from corrupt Philadelphia that he, too, "was a Progressive" (*Roosevelt,* 299). Wister's mentor Theodore Roosevelt, of course, also came to be identified with the general spirit of reform associated with Progressivism. But that movement was ill-defined, and its umbrella covered a varied group, mostly Protestant and financially secure, who shared a distress at what they saw as the loss of values in an America increasingly industrial and urban. The general principles of Progressivism were commendable but vague: citizens should be active and well-informed; politics, especially urban politics, should be less corrupt; both big labor and big business should be reined in; a strong government should serve as a benevolent, perhaps paternalistic, improver of social conditions. From the smorgasbord of specialized and sometimes conflicting goals held by the many stripes of Progressives, Wister would have found the following ones particularly appealing: universal use of the secret ballot; direct primary election rather than selection of candidates by political bosses; restriction of immigration and "Americanization" of those already here; emphasis upon a meritocracy of talent rather than on a leveling equality. Education historian Lawrence A. Cremin has written that "Progressivism implied the radical faith that culture could be democratized without being vulgarized."[17] That faith—or, better, that hope—pervades Wister's *Romney.*

Roosevelt's stinging criticism of *Lady Baltimore* determined many of Wister's actions between the publication of that novel in 1906 and the beginning of *Romney* in 1912. "Roosevelt rose in my mind like an accusing shape," Wister wrote; the President "thought little of the citizen who talked and talked and found fault in his comfortable arm chair, while others got into the

---

17. *The Transformation of the School: Progressivism in American Education, 1876–1957* (New York: Alfred A. Knopf, 1969), ix. Wister's wife, Mary, served on the Philadelphia Board of Education.

fight" (*Roosevelt,* 266). So Wister did get into the Progressive fight, writing in 1907 a long article ("The Keystone Crime," see Appendix II) castigating the graft involved in building Pennsylvania's state capitol and expressing his hopes for reform. In order to keep the Progressive agenda before the public, Wister agreed to run in 1908 for Philadelphia's Select Council on the ticket of the reformist City Party; he lost to the Republican Party machine candidate by a vote of 3,458 to 646. In April 1912 he introduced Roosevelt, then campaigning for a third term as president, at a Philadelphia campaign rally, shouting to the audience in the unamplified hall that the "battle is against the secret inner circle of privilege that would defraud these American people and turn the very Constitution that they made into a weapon for their destruction" (quoted in Payne, 279). And when Wister once again came to write fiction about the social structure of the North, in *Romney* between 1912 and 1915, he planned a work very different from *Lady Baltimore* in presenting his hopes for reform.

After publication of *Lady Baltimore* in 1906 and of his biography *The Seven Ages of Washington* late in 1907, Wister next intended to write a collection of short stories and a novel.[18] But there were distractions: his unsuccessful campaign for a Philadelphia Select Council seat, his mother's death, his relocating of the family to Butler Place, the ancestral home that he then inherited. In addition, the nervous ailments and depression that had struck Wister in the 1880s recurred, leading to trips to California, Virginia, and Wyoming in search of renewed health. Despite his illness, the planned short-story collection (*Members of the Family: More Stories of the Virginian*) appeared in April 1911. Wister's thoughts then turned to his new novel, already about two years past Macmillan's suggested due date for the

---

18. Owen Wister to M. A. De Wolfe Howe, 20 and 29 August, as quoted in Payne, 253.

next full-length work of fiction from its phenomenally popular author.[19] There were false starts as Wister tried to find his subject, but the process that would eventually produce *Romney* was now under way.

On 19 September 1911, at the J. Y. Ranch in Jackson Hole, Wyoming, Wister drafted a prospectus for a "short novel" to be called "The Star Gazers" (see Appendix 1). That outline did not become the story of *Romney;* instead "The Star Gazers," if written, would have been the story of a female astrologer who begins in cynicism but gradually comes to believe in her own powers, and of two couples who switch partners. Even though "The Star Gazers" never advanced beyond its prospectus, Wister nevertheless had made crucial decisions that affected the next novel he did write. "Augustus—the same person who had narrated *Lady Baltimore*" would have recounted the events of "The Star Gazers," set in a "large place like New York, Boston, or Philadelphia." When Wister abandoned "The Star Gazers" for *Romney,* he kept Augustus as storyteller and a major eastern city as setting.

Several reviewers of *Lady Baltimore* commented on the influence of Henry James on the plot and especially on the character of Augustus.[20] Those comments were apt. The old-money, aristocratic, gentlemanly Augustus—twenty-eight in *Lady Baltimore,* forty in *Romney,* and unmarried in both—is so similar to James that Macmillan editor George Brett cautioned Wister

---

19. Owen Wister to M. A. De Wolfe Howe, 29 January 1913, which indicates that the novel is, as of that 1913 date, four years overdue. This manuscript is referred to by permission of the Houghton Library, Harvard University: bMS Am 1524 (1724).

20. See, in particular, "Some New Novels of the Spring: Owen Wister's Story," *New York Times Book Review,* 21 April 1906, 254; review of *Lady Baltimore, Public Opinion* 40 (5 May 1906), 572–73; Edward Clark Marsh, "Owen Wister's *Lady Baltimore,*" *Bookman,* 23 May 1906, 296–97; "Summer Reading," *New York Times Book Review,* 16 June 1906, 383.

about "some phrases which sound like Henry James."[21] After reading sections of *Lady Baltimore* aloud to James, Wister tried out on him Brett's criticism: "Look here, while I was reading my stuff aloud, Augustus sounded remarkably like you. That'll never do." James countered with a typically Olympian (and Jamesian) remark: "Well, my dear Owen, may I in all audacity and sincerity ask, what could Augustus better sound like?"[22]

The social attitudes of Augustus also influenced the plot and themes of *Romney.* Wister described those ways of thinking in his original 1906 preface to *Lady Baltimore:*

> Whence came such a person as Augustus?
>
> Our happier cities produce many Augustuses, and may they long continue to do so! If Augustus displeases any one, so much the worse for that one, not for Augustus. To be sure, he doesn't admire over heartily the parvenus of steel or oil, whose too sudden money takes them to the divorce court; he calls them the 'yellow rich'; do you object to that? Nor does he think that those Americans who prefer their pockets to their patriotism are good citizens. He says of such people that 'eternal vigilance cannot watch liberty and the ticker at the same time.' Do you object to that? Why, the young man would be perfect, did he but attend his primaries and vote more regularly,—and who wants a perfect young man? (viii)

This Augustus sounds rather like Henry James crossed with Owen Wister, with a dash of Theodore Roosevelt. That there is indeed much of Wister in the narrator of *Lady Baltimore* and

---

21. Owen Wister to his mother, Sarah Wister, 21 January 1905 (OWP), quoted in Julius Mason, "Owen Wister: Champion of Old Charleston," *Quarterly Journal of the Library of Congress* 29:3 (1972), 168.

22. Owen Wister, "Preface" to *Lady Baltimore* (New York: Macmillan, 1928), ix.

Romney is suggested by the author's calling himself "Augustus George" as early as in a schoolboy poem written to his parents.[23]

Wister made no progress on "The Star Gazers," eventually abandoning that subject and seeking advice from Roosevelt on three other possibilities. By late 1912, when Wister went to visit Roosevelt at Sagamore Hill, both men faced a crisis in their lives. Roosevelt was a defeated politician. Feeling that his presidential successor, William Howard Taft, had betrayed the reformist goals of the Republican Party, Roosevelt had run and lost in 1912 as the Progressive Party candidate against Taft and Democrat Woodrow Wilson (the winner). Progressives worried that Wilson's victory threatened their goals: would big business and big labor be checked, corruption stopped, and democracy reformed? As for Wister, despite his first two very successful novels, his writing career had reached an impasse. His new novel was not only several years overdue at the publisher, but he had not even determined his subject.

In the north room of Sagamore Hill, beneath the vaulted ceiling, surrounded by stuffed trophies of the hunt, and before the massive fireplace, the blocked writer discussed subjects for fiction with the defeated presidential candidate. The first possibility, "The Fixed Star," would portray a young actor and his wife, he at first the tremendous success but she in the end casting him into the shade through her talent and hard work. In a second option, "The Marriages of Scipio," a character from *The Virginian* would face the tragedy of outliving the era of the Wild West and being unable to cope with the civilization that follows. There was one final alternative: "I sketched it. A picture of Philadelphia, and its passing from the old to the new order; the hero of no social position, married to a wife of good social position elsewhere, and turning out superior to his wife. Possible title: *Dividends in Democracy*" (*Roosevelt,* 319). "Which of these

---

23. OWP, Box 102, folder "Notes of Florence Kane."

FIG 4
North room of Sagamore Hill, Theodore Roosevelt's home in Oyster
Bay, New York, where in 1912 the ex-president told Wister that he
must write the novel that became *Romney*.

books," Wister asked Roosevelt, "shall I write?" Roosevelt, who
had rebuked Wister in 1906 for his cynicism about the possibilities for meaningful social change in a democracy, and who now
worried whether the Progressive movement could outlast his
defeat at the polls, urged his friend to write all three. Wister
should start, however, with the Philadelphia novel and make
clear those "dividends in democracy."

   That mandate from Roosevelt seemed to spur Wister to action:
he began and made good progress on what he eventually decided
to call *Romney*. Wister probably selected his original title, *Dividends in Democracy,* in response to Roosevelt's accusation that

Lady Baltimore was too much like Henry Adams's popular—but disliked by Roosevelt—novel *Democracy* (see page XXXIV above). Wister's title *Dividends in Democracy* makes clear that his work, unlike *Democracy,* aimed more at reforming the democratic process than lamenting its failures. Setting the first part of *Romney* in the 1880s, the same time period as *Democracy,* further emphasizes the contrast between the two novels. In *Romney,* therefore, Wister takes on Adams, one of the central cultural figures of his time.

Beginning in 1912 and continuing into the summer of 1913, Wister worked on *Romney,* writing it in a minuscule pencil script that sometimes squeezed 1,800 words onto a sheet 7½ by 12½ inches. With the creative dam opened at last, Wister worked quickly, telling a publisher friend, "I want horribly to complete the novel."[24] The book opens in the present with Augustus discussing his novel-in-process *Romney* with his Aunt Carola and setting forth a long and insightful analysis of what characterizes life in Philadelphia, called Monopolis in the novel to provide the same "slight disguise" that Wister gave to Charleston/Kings Port in *Lady Baltimore.* The story of Romney then begins in a flashback to the mid-1880s, first at the suburban railway station of "Ap Thomas" (Bryn Mawr on Philadelphia's Main Line), where old-money and new-money families mix in the gilded age of booming capitalist fortunes. Wister once suggested to students at Philadelphia High School for Girls that they begin writing fiction by observing people at a railway station,[25] and he assembles a rich cast at Ap Thomas, including the Hythes who have used their new fortune to erect a grandiose mansion that appalls the old families of Monopolis. A young visitor from Boston, Henry

---

24. Owen Wister to M. A. De Wolfe Howe, 29 January 1913, is quoted by permission of the Houghton Library, Harvard University: bMS Am 1524 (1724).

25. Wister's address to the students is included in a monthly publication of the school: *The Iris* 2 (February 1899), 3–5; a copy is preserved in OWP, Box 52 (Folder: "Fiction").

FIG 5
Bryn Mawr railway station on Philadelphia's Main Line, site of several scenes in *Romney*. "Ap Thomas," however, is the name Wister gives Bryn Mawr.

Sumner, allows Wister to present Monopolis through an outsider's eyes, to contrast the two cities, and to introduce the voice
of a reformer. There are fine set pieces at the Buena Vista (actually, the Bellevue) Hotel and at Independence Square. Hovering
over the entire novel are the interrelated power of the Pennsylvania Railroad and the effect of political corruption, the latter
compellingly embodied by city boss Mark Beaver (an obvious
portrait of the actual politician Matt Quay). What we do not get
is the story of Romney himself, however, since the extant text
ends before his birth.

Wister's novel came to an abrupt halt on 24 August 1913, the
day his forty-four-year-old wife (and second cousin once removed), Mary Channing Wister, died giving birth to their sixth
child. Not until the beginning of the following year could Wister even look at the novel again, as he recorded in his journal for
3 January 1914:

> A tempest of wind and rain. Sat in office and revised a few
> pages of Romney. I hope by revising it to become able to go
> on with the book. I have written nothing of it, since Friday
> morning August 22nd 1913. She came into my study & told
> me not to be worried that I had been able to write so little
> that morning—She said "In September I think you will
> write easily and well." I can see her smile as she stood beside
> me at the table. (OWP, Box 101)

On 5 February 1914, the long-suffering publishers asked about
the novel, and that inquiry produced some additional activity.
The first seven chapters were typed from the pencil manuscript of
Romney. Then Wister heavily revised that typescript. "Revision,"
he wrote in his journal for 10 April 1914, "is a process I don't like
to begin until I have completed the work I want to revise. But my
case now is different—I have no heart, no strength, no seclusion"
(OWP, Box 101). Finally, the revised seven chapters were retyped

FIG 6

Rathalla, a Main Line *château* built about 1889 in Rosemont,
Pennsylvania. It was homes such as this one that so irritated the ladies
of "Ap Thomas" in *Romney*.

and sent to George Brett of Macmillan on 27 April. After Brett
read those 100 pages in a single day, he telegraphed the author
that his chapters were "magnificent" and later told Wister that he
found a "new touch" in it.[26] Wister sailed for Europe on 2 May,
resolved to "keep up the pace," and there are indeed additional
entries in his journal recording work on *Romney*. But at the end
of May the doctor at Nauheim in Germany forbade additional
writing while Wister was there taking the baths and the "cure."
The last journal entry about *Romney* comes at the end of June
when Wister observed a couple's "lame honeymoon" and planned

26. OWP, Box 28 (Folder: "Macmillan Company"); Box 101, journal entry of
7 May 1914.

"AMERICA'S GRANDEST RAILWAY TERMINAL"
— PENNSYLVANIA RAILROAD —
NEW PASSENGER STATION, BROAD STREET, PHILADELPHIA, U.S.A.

FIG 7
Broad Street Station, opened in 1881, a monument to the power of the
Pennsylvania Railroad. At this time, the PRR corporation was said to
be the largest industrial employer in the United States, controlling the
most lines of rail in the world.

how he might use it in his novel. Unrelated jottings Wister wrote
on a single sheet used to revise the novel's opening suggest that he
may have returned to the book briefly near the end of 1915 (see
Appendix 1, below). The author lived on until 1938, but no further references to his Philadelphia novel are known to survive
among the family papers. What remains of *Romney* in its various

manuscripts comes to 48,000 words, just over half the length of
Lady Baltimore.

Wister's setting the first part of *Romney* in the 1880s makes the
novel an Eastern counterpart to the same Wild West time period
depicted in *The Virginian.* In 1895 Wister had just such a direct
regional comparison in mind when he decided to append an
"Eastern chronicle" as a "postscript" to his journals about the
West.[27] The author in his three novels (*The Virginian, Lady Baltimore, Romney*) thus provides an all-inclusive picture of America
and its people in the West, the South, and the East. Although the
incredible success of *The Virginian* may understandably make us
think of Wister as chiefly a Western novelist, he is better considered as a novelist of manners, whether those manners be of
Wyoming cowpunchers, of the fading aristocracy of Charleston,
or of the upper classes and the rising industrialists of Philadelphia. Character is the real issue in all three of these regional novels: what future for America, in its regional sections and as a
whole, can we hope will be built by those true "aristocrats," the
coming democratic meritocracy? The tenderfoot narrator of
The Virginian sees the kind of person who could be the hero of
that future: "Here in flesh and blood was a truth I had long
believed in words, but never met before. The creature we call a
gentleman lies deep in the hearts of thousands that are born
without a chance to master the outward graces of the type" (*Virginian,* 12). People such as the Virginian, Wister wrote to a friend,
embody "something I have felt the throb of far and wide in our
land—the best thing the Declaration of Independence ever
turned out,"[28] and the hero of *Romney* promised to transplant

27. OWP, Box 89, entries of 15 and 16 October [1895], in notebook entitled
"Journal and Notes 1895" in section entitled "A Postscript," as quoted in Payne,
160.

28. Owen Wister to Hamilton W. Mabie, 4 June 1902, Hamilton W. Mabie
Papers, Library of Congress, as quoted in Neal Lambert, "Owen Wister's *Virginian:* The Genesis of a Cultural Hero," *Western American Literature* 6:2 (1971), 107.

those characteristics of the Virginian from Wyoming to the Delaware Valley. Both books (one in actuality and one in potentiality) celebrate the "Dividends in Democracy."

Why did Wister stop writing *Romney,* a novel that his publisher thought to be so "magnificent"? The simplest answer is that he wrote other things instead. In August 1914, when Wister was aboard ship returning from his European trip, war broke out between England and Germany. Now began what his biographer Darwin Payne has called Wister's "personal obsession" (285): awakening Americans to the German threat and convincing his countrymen to put away old prejudices against the English, now struggling to preserve civilization and humanity. On New Year's Eve, 1914, Wister summed up the year in his journal: "When has the world known a year more terrible than this, which in 90 minutes will be ended? There is none in the whole recorded memory of mankind. . . . Will 1915 be any worse? It may be much worse" (OWP, Box 101). For Wister, "The war had set aside all plans of fiction" (*Roosevelt,* 341). A trilogy of political and moral polemics instead occupied him over the next eight years as Wister tried to rouse his nation to action and then meditated upon the meaning of the Great War: *The Pentecost of Calamity,* 1915; *A Straight Deal,* published as a long magazine article during the war and as a book in 1920; *Neighbors Henceforth,* 1922. Thus it was not simply *Romney* that Wister abandoned at the beginning of World War I. He published no new book of fiction whatsoever until *When West Was West* (1928). In nine elegiac short stories, he returned in his last published volume of fiction not to the Philadelphia narrative but to his Western plots and themes.

The death of his wife, Mary, also made it hard to resume work on *Romney.* Entry after entry in Wister's journal makes painfully clear his devastating loss. After her death, his life had "begun the final volume—And the thought is not unwelcome" (OWP, Box 101, journal entry of 8 January 1914). A loose sheet among the family papers preserves Wister's 1914 drawing of his own tomb-stone, on which he has written, "The Lord is nigh unto them that are of a broken heart" (OWP, Box 101). But terrible as these evidences are of Wister's overwhelming depression, they do not record still another reason why it was so difficult for him to finish *Romney*. During the entire time he was at work on the novel in 1912 and 1913, Mary Channing Wister served as president of the Civic Club of Philadelphia, a women's political action group she had co-founded in 1894. Her civic activities and battles against Philadelphia corruption predated those of her husband and found their practical testing in her daily work. Articles she wrote for the various annual reports of the Civic Club could be statements of the themes of *Romney*:

> There is no compensation for dishonesty. Its honor is the only thing Philadelphia cannot afford to do without. Material greatness means little in the world's history, and less to the people in the cities who make it their goal. The poets of the ages repeat for us this eternal truth. Walt Whitman says: "A great city is that which has the greatest Men and Women. If it be a few ragged huts, it is still the greatest city in the whole world."

> Shall we not support the Mayor in his efforts to free this city from a corruption which has established our great community in the eyes of the outside world as "The City Corrupt and Contented"? A crisis is at hand and must be met.[29]

At times after her death (such as when Wister addressed the Logan Improvement Association on the subject of James Logan,

---

29. *Seventh Annual Report of the Civic Club of Philadelphia,* 12 January 1901, 17; *Nineteenth Annual Report of the Civic Club of Philadelphia,* 29 April 1913, 28–29. Copies are preserved at the Historical Society of Pennsylvania among the archives of the Civic Club.

his wife's colonial ancestor), he felt that he was carrying on her civic work (OWP, Box 101, journal entry for 12 February 1914). But, inevitably, work on *Romney* reminded him of his wife and of his pain. Whatever the reason, Wister shifted from a local, Philadelphia stage to an international one; he dedicated one of those international volumes to which he now turned, *Neighbors Henceforth*, "To the Memory of M.C.W.," Mary Channing Wister.

And it was not his wife's death alone that darkened the years 1912 to 1915. It seemed to Wister that an entire generation of his Philadelphia relatives and acquaintances was disappearing. The roster of the dead included two of his cousins, the novelist S. Weir Mitchell, to whom Wister had dedicated *Lady Baltimore*, and the Shakespeare scholar Horace Howard Furness, whom he considered to be his mentor. These two were "the kingpins of Philadelphia's late-nineteenth-century literary flourishing" (Burt, 381), and Wister delivered memorial addresses for each of them. "What a chain of awful events has run through the months, beginning with August 24, 1913! Anguish after anguish," lamented Wister in his journal on 30 November 1914 (OWP, Box 101). Strangely, Wister could posthumously contemplate even his own death, as newspapers across the country mistakenly reported his demise in 1911. Neatly pasted into one of Wister's albums are his premature obituaries, "couched," he wrote, "in that faintly patronizing tone into which the living unconsciously fall when they speak of the dead" (*Roosevelt*, 296). *Romney*, Wister had told Roosevelt, would be about the "passing from the old to the new order." As long as the author was dealing with the mid-1880s, he could treat his material with aesthetic distance; but the unwritten parts of the novel were to bring the story up to the present, when Wister shuddered at this passing of the old with "anguish after anguish." *Romney* poses dilemmas: How can Americans reconcile the aristocracy of gentlemanly birth and behavior with the practices of democracy that at times seem to pander to the lowest common denominator and encourage crass materialism? In a democracy, what is the responsibility of

FIG 8
Wedding picture of Frances ("Fanny") Kemble Wister Stokes, with
her father, Owen Wister, and her siblings, 21 May 1928, in front of
their home in Bryn Mawr, the "Ap Thomas" of *Romney*.

such wealthy social classes as Wister's own toward the masses of
the American people? How can there be a true democracy when
money so controls the political process? Ambitious, captivating,
funny, angry, and the best fictional portrayal of Philadelphia in
the nineteenth century, *Romney* nevertheless remained a fragment perhaps because Wister could not, ultimately, solve those
dilemmas. Nor, a century later, either in Philadelphia or the
nation, have we.

In the first chapter of *Romney,* Augustus, at least some part of
him Wister's *alter ego*, makes a confession: "I wanted somebody
to read my book very much! I wanted praise, I wanted appreci-

ation, I wanted to discuss it. Nobody had seen this thing that I had toiled over during so many hundreds of hours." Nearly nine decades after Owen Wister's "so many hundreds of hours" of toil leading only to a thing that "nobody had seen," readers can at last judge for themselves what survives of his Philadelphia novel.

The Owen Wister Papers at the Library of Congress contain
three manuscripts of *Romney,* which I here designate by order of
use as *Romney* MSS. 1, 2, and 3.

Romney MS. 1 is the earliest known draft of *Romney,* written
by Wister in pencil (except for ink on the final half of the last
page), on one side only of forty sheets of lined paper measuring
7½ by 12½ inches. The manuscript has been extensively corrected by erasing and rewriting in pencil; only isolated letters of
what has been erased remain visible. The most complete of all
the manuscripts of *Romney,* MS. 1 begins with Chapter I and
ends with Chapter XIII (breaking off in mid-sentence). A loose 5
by 8-inch sheet included with MS. 1 presents two stages of a
revised opening to Chapter I; external evidence dates this loose
sheet as late 1915 (see Appendix 1, below). OWP, Box 74, folder
entitled "Romney."

Romney MS. 2 is a carbon-copy typescript of sixty-four pages,
contained in two folders. No doubt prepared from MS. 1, MS. 2
provides most of the opening seven chapters of *Romney* (the
typescript ends in mid-sentence in the fifth paragraph from the
end of Chapter VII, suggesting the last page may have been lost).
Wister extensively revised this typescript in pencil and ink,
sometimes by pasting new handwritten passages over the old
typed ones or adding handwritten foldout flaps affixed to the mar-
gins. Preceding page 1 is a sheet handwritten in ink by Wister, giving the heading "BOOK FIRST" and its one-sentence summary. As is
true of MS. 1, MS. 2 has no title for the novel. Most of the sheets
are 8½ by 13 inches, but the text of MS. 2 includes two other
kinds of paper: (1) filed as the first sheet in Folder 1 is a typed
8½ by 11-inch page preserving what Wister may have intended
as a preface (see Appendix 1, below); (2) inserted before page 22

in Folder 2 are four 7½ by 12½ sheets containing Wister's hand-written revision of the opening of Chapter IV. Laid in to Folder 1 is an additional scrap of paper upon which Wister has written "Unfinished novel about Philadelphia started about 1912, I think." OWP, Box 83, two folders (the second starting with "Book Second"), each folder entitled "Unfinished novel about Philadelphia, ca. 1912."

Romney MS. 3 is a typescript of one hundred and four pages of 8½ by 11-inch sheets, contained in three folders. Incorporating the revisions made in MS. 2, MS. 3 is a clean copy, except for a few ink revisions by Wister, of the opening seven chapters of the novel. A handwritten sheet precedes the first typed page, and on it Wister has written in ink "ROMNEY by Owen Wister." OWP, Box 74 (Folder 1, 1–28; Folder 2, 29–61; Folder 3, 62–104, each folder entitled "Romney").

These manuscripts correspond well to what we know of the composition of *Romney* from Wister's various accounts (see the Introduction, pages XL–XLV above). He clearly used the sheets of MS. 1 to draft the novel, probably beginning in autumn 1912 after Theodore Roosevelt recommended the writing of the Philadelphia novel. Between the time Wister's publishers at Macmillan asked about the novel on 4 February 1914 and the dispatch of the first one hundred or so typed pages to editor George Brett on 27 April of that year, MSS. 2 and 3 were proba-bly prepared, with MS. 3 a duplicate of what was sent to Brett. One anomaly in this sequence of composition is that Wister con-tinued to use MS. 1 to draft new material even after MSS. 2 and 3 provided a more finished state of the first seven chapters. For example, in MS. 2, Wister changed the names of a number of his characters (the Galts to the Hythes, the Floxes to the Lawnes, Mark Davis to Mark Beaver, Tom Atterbury to Tom McNary, and Timothy Tingle to Timothy Chace—the last altered back to Tingle by handwritten changes in MS. 3). MS. 1 has the unrevised names in its text up to Chapter xi, but then begins to introduce the new ones. (In ms. 1, Mrs. Brielle originally had the name Mrs. Rillet, and Wister did not go back in that manuscript to revise references to "Rillet" after he changed her name.)

Owen Wister recorded in his journal for 10 April 1914 that "not one new word [of *Romney*] has been written since last July [of 1913]" (OWP, Box 101). Since Chapters 1-x in ms. 1 have the names as they stood before the revisions undertaken between February and April 1914, and since Wister indicated that nothing new was written between July 1913 and 10 April 1914, those ten chapters were almost certainly composed between autumn 1912 and July 1913. Since Chapters xi–xiii of ms. 1 begin to include the names as revised in ms. 2—and as sent to Brett on 27 April 1914 in the form of ms. 3—those chapters must have been written after the journal entry of 10 April 1914. The last journal reference to work on *Romney* occurs on 28 June 1914, but there are blank pages for many dates thereafter. Nevertheless, 10 April to late June 1914 seems the most likely date for Chapters xi–xiii of the novel. The final page, numbered "40," of ms. 1 ends in mid-sentence; it is possible that one or more additional pages once followed. The shift on page 40 from tiny pencil script to a larger ink script does indicate, though, that Wister's usual process of composition for *Romney* was starting to break down.

The text of *Romney* here presented comes from two different manuscripts. For the first seven chapters, I draw the text from ms. 3, since that manuscript records Wister's most finished state of them. Because it is unclear whether Wister's possible preface (filed with ms. 2) or his late-1915 revisions of the opening chapter (filed with ms. 1) represent his final intentions, I include those materials in Appendix I rather than incorporating them into the main text. For Chapters viii–xiii of the novel, there is no choice of text: ms. 1 is the only place where those chapters exist. Notes and commentary, at times identifying the people and places

Wister draws upon, are bundled together after the novel (see pages 177–208 below); an asterisk in the text of *Romney* signals the presence of such a note.

In editing MS. 1, I made the names of characters consistent with Wister's revised intentions in MS. 3 (or, in the case of Mrs. Brielle, with the final aim in MS. 1). I have altered chapter numbers in MS. 1 so the numbering carries on from the revised count in MS. 3, and I have placed in italic type all Wister's references to the titles of published books. Wister's typist for MS. 3 sometimes misread the author's handwriting or introduced other errors; the manuscript wording has in these cases been restored. If the typist changed manuscript spelling, Wister's preferred forms (for example, "to-day," "well-fare," and "skilfully") have been reinstated in my text. If Wister used different spellings in the *Romney* manuscripts (for example, "for ever"/"forever," "grey"/"gray," "towards"/"toward"), I have employed the spelling imposed by Macmillan's house styling for *The Virginian* and *Lady Baltimore.* My intent throughout is to produce a text as close as possible to Wister's preferred forms (which frequently favor British spelling) or, if it could not be determined with certainty, to that of his publisher. The resulting text does not, then, always follow modern practices in spelling and punctuation. It does, though, have the advantage that the text of *Romney* here given is close to what would have appeared if Wister's novel had been published when it was written: in the second decade of the twentieth century.

ROMNEY

by

Owen Wister

BOOK FIRST

Though very short, nevertheless introduces
a lady of importance
and covers almost two hundred years.

I

*In which Aunt Carola gives a warning to her
nephew, who gives another to the reader.*

"Augustus, I desire to speak to you in the library for a few
moments."

When Aunt Carola said this to me the other day as we rose
from the lunch table, my cheerfulness fell at once a number
of degrees. So does it always fall when my Aunt addresses me
in this particular formula. She has never varied it since I was
eight. No doubt she used it still earlier, but that day I remember clearly. I had been found in the pantry; it was a matter of
disobedience connected with a pot of apricot jam, and Aunt
Carola's disagreeable footman (the butler would never have
done it) told her. The look of her back as she preceded me, the
tone of her voice, and the sort of time I had in the library, have
been recurring for thirty-two years without any change either
in them or in the apprehensive faintness of my stomach.

"Oh Lord!" thought I, "what has she found out now?"
When a man is forty he is never innocent. I left Uncle Andrew
picking out a cigar and pouring out a glass of cognac for himself at ease, and I slowly followed after Aunt Carola with the
forlorn and hang-dog spirit that I had inherited straight from
the days of apricot jam.

"Sit down, Augustus, if you please."

Of course I did so, and in silence, as the footman came in.

My Aunt remained standing, and took a cup of coffee from his tray; I took one also, and the man, who had brought it upstairs behind us, departed, shutting the door with a quietness that seemed to increase my apprehension.

Aunt Carola had been looking out of the window as if I wasn't there; she now turned her eyes upon me. "Have you understated your age again?"

When my relative begins obscurely, like this, it is apt to portend that she will presently rise to her chilliest heights. I drank my coffee all down at once, set the cup on the table, and resorted to flippancy. "Well, who do they say is the lucky girl now?"

"It is no question of your being engaged, Augustus, I wish it were—if the choice were fitting. So much depends upon your having children, and your Uncle Andrew is disposed to be so generous. No; think a little." She had shaken her head at me all through this lecture. "Think," she repeated.

"I can't. I'm too alarmed."

This failed to soften her. "I liked nothing in that whole book so little, Augustus, as your not being candid about your age."*1

This speech started in my mind a glimmering both of hope and of relief; but it wasn't yet bright enough, and I sat in suspense unrelaxed, looking at her during the pause she made before she continued:

"In that account of your visit to Kings Port, you said that you were twenty-eight." Again my Aunt paused; then finished sternly: "and you were actually thirty-five. Thirty-five that March."

---

1. An asterisk signals the presence of an explanatory note on pp. 177–208, below.

Shameless pleasure now relaxed me. "People did often take me for twenty-eight then, you know."

She gave me a cold gleam of reproof—but I didn't care, I pranced on:

"And they often take me for thirty-five now. It's my nature to be well preserved."

"Psha, Augustus!"

"All right, Aunt."

"In a woman," said she, "concealments about age are non-sensical enough, but one expects them. In a man—."

She allowed me to imagine her opinion of such a man— but what did I care now? Aunt Carola comes undiluted from the old New York families of the Hudson River, and when she chooses, she can call a spade a spade just as nakedly as if Queen Victoria had never lived. One or two delicate matters had started up from the cushions of my softly upholstered conscience—but she didn't mean these, after all. I knew now what was coming, and I was braced for it—it needed but little bracing.

Yet still she didn't come out at the place where I was ready for her. "Speaking of being engaged, Augustus, I suspected once or twice from the letters you wrote me while you were in Kings Port, that the girl—that very nice girl who made the cake, and of whom you seemed to see so much—that she might turn out to be the one, you know. It would have been acceptable to me—very."

"Alas, Aunt Carola, it wasn't acceptable to her!"

"Well; well; such disappointments may be wholesome for a conceited young man. What is this I hear about your having written another book?" She had come out now!

"I have."

"I am told that it is about—ourselves."

"It is."

I don't think she had looked for such prompt acknowledgement on my part, she did not speak at once, and something of speculation came into her steady eyes, rendering less keen the penetrating glance she had been fixing upon me.

"Now ourselves at the time of the Revolution," she said presently, "with George Washington and all those picturesque figures introduced—that would be something I could understand."

"Dear Aunt, you wouldn't have me try to rival *Hugh Wynne?*"*

"But Augustus, what can you find to-day in this dismantled town?"

"What can I find? Good gracious, what can't I find! Don't you see that it swarms and teems with things that for interest make the Revolution look absolutely evaporated in comparison?"

"No," declared Aunt Carola decidedly, "I don't see at all."

"Well, to me the present spectacle is vertiginous. The ferment, the unrest, the transition, the ebb of the old, the flood of the new, the uprooted tradition, the quickened pace, the diminishing serenity, the increasing roar! Where else in such abundance as here can you find Autumn and Spring so intermingled—the exquisite hues of decay stirred right in with the strong, glaring tints of the coming thing—the beautiful old colonial house torn down to make way for three dozen or four dozen or five dozen up-to-the-minute American 'homes'? No Declaration of Independence signed in any of 'em—but they've got a bath-room on every floor! Why the very insurance companies are a barometer of the times. They register the economic destruction of the old American family, and the invasion of the Hun, the Vandal, the Croat, and all the rest of the steerage. The 'perpetual' insurance policy that everybody used to put on their houses, has been entirely supplanted by the 'five-year' policy, because nobody feels sure he's going to be able to stay anywhere longer than that any more. Don't you think all this pretty interesting?"

As I came down from my flight of enthusiasm, I noticed that Aunt Carola's face had become rather fixed and rather pale.

"The exquisite hues of decay," she repeated very quietly to herself, and sat a little while without speaking. "The exquisite hues of decay!" And she nodded. Then her face regained its usual quality of decision, and so did her voice.

"Well, Augustus, I think I should prefer George Washington and the battle of Monmouth Court House, even if you put in the strong language he used to General Lee upon that occasion."*

"Oh, my hero can swear!" I laughed.

"Can he indeed!" exclaimed Aunt Carola with a note of disapproval, as if she felt that the oath revolutionary was permissible because it was a long time ago, but that the oath contemporaneous should be discountenanced. "And who, if you please, may your hero be?"

"Then you haven't heard that? Rummy Hythe is my hero. Of course I shall not print all the words that he—and most of us—will sometimes use during intimate talk."

"Romney Hythe!—That's a nice nick-name you give him."

"He got it in college—not that he drank so awfully much, but because Romney, as the family pronounce it, naturally suggests Rummy to the undergraduate mind. I believe he tried to object, but they told him he deserved it for pronouncing Romney like the famous marsh instead of like the famous painter."*

"But you surely have not dared to tell the story of that—that very" (my Aunt sought for an adjective and found it) "that odd young man?"

"Oh yes I have!"

"You haven't gone into the whole thing?"

"The whole thing. There's not one of the Ten Commandments that isn't broken, I believe. And at least two female reputations are cracked into fragments and powdered to the finest dust."

My Aunt thought it over—or seemed to be thinking of it. "I cannot see how a hero is to be made of that—odd—young man."

"Perhaps that's because you don't know him, Aunt. I've known him for a long while, and I'm very fond of him."

It struck me now that there was less attention in my Aunt's face, and I began to feel that perhaps she hadn't come out with everything yet, that something still remained behind. Her eyes had become singular, and her tone was not quite so direct as is usual with her—especially when she speaks to me.

"What else have you told?" she inquired.

"Oh, things—things—lots of things."

"You can't publish it till you're dead."

"Dear Aunt, I've been dead for a number of years, but I don't wish it generally known."

"There would be a great deal to tell, I suppose," my Aunt musingly remarked, "if one came to think it over. A great many people, agreeable and otherwise, have lived in Monopolis. And there have been many sorts of occurrences—better worth recording than your Romney Hythe, I should think. But perhaps you have?" She said this last searchingly.

I still felt that something more was coming, and still I failed to guess what it was.

"Coming from another place and society to live here in Monopolis," Aunt Carola pursued, "enables me to look at the town in a more detached way than if I had been a native. I can see, for instance, that here none of our respectable people are enterprising and none of our enterprising people are respectable."

I laughed heartily. "I wish I'd made that remark!" I cried.

But she hadn't made it with any idea of laughter, she remained serious and musing, and now and then her small, steady eyes looked at me hard. "Monopolis has produced a number of types," she said. "Characteristic types. Types with background."

I said nothing; a new glimmer was suddenly twinkling in my mind as she proceeded:

"It's a pity that these types will all be gone in a very few years.—I don't see how you can know the whole story of this Mr. Hythe."

"Remember how well I know him."

"Well enough for the intimate secrets he must hide?"

"No, but I have heard a good deal too, and the rest is easy to infer. Whatever may perish of our types, the Gossip is deathless."

Aunt Carola listened to my words, but she wasn't really attending to them: this I knew because I was watching her with increasing secret entertainment; I had guessed what she was still holding off from, what was her real point.

She now manufactured one last piece of conversation. "I don't know any town richer in its people—by people I mean personages, Augustus—than Monopolis has been. And I don't understand what has changed this. One would suppose that in a society easily five times as large as it used to be when I was a girl, there would be more instead of fewer people— individuals, I mean—but everybody is getting just like everybody else."

To this I did not choose to manufacture any answer. She wouldn't have listened to me—and she wasn't listening to herself. Her pretty hands had been folded in her lap as she sat on her sofa delivering herself of these sentiments; she now placed her hands at each side of her, slightly grasping the sofa's edge, and so rocked herself forward and back about an inch, while she spoke.

"Your book has a great many characters in it, I suppose, Augustus?"

I simply nodded, watching the sparkle of her rings on her fingers. That last remark had much less of manufacture about it; she still rocked back and forth, and the point was upon us.

"Augustus."

"Yes, Aunt?"

"Augustus, have you put me into this book?"

"Yes, Aunt." I brought it out whack! like that.

The rocking stopped. She folded her hands in her lap again, and sat far back in the depths of the sofa. My guessing was quite at an end; what turn our interview would now take, I made no attempt to surmise; only one thought seemed to be in my head, and this was, that it would mar the book lamentably if Aunt Carola had to be taken out of it.

"Well, Augustus!" This was what she next uttered, very quietly, with a long exhalation of breath upon which the words floated across our silence.

No; it would be impossible to leave her out, I thought.

"I suspected something of this directly the rumor reached me." This she said in a tone so little expected by me, that I raised my eyes to her face. Would you believe it? She wore an expression—yes, it was something like gratification—as of one who had merely received a tribute that was due to her station and prominence.

I thought that she would keep to the point, now that she had so successfully come to it, but she didn't, she veered off— I suppose to give herself a little more time for thinking it over.

"You say you know the whole story?" she observed. "Do you know, then, the truth about his grandmother, and how that all came about?"

"But that wouldn't exactly be the story of Romney, would it?"

"I think it would probably be much more romantic and better worth while than—anything about me, for instance."

"But dear Aunt Carola, any true picture of Monopolis couldn't do without you. They'd all be inquiring where you were!"

"She never got over the foreign accent, did she?"

"The old lady? Romney's grandmother? No."

"It must have been a romantic story—how she ever came to cut herself loose from all those great Austrian relatives, and renounce her place in the highest society of Europe for the sake of that American nobody—a mere commercial buccaneer."

"Well, Aunt, you know that they say that when he was twenty-five, he was the handsomest creature that anybody ever saw. And probably he had something about him that to her—with her strict continental bringing up, and the sort of men whom she was allowed to see—must have been wild and—well, engulfing."

"Engulfing indeed!" my Aunt assented with emphasis.

"They say she wasn't nineteen," I pursued. "And what with reading Chateaubriand,* and growing exalted over the anti-slavery agitation here, she fell in love with the idea of America and freedom—"

"Psha!" interrupted my Aunt. "It was the buccaneer."

"Well, she was ready for him to appear—and he appeared."

"But how was she ever allowed to see him?"

"Business relations with her father, I believe. The family was poor, American enterprises were a temptation, the buccaneer was seeking foreign capital, they had him freely at the palace or castle or whatever it was—it never entered their heads that he would dare to look at a daughter of that house, or that a daughter of that house would deign to look at him. So it all flared up suddenly between the young people. She ran off with him. I don't really know much about it; nobody does."

"It ended everything between her and her people, didn't it?" asked my Aunt.

"I believe so. And the buccaneer's venture failed too—the financial scheme."

My Aunt nodded her head in silence. "She had her lover," she then said slowly, "and great poverty in a strange land for many years, and at last great riches. But when these had come, the lover"—she didn't finish this sentence, but said to me: "Now that would be a story worth writing down."

"It has but a single objection, Aunt—my well-nigh total ignorance of it—until the grandson appears on the scene."

"Oh, your Romney! Well, he's a great improvement on his nameless grandfather."

"Hardly nameless, do you think?"

"You know what I mean, Augustus. Society never accepted that scamp."

"He never lifted a finger to make it accept him!" I cried. "And I'll tell you one thing; he couldn't possibly have been more striking or more interesting as a young man than he was as an old one."

"I understand that many persons of *all sorts* have thought so," said my Aunt with remarkable severity.

In this I could but acquiesce; old Jacob Hythe had taken small pains himself to veil his doings. Still, I felt pleasure in remarking: "I'm always so interested to notice how public a man's private life seems invariably to be to you women."

But Aunt Carola had her retort also: "Our husbands are careful to tell us all the scandals, Augustus. The Gossip is deathless, as you truly observe.—To think," she went on, "of a Boston Chippendale's marrying into that family!"

"Romney's wife was named Alix Sumner," I said.

"Certainly, my dear. Her father was Henry Sumner, and his mother was a Chippendale."

"So she was! I remember now. My friend Robert Grant has written a delightful account of that family."*

"The girl Alix must have been a great-niece of my old friend Miss Georgiana Chippendale, whom I used to like so much at Newport before the war. She was one of the group of Bostonians who came there. Some of the St. Michaels of Kings Port used to come too. But the war broke up all that agreeable society. The Southerners never came again."

We had wandered so far from my Aunt's real point, that I had forgotten there was one, when she rather suddenly brought us back to it.

"Well, Augustus, if you're ridiculous about your age, you've been straight with me about your book."

"Thank you, Aunt."

"And now—when are you going to show me your book?"

"Whenever it shall be your pleasure to name the day."

"Don't you think you had better bring it to me soon?"

"Certainly I will."

"Because I'd like to see what you have done with—me."

"Yes."

"Perhaps mine is one of the female reputations that you have 'cracked to fragments.'"

"Oh, Aunt Carola!" But she was now in such a gracious humor that I ventured to add: "Yes, I've reduced you to powder." Whereat she laughed. "Hadn't you better wait," I continued, "until I can get it type-written?"

"Nonsense, Augustus. Your hand-writing is one of the few legible things about you. Bring it this afternoon, and I'll read it after dinner. Bring it this afternoon, Augustus, if you please."

To this command—for it was nothing less—I responded: "With all the pleasure in life, Aunt. But don't imagine you can finish it in one evening—or in five—unless you sit up all night."

"I hardly expect to pay you that compliment," said my Aunt.

"I wish I could think that the book deserved it," I replied.

"And so I can't finish it in five evenings?" she remarked. Her eyebrows were raised as much as she ever raises them; she doesn't allow her face to express much. "Isn't that a pretty long book, Augustus?"

"I've not written it for people with the head-line habit," I said. "Or for the tired business man."

"But don't you risk having a very limited audience?"

Then I broke my reserve. "I've written it at leisure for readers of leisure. If the organ of attention of the entire American people has atrophied into a mere non-functioning survival, like the vermiform appendix,—why then I'll have no readers, except you!"

"And perhaps I may not be able to finish it," suggested Aunt Carola.

"I dare only hope for the best. I think, at any rate, that you wouldn't agree with the up-to-date critic who saw *Othello* somewhere out West and wrote in his review next morning that three hours had been wasted in what could have been told in three lines: 'Jealous Othello, colored, husband of Desdemona, white, instigated by scheming Iago to suspect his wife and her young military friend Cassio, smothers the innocent lady, afterwards committing suicide!' That was all he said."

My Aunt smiled. "No, I don't agree with that. But I am more likely to finish your book than to wish to see that terrible play again.* I'm too old for tragedies." She rose from the sofa. "I think I hear the carriage. I must get ready to go out with your Uncle Andrew."

I looked out of the window. The victoria was there,* clean and bright, the handsome harness shone, the coats of the horses were sleekly resplendent; with the coachman and footman in their sober, suitable livery, the whole made as excellent and dignified a turn-out as could be seen. It was almost the last of its kind in Monopolis.

"Augustus!" Aunt Carola was shaking a finger at me, though not seriously. "If I find you have given me a vulgar automobile in your book, all is over between us.—This afternoon, Augustus. Don't forget."

Many laws have I disobeyed, but seldom my Aunt. (She is my Great-aunt by marriage, to speak strictly, but she has been so long a severe yet affectionate corrector of my ways, that I count her a parent and hardly ever remember that the same blood does not flow in our veins.) Therefore, even before she had returned from driving, I had carried round to her house my bulky manuscript, wrapped up preciously; and thereafter much expectation daily filled my spirit, for I will confess something here: I wanted somebody to read my book very much! I wanted praise, I wanted appreciation, I wanted to discuss it. Nobody had seen this thing that I had toiled over during so many hundreds of hours, though I hadn't been able to help speaking of it now and then to a friend. Aunt Carola might help me to see and correct some faults. Unless she had demanded that I should bring her the book, I had never dared to do so. So my obedience to her word was not reluctance on this occasion—it has been reluctant pretty often!

Not a sign did she make for what seemed to me a long time; I believe it was only from a Tuesday to a Saturday. Then she wrote me one of her little notes in that clear, elegant hand-writing of hers, and this also I obeyed with alacrity and with numerous expectant tremors. People think I am indifferent to what they say; perhaps I am to what *they* say—but Aunt Carola is not 'people' by a long shot.

She was seated on her sofa, and her first words gave me a disappointment. "Augustus, I sent for you because I expected to talk to you about your book. I have finished it. Oh, yes; I have read it all through. But" (here she displayed a note she was holding) "some Italian people from Florence have brought a letter to me from Lady Brestford, and I've got to call and ask them to dine.—Yes, I've read it through." And she looked at me from her sofa.

"Well, Aunt?"

"Well, Augustus, I have decided to stay in your book."

"Thank you so much, Aunt Carola!"

"It needs me very badly."

"It couldn't do without you; I said so before."

"Yes; you said so from what I suppose you would call your artistic point of view. That is not my reason for saying it—I don't know anything about such things. But I know what I like."

"Then—then—you don't—?"

"Don't ask me that, Augustus; I am not a critic. I am an old-fashioned woman. When I was young they didn't write such books. Or if they did, we weren't allowed to read them. Imagine dear Sir Walter!*—but I'll not pretend to be a judge."

"But you did finish it?"

"I did—yes. And I allow you to keep me in it because it can't spare a single—decent—person. Your Uncle Andrew will allow you to keep him too—for the same reason. I hadn't known before about your Uncle and Romney and the Madeira. He tells me that he has always liked that young man. Well. But what I

can't like, Augustus, is that you should tell us about—certain things at all. I will say at once that I found other passages entirely to my taste."

"I'm only telling what happened, Aunt. I can't make things up in a way that didn't happen."

"Then it would be more agreeable if you left them out. And now I must send you off, because I have to dress. Leave the book here for a few days, until I can speak to you of certain points."

I rose to take my leave.

She sat on the sofa, quite still, and her face began to wear its fixed look. "I am perfectly satisfied with what you say about your Uncle Andrew and myself." She spoke slowly, enunciating each word with clear precision.

"I am very glad," I returned, "that you find—." She stopped me with a slight gesture of her hand, and continued:

"It is true. Exactly true. I knew it already, of course. But perhaps you have made me see it more clearly, or in another light, at any rate. My generation is gone. Only three or four are left who have the right to call me by my first name. We are at the end of an era. We have nothing to do with what is going on, what is going on has nothing to do with us. You are perfectly right."

Still she sat on her sofa, upright and stiff, and I stood in front of her.

"Things have to pass," she resumed. "But I am quite ready, Augustus, I don't want to stay any longer than it is intended that I should." Her voice now reached its quietest, and hardest, and most matter-of-fact tone, beneath which, as I have learned to understand, deep emotion is firmly repressed. "The world has to be carried on by the young. And that is right. I am perfectly satisfied that everything will be right, no matter when we come, or when we go, and no matter how wicked the world seems. Nothing but our own duty is in our hands.

'Change and decay in all around I see;
O Thou who changest not, abide with me.'"*

She stopped. I tried to say, Amen, but my lips merely shaped the syllables; no sound came.

"And now, Augustus, you must go, for I must dress at once."

She rang the bell that was within reach from her sofa. I found a difficulty in speaking to her, in uttering any more words after those which she said to me in that compact, decided, self-controlled voice of hers; and so in silence I bade her good-bye and left her still sitting on her sofa, motionless and erect, her steady glance following me with a sort of severe kindness.

II

Shows what Nature did for Monopolis.

I speak like Lucio, "according to the trick,"* when I here
state that upon several points Aunt Carola corrected me, and
I made changes; but what I had to say about our earliest settlers she found true. What our earliest settlers saw first when
they looked upon their new land, we their descendants see
now. What they felt when the first April warmed their new
land into green and blossom, we feel now. Some of them had
come from regions all flat, with no hill to look up to, and
some from where the world is set on edge up and down, with
no wide, comfortable lap of fertility. Their new land spread
for these colonists a broad table of promise, open meadows
rich in soil, rolling to hills of woodland beneath a temperate
and gentle sky. The earth wore no cloak of stones or barren
sands or malarial swamps. Moderation, amplitude, fecundity,
these were the promise that breathed from the gracious landscape which the settler saw. Winter would seldom be excessive,
nor summer, nor many seasons too wet or too dry. Moderation,
amplitude, fecundity! They flowed in the two rivers* and in
the plentiful brooks; they floated upon the quiet winds from

the woods of chestnut and oak; they shone in the gleaming white of the dogwood, the pink of the laurel, the blue of the quaker-lady*; they perfumed the air with mild and teeming odors of moist earth and honeyed flower; they stretched over the large round hills deep in thick grass, back beyond sight through days of journey to the forests and the mountains. Nature forbade nothing here to man, her hands did not need to be pried open, they were open wide already, and full of gifts. In the midst of moderation, amplitude and fecundity did the settlers found their city.

Quarrel amongst themselves they might, and did; but nature never lost her temper with them. No tropic violence or polar chill brought them any devastation; the crusted planet never shook their city down or sank it beneath a tidal wave. Whatever they were doing of right or wrong—and how should they not do plenty of both, like the rest of mankind?—whatever they did, their landscape looked upon them with an unclouded brow.

With an unclouded brow. Colonists to the north and south of them did not find it so; so was it by no means everywhere. Some came to regions where the landscape's brow, though lovely, seemed vexed or anxious, as if troubled about ways and means, and the coming hard Winter, and whether both ends could be made to meet. Its soil was not deep, its rocks were many, its snows came early and lingered late. The earth here did not hold out her gifts ready to be taken, her hand must be forcibly opened, and then it did not contain any too much. These colonists must fight for their living; they won their ease through hardship. And southward there were other founders of cities whose crops had to encounter hurricanes from the West Indies, or submerging floods from a great river. They also were in frequent battle for their livelihood. But around Monopolis hung a calm veil of safety. It wrapped the summer fields in its blue haze that hung over wheat and corn and distant dairies full of cream. In winter it cast its violet hues upon the woods, and through their interlacing branches the eye looked beyond to the ploughed fields, the great stone barns, the comfortable farm houses. Not much battling for livelihood was needed here; ease won with ease was the lot of Monopolis amid moderation, amplitude and fecundity.

III

Shows what Monopolis did for herself.

The ironic gods now looked down upon the City of Moderation, and forthwith planned their jest;—or so a pagan Greek would put it, and we Christians may let it stand so. The task for the ironic gods was, How in a city that was bathed in a moderate climate and itself dedicated to religious moderation—how to bring about Excess? Plenty of good wine and good food were a temptation, and plenty of good citizens would fall in consequence; but this was not enough, this happened anywhere, the excess must be deeper and more subtle to satisfy the ironic gods.—Yes, and to teach a humbled city at last a vision higher than moderation! So the gods in their mills ground their jest slowly, taking well-nigh two centuries to it.

They allowed it to lurk and germinate through colonial vicissitudes, and the convulsion that wrenched a young people free from their Mother Country. In that most burning hour of her life, Monopolis shone many degrees brighter than moderation, a lustrous storm-centre for the spirits that in the name of liberty gathered from north and south within her gates. Then, when the storm was over and the strangers gone, the City of Moderation settled down again with nothing but her usual light by which to pursue her usual path of ease and comfort. Two wars we had in the next fifty years*; these passed without visibly affecting the serenity of the town. Then came the death-grapple of the Union, and once more Monopolis burned with wholesome excess of faith and fervor, until that war's successful end let down the city's spiritual fires again to a combustion harmonious with the normal moderate temperature of her soul. Now followed the fat years of increase, filling many new purses—an era that quietly ripened the jest of the ironic gods.

A sharp eye could have seen it already established in the faces of the citizens of Monopolis, of whom something should here be said.

Remember three things: they lived in a climate seldom too hot or too cold, a soil gentle and generous. From England the first earnest band of them had brought a religion of simplicity, a protest against worldly luxury, a faith as pure as crystal. And lastly, into the farm country behind them had come a phlegmatic foreign race,* whose ideal reached the height of a clean floor and a full larder, whose stolid political vote was still cast for General Jackson after he was long dead, and whose immoveable intelligence after a century-and-a-half had not yet chosen to master English, but still tenaciously spoke its foreign dialect. In the old country, wars and tyrannies had welded this race into heroes; in the new, no adversity ever came to strike sparks from this rustic brain; it lay like a lump of metal, ponderous and valuable, awaiting the white-heat, and the hammer, and the anvil.

In circumstances such as these—moderation everywhere—certain virtues were sure to flourish. The town was kind, the town gave liberally to the poor and the sick, neighbors took

thought for neighbors who were in trouble; there was much
sending about of home medicines and home delicacies. Furthermore, the town was of sane judgment, well balanced, not
a place to meet any form of public hysteria. If no poet with a
high song was generated in this temperature, neither was any
tribal enthusiasm for oriental cults or free love. The unusual
fell under a proper suspicion; the town's mind was something
like the quiet buff and gray prescribed by its traditional religion. A great seat of learning might hardly be expected in
such a zone, but good doctors and lawyers ought to grow—
and they did. The traditional religion leavened many people
and customs outside of its own creed, and lay at the bottom of
the perfect courtesy and consideration that marked the good
manners of a people whose particular and distinctive vision
was religious toleration. Where there is no vision, the people
perish;* with this one Monopolis began.

It all did better for the women, they in those times being non-
combatant. In a few generations they had surpassed the men.
The simplicity of their crystal faith and their unworldliness
made them into something spiritually so gentle and serene, that
America has seen nothing lovelier in the shape of womankind.
When the breath of the cock-tail and the cigarette blew them
away, Monopolis was not a gainer by this change of wind. It was
the men who suffered through their creed of non-resistance,
their life without battle, their religion's ban upon Arts and Letters. Money-making was the single outlet for their energy, this
choice of occupation being forced upon them. Thus do we
return to the ironic jest, established visibly by mid-nineteenth
century upon the faces of these folk beneath their broad-
brimmed hats, as they are seen discreetly entering the doors of
their banks, demurely passing up and down the business streets
of their city. By mid-nineteenth century something is perma-
nently written upon their faces—too many of them.

"We keep on the Safe Side."

Upon too many did it come to be written. Caution, caution, and yet more caution: it was the version of a notable Frenchman's remark, translated by unmitigated bankers. In their voices it was to be heard. They waked with it, they slept with it, they walked with it, sat with it, ate and drank with it. To look at them, shrewdness was to be plainly observed, but where was imagination? Hardness was there, but where was daring?

"We keep on the Safe Side." The habit, in the end, becomes dangerous.

And so, by mid-nineteenth century, toleration had degenerated into acquiescence; acquiescence, fold upon fold, had wrapped up virile independence. It spread from the men of the broad-brimmed hats to the world's people who did business with them, undoubtedly assisted by the climate; and the sluggish rustics in the farm country had it already. Why complain if a senator was stealing a canal? The larder was full. The farm-house floor was clean: dinner could be eaten on it— so they said always, finding this enough answer to everything. In town, all was well with the bank account. Why complain if the water gave typhoid fever? Why quarrel with the gas, or the paving, or the drainage? Why examine too closely into somebody's profits in a municipal contract? You might make enemies. These might hurt your business. Be moderate.

Thus grew Monopolis from a village to a large city full of big buildings, good institutions and comfortable citizens; hospitable, agreeable, well mannered and well fed; some going to Meeting and some to dances; few of them large-spirited, most of them too careful with their purses—which might open readily to pay for green-turtle soup, but got lock-jaw in the presence of any enlightened public appeal; and all keeping on the Safe Side. And thus was the jest consummated by the ironic gods. During a hundred years the town had called itself the historic cradle of liberty—and liberty in her historic cradle had collapsed. Revolutionary ardors had died down; in politics and business scarce a spark of liberty was left large enough to light a cigar. Here then was the jest: out of moderation's very heart excess had been created—too much moderation.

BOOK SECOND

Might in ordinary circumstances have contained more
but does contain less than nine months.

IV

For which Aunt Carola is responsible.

The nine or ten people whom I was now ready to present to you must be put off, because at this point Aunt Carola stopped.

"You should say something about San Domingo,* Augustus."

She was quite right. How had I come to forget San Domingo? Even in so summary an historic account of our town and her people as I had given, San Domingo should have a word said of it. More than ever was I glad of submitting my story to the searching scrutiny of my Aunt.

"And aren't you going to speak of the French refugees?"

"Gracious! I'd forgotten them too."

I made a note of these two corrections, but my Aunt had more to say.

"I think you touch too lightly upon the climate, Augustus. Of the three chief influences that have—well—held us down too close to the earth, do you believe the non-resisting religion and the sluggish immigrants count for more than our very damp, enervating climate? And aren't you rather severe upon us?"

"Too severe, Aunt?"

"Well, in portraying one's own people I—but you needn't keep looking at me like that, Augustus; the tone of your voice suffices."

"Suffices for what?"

"To express invincible obstinacy. Keep your opinion. But our climate is a fact. Haven't we humidity and heat enough to take the starch out of many ideals?"

"Then you admit we're limp!"

She merely rebuked me with her eyes. "They tell me we're all living on top of what for some geological reason which I don't pretend to understand, is a perpetual pond.—And yet we *have* produced distinguished painters and poets and scientific men." She named them to me.

"Yes," I retorted. "And they went to other places because they couldn't bear it here. And those who stayed were never valued until Europe recognized them. Mediocrity's the only thing we recognize."

"Keep your opinion, Augustus. But I think the pond is largely to blame. And that is enough for to-day. I shall send for you when I have been able to read the next chapters again. You will have to wait, because—(here Aunt Carola suddenly became shy) because it is Lent; and during Lent I always give up what I enjoy most."

"And you like my book so much?" I cried.

She was now blushing a little. "It is not that, Augustus. During Lent I always renounce reading after I have gone to bed."

I kissed my little Aunt very affectionately. How dear she was! What rectitude and grace and perfume of character the strict old-fashioned Christianity imparted! Is it gone forever from the world?

I saw that she was right about the climate; and much in the admirable cooking and in the graceful and gracious manners of Monopolis is owing to the refugees who came from San Domingo, driven thence by Revolution. These hapless and gallant French folk—such of them as escaped bloody murder upon their island of distraction—were fluttered upon our shores like birds flung by a tempest. They arrived in every sort of plight, mothers who had heard their slaughtered children's last cry, daughters who had seen their parents torn to pieces, bereft sisters and brothers, the surviving tatters of gentle families packed secretly (some of them) in great baskets and barrels, and so put on ship board and rescued. Certain of the men saved from the butchery came too. All being penniless, and of that high French courage which can forever begin again gaily, set about teaching what they knew for a livelihood. Thus into Monopolis at an early day came an excellent enlightenment, following that already brought by those refugees who fled to us from the French Revolution while Washington was president. The tradition of our chicken soup and croquettes still haunts the palate.* Fencing and dancing were taught to youths whose too plain deportment could well bear some ornamentation. The sisters of these youths learned to sing, to curtsey, to turn conversation lightly, to make the occasion pleasant. Urbanity was promoted, and wit, flavored at times with a good deal of spice.

It is plain that poets with a high song, thinkers with an exalting message, even statesmen with a daring conviction, are unlikely to be made from such ingredients: this were asking too much of moderation, amplitude, fecundity—even with fencing, singing and croquettes thrown in. But mahogany, silver, and family portraits, together with libraries sure to contain the Works of Pope, Addison, Fielding and Smollett,* abounded indoors in Monopolis, while out-of-doors prosperous manufactories were to be seen, iron works, banks of coal, and the greatest railroad conducted anywhere by mankind.*

If a monument be your quest, look at the railroad: surely a work necessitating imagination, the highest flight taken by the genius of Monopolis. Along its suburban curves and sweeps many were drawn to dwell, drawn away from older homes longer established: merely to buy your ticket on this road conferred, it came to be felt, peculiar social sanctity. Some indeed resisted its spell; compassion was evinced for these by the kindly disposed. Few comedies in our Democracy (which has not so far produced many comedies) surpass this one of Monopolis and its Railroad. Allusions to The Railroad were generally made with that bating of the voice observable in the godly as they approach the church-door on the Sabbath.

Some twelve miles out from the city of Monopolis—or perhaps it may be a little further—and to the west thereof on The Railroad, is the suburban station Ap Thomas.* This is one symbol of the Road's genius: at an era when other roads had hovels for their way-stations, along this far-seeing line neatness, architecture and landscape-gardening were already established as a principle in maintenance. This station was one of a dozen or more. A bland smooth sweep of gravel, cleanly framed by bland, smooth stretches of sward, made a driveway wide enough for a large concourse of vehicles meeting the trains. The sward was close-trimmed, and green with daily sprinkling. Compact beds of geranium radiated scarlet and exhaled perfume.

"So like the lawn of an English vicarage!" This is the recorded rhapsody of Mrs. James Cuthbert, a patroness of The Road.

Aunt Carola said: "The woman's an ass!" It is one of several occasions when I have heard my Aunt snort.

The sacred geranium-beds were so artfully shaped and disposed that, even for a passenger whirling by at sixty miles an hour, they formed letters spelling Ap Thomas unavoidably—unless the passenger were a perfectly illiterate person. Almost no families save the best got in or out at Ap Thomas in those days, and in those days you could tell the best from the others. Their neighboring country places with their thick-planted gardens made a sort of gigantic bouquet over the hills and dales, and that new-comer who would push in among these sumptuous land-holders must pay a pretty penny for each acre that he acquired. So it is to-day, even more than it was then, on the afternoon that we shall now particularly consider.

V

In which some of our best people forget their manners.

What year it was by the calendar needs not be too precisely told—it was a little less, or perhaps a little more, than a generation before that brilliant season, which we shall reach in due time, when the richest of our yellow-rich ladies, aped by a horde of entirely respectable females all over the country, discarded those hats which made them look like strumpets, and adopted those hats which made them look like assassins: to American virgins and matrons Paris had not yet offered Venus Astarte* as their fashion plate.—Hither to Ap Thomas comes Mrs. George Delair, driving her ponies. She drives well, sits well in her basket phaeton.* This smart vehicle with the bay ponies, and Patrick Gass, her trim groom, in the rumble with the correctly folded arms, makes an agreeable setting for the lady, whose good looks are an institution in Monopolis. She is much sought after, she gives a better dinner than most people, she is a widow and her only child, a daughter, is abroad, perfecting her education under the care of a useful Aunt. She is clever, she is even cultivated (she has called her ponies *Sturm* and *Drang**), but when her name is mentioned, some men whose discretion does not equal their valor, smile. Mrs. James Cuthbert, who has now appeared in her surrey, also on her way to the station, has been heard to call Mrs. Delair a demirep.* Yet, to look at the aspersed lady, who would dream it? The propriety of her veil, her gloves, her whole dress, forbids such a suspicion. How does it happen that such spotted dames as we produced in the last generation strove for a spotless appearance, while now many of our truly immaculate ladies seem to strain their ingenuity to suggest that their virtue has exploded amidst paint, smoke and champagne?— Mrs. Cuthbert manages so to hold her parasol that she can't see the other lady, escaping thus a bow of friendship otherwise unavoidable.—If fifty years be old, here comes old Evans Gwynedd, riding his horse to the station; crisp gray side-whiskers, a keen if merry eye, ruddy cheeks, riding clothes from London, boots the same. He is long a widower. By his various children, all married and settled, he is frequently made a grandfather; this does not at all disconcert his well-preserved youth. Youth well-preserved is hereditary in his gallant and distinguished family, in which young marriages are also a traditional custom. He lifts his hat to both the ladies; but as he happens to greet Mrs. Delair first, Mrs. Cuthbert acknowledges his salute with the precise quantity of unuttered comment that her skill, delicately versed in social half-tones, knows how to convey. This finely shaded resentment is not a whit lost upon the gentleman and the other lady, who in consequence exchange a glance more finely shaded still. Had I a cub for a son and saw Mrs. Delair licking him into shape, I'm afraid I shouldn't discourage it; but had I a boy of twenty, likely and precocious, whom I was anxious to hold back from, rather than push into, a full knowledge of the world, I don't believe I should care to see him driving about too constantly with this lady and her ponies.

She could do Gwynedd no harm and he none to her, both being equally expert at the game. Old Evans Gwynedd has been leader of the Monopolis bar since the death of a great predecessor*; he too gives admirable dinners, and his cellar contains Madeira, and the blue seal Johannisberger,* to say nothing of its clarets and ports; vintage champagnes were not yet known. The station and railroad employees, and such farm folk as remained hereabouts, stared at the eminent lawyer on his horse, although they saw him every fine day and on many rainy ones thus taking his exercise. Here, then, are many facts to place quite nearly the era to which this summer afternoon belongs: the ladies came in carriages, not in automobiles, to the station; blue seal Johannisberger was not yet drunk up; the sight of an elderly well-dressed horseman was still uncommon enough for rustics to gape at, and the horseman, though a gentleman and a scholar, was leader of the bar of Monopolis.

Now Evans Gwynedd is speaking to both ladies: "You will find notes from me when you reach home—prayers in essence."

"Can we grant them before heard?" both said.

"Have I ever asked too much?"

"I'm not sure," said Mrs. Cuthbert.

"Never," murmured Mrs. Delair.

The remark—who knows why?—went wrong with Mrs. Cuthbert. "I think I'll wait!" she smiled.

Gwynedd spread a deprecating hand. "Why so little faith?"

"Do you make the same prayer to both of us?" Mrs. Delair asked gently.

It brought heavy syllables from Mrs. Cuthbert before she could stop herself. "Of course he doesn't!" Then, to recover from the stumble: "Isn't the train late?" They that are too conscious of virtue lack lightness at times.

"Eleven minutes yet," said Gwynedd, slipping back his watch in his waistcoat. He was counsel for The Road. He now dwelt on his prayer. "Merely a humble house-warming next Monday. Yesterday I opened my farm for the summer. You must help me amuse my son Joe and his wife, and a younger guest, known to Joe it appears at his club in Harvard. The boy was a sophomore during Joe's last year at the Law School. I somehow dread him. My meal is at seven. Call it high-tea, rather than dinner."

"How d'ye do, girls, how d'ye do! How d'ye do, Evans!"

Thus a new voice, cheery, dominating and melodious, adds its tones to the growing concert. It is Mrs. Charles Ronald, hailing her friends and neighbors from her well-set-up victoria. She is Mr. Gwynedd's sister, somewhat younger than he, but a mature matron of agreeable, valiant countenance, and comely figure. No living member of high society in Monopolis is more delightful good-humored company. She possesses, furthermore, a wisdom and a wit that those but partially informed as to the many qualities of woman would call masculine.

"Really," she declared, "this afternoon train-meeting at Ap Thomas is becoming such a function that somebody ought to bring a table with a tea-kettle and thin bread-and-butter." Mrs. Ronald was a pioneer of the very new fashion called "afternoon-tea," which was just beginning to displace the "kettle-drum."* "John, you may stop." (This was addressed to her coachman, and she continued to her friends), "I'm taking a basket of our fresh strawberries over to mother, but I have plenty of time. Well, girls," she exclaimed, "I've just seen it, and I'm still breathless!"

"Isn't it shocking?" said Mrs. Cuthbert.

"You hadn't seen it before!" cried Mrs. Delair. "It's the first thing we all did."

"My dear, I only moved out on Wednesday. Think of spending half of this lovely June cooped up in our town house! But Charles insisted upon his new library being finished and the books on the shelves before we closed the house. Of course you know what that meant. Directly the hammering and falling of plaster began, Charles went fishing in Maine with a peaceful conscience (but I'm glad to say that the black flies are driving his body mad, and everything bites except the fish) and I stayed alone, coping with the carpenter and spotted with white lead. I've been walking up and down step ladders until level ground feels positively unsafe.—I shouldn't call it exactly shocking, Mary."

"I call any private house as large as that shocking,"* repeated Mrs. Cuthbert.

"The rumor is, that they told the architect nothing, except to build as big a thing as he could," said Mrs. Delair.

"He needn't be ashamed of his work," observed Gwynedd. "I'm too ignorant to be sure whether it is a copy of Amboise or Azay-le-Rideau.* There was a moat—"

"Now Evans," interrupted his sister, "your ill assumed ignorance is really in order that we should pat your knowledge on the back, moat and all. There shall be no patting while I'm present."

"I think you must be talking about the new—the new— what should one call it?"

A fresh arrival had thus spoken, Miss Laetitia Lawne. She had drawn up quietly in her reserved, spinster-like equipage, driven by an ancient colored coachman. Miss Lawne usually said nothing. She was the eighth generation of Lawnes who had usually said nothing. The Lawne men had steadily added to the family fortune, and had seldom voted. To cast a vote was vaguely held by the Lawne ladies to be something that perfectly nice people didn't do. Laetitia Lawne was not

thirty; but as far back as Madison's administration somebody
in Monopolis had remarked that the women in other families
were born maids, Lawne women old maids. It should be said
that plenty of Lawne men had fought in our wars on land
and sea with distinguished gallantry.

"What is one to think about it?" inquired Miss Lawne.

"Now Letty be bold for once, and tell us you hate it." This
was Mrs. Ronald.

Miss Lawne turned her soft eyes from one friend to another.
She made one think of some folded moth, settled on clean
fresh chintz. Her voice resembled the placid colors of the
moth.

"Don't you think," she said, "it's queer?" Now among the
old families of Monopolis, "queer" was as damaging an adjective in those days as could be used. Its meaning was extraordinarily special and indigenous; for instance, if you walked
up the north instead of the south side of Magnolia Street after
church on Sundays, those walking on the traditional side
would feel sure you must be "queer."

"Yes," said Mrs. Cuthbert, with decision, "it is queer."

"When we moved into town last Autumn," Miss Lawne
continued, "Pa and Ma never dreamed that we should come
back to find it all done, and standing right up in our midst."

"Staring at us," said Mrs. Delair.

"Night and day," added Mrs. Cuthbert.

"I'm told hundreds of workmen were employed, some of
them foreign," pursued Mrs. Delair.

"There are said to be eight bath-rooms," said Mrs. Cuthbert.

"Ten, my dear," corrected Mrs. Delair.

"Of course we shall never know the exact number," said
Miss Lawne.

"Well, at any rate they wash!" exclaimed Mrs. Ronald.

"Of course Pa and Ma will not call."

"Professionally, Miss Lawne, your father does know them," remarked Evans Gwynedd.

"Oh, in his office, perhaps," Miss Lawne assented, distantly.

"Well," declared Mrs. Ronald, "I think it beautiful to look at—and our poor old antiquated family abode would go inside it five or six times."

"Oh, Mrs. Ronald!" murmured Miss Lawne, "your lovely house where Washington dined!"

"That honor didn't enlarge it physically, Letty," replied the lady.

"Washington will never dine with those people," said Mrs. Cuthbert; which nobody could deny.

"Who will ever dine with them?" demanded Mrs. Delair.

Evans Gwynedd laid a hand upon his heart. "Behold a culprit. I plead guilty. The bride, moreover, is a sweet, pretty little girl."

"Then you *know* her!" Mrs. Cuthbert fairly shrieked it.

"Evans, why have you concealed this from us all?" His sister's voice spoke in mock reproof.

The lawyer smiled; his strong teeth were excellently shaped. "Where's the concealment, since I tell you?"

"Then tell us more at once, Evans."

"Oh, don't leave us out!"

Gwynedd turned, they all turned, Gwynedd made his very best bow; for here were Mr. and Mrs. Andrew Adair just arriving—and adding greatly to the distinction of his already distinguished audience.

"Gracious, Carola!" exclaimed Mrs. Ronald. "What are you and Andrew doing so far from home?"

"On our way to see you, Maria."

"And I'm on my way to mother's! Never mind! Just stay here and listen to the awful things Evans is going to disclose to us,—and I'll consider you've called!"

"Very well, Maria—and I'll consider you've returned the visit. Now Evans, go on."

He sat on his horse, smiling, ruddy, diverted by their clustering eagerness. Even Miss Lawne leaned out of her prim vehicle, lest a precious syllable be lost; if the Lawnes had generally said nothing, they had always heard everything. It is to be doubted if Evans Gwynedd (who could even keep judges awake in court) had ever had listeners hang on his words more than now.

"Come and hear this!" one of the ladies called to a latecomer just arriving at Ap Thomas, where some dozen and more had now collected to meet the train. All were acquaintances, most were friends; the good dressing was to be noticed; men were few—since it was the men coming from their business that wives, daughters and sisters were there to meet. First names and pleasant familiarity filled the air. Much greeting and bobbing of heads and inquiries as to domestic affairs went on. Freddy was over the measles. A New York man was attentive to Alice, who wouldn't look at him. The cook had gone crazy at ten o'clock last night. The girls were in Baltimore. The boys would be home from boarding-school next week. What lovely weather! In truth, a tea-table was the one needful accessory in this gathering upon the bland gravel drive, by the geraniums and the grass so like the lawn of an English vicarage.

The happy few who could hear Evans would listen to nothing but his tale—yet the tale, set down here, seems hardly portentous. Gwynedd, as leader of the Monopolis bar, had been giving advice to the bridegroom's father in his vast business operations during several years. Upon this father, Gwynedd expatiated. A remarkable man. A force. On the whole, the strongest brain he knew. A great benefactor to the community.

"Benefactor, Evans?" Mrs. Ronald failed to see how.

Her brother's hand waved explanations aside. These were intricate economic questions, not for women. The said benefactor deserved the name of genius. An imaginative constructor on the grand scale.

"He has the handsomest nose in Monopolis," said Mrs. Delair; "I have seen him in the street."

"To think of beauty being wasted on persons of that kind!" murmured Miss Lawne.

"Scarcely wasted, Letty," said Mrs. Ronald; "since he bestows it on so many." Miss Lawne cast down chaste eyes.

The tale of Evans continued. Benefactor's wife was also remarkable. She came originally from Vienna. Of late years she was but little to be seen. Lived much in privacy. Was apt to excuse herself and dine upstairs in her own apartments. Of course she now had everything in the world that money could provide; but—well—um—perhaps she wasn't quite happy. The ladies would of course consider this spoken in the strictest confidence.

"Of course," promised the eight ladies now listening to him.

But Evans was telling them nothing they did not know; it was merely that they loved to hear it again; he knew this, knowing them; therefore, being a flatterer, he put it in the guise of a secret imparted. This bridegroom who had invaded them with his new palace, was the ablest of all the benefactor's sons. He was the mother's favorite child, and perhaps—well, perhaps—this was because he was the youngest, or—well, perhaps—because his father had at one time not shown him that affection which—but this was all coming right now. Ah, well, these were family matters into which—the ladies would understand his reticence— Gwynedd could not enter. He had seen all those girls and boys grow up from childhood.

His confidential and fiduciary relations with his father led inevitably to his knowing more than he could tell. The revelations between client and lawyer were of necessity sacred.

Mrs. Delair interposed with a theory: was the father perhaps jealous of his youngest son's ability? She had heard something about the son's getting something in South America, or Mexico or one of those places, that the father had intended should be his own.

But in this remark the lady came shrewdly near ground upon which the counsel for the benefactor had no intention she should tread. He had carefully uttered nothing, suggested nothing, which they could not hear in the general air of rumor. Therefore his manner became a perfect representation of indulgence to credulity. Where had such an idea come from? Nothing could be wider of the mark. Here he allowed a smile to finish for him. He was glad to be able to set such an impression at rest. At this very moment father and son were together in an immense enterprise.

Mrs. Ronald had her theory: did the father, by any chance, prefer filial drunkards?

Indulgence smiled all over her brother's face. With another gesture of his hand he waved drunkenness away. Had not the best families in Monopolis seen young men whose youth had lured them to occasional indiscretions. "Drunkards" was an excessive term, undeserved. The boys were full of life, of course—with such a father!

"And marriage," said Mrs. Ronald, "doesn't seem to have diminished their vitality."

A kindly laugh from Evans Gwynedd indicated that this, too, was a myth. He said to his sister: "My dear Maria, such a thing as you suggest couldn't have escaped my observation. The year round, they are in and out of my office. Steady young men! Before they married,—well, think of the money they had!"

"Evans, perhaps you call it steady when a man—is there one they call Dug? With several children?"

"Douglas—yes. Three children."

"Last summer Charles was driving home from the Boston night train along Great Street at six o'clock in the morning. As he passed the Free Soil Club,* they were carrying Dug down the steps to a carriage. They put him in and told the coachman where to deliver him. As the carriage drove along beside Charles's cab, its door was opened, a pair of boots was put out on the step, and the door shut again. Charles couldn't see how much more undressing than this went on, but neither he nor I consider that being steady."

To this Evans answered easily: "An exception. One must grant exceptions."

"But they say," said Mrs. Cuthbert, "that this one was just like his brothers." She meant the bridegroom with the new *château.*

Evans turned gently and gravely to her. "When my boys were twenty, I talked to them as a father should, and abstained from too close inquiry. So will your boys' father do when they are twenty. Keep your son's confidence" (the lawyer grew sententious) "always keep his confidence; let him tell you, never ask him." No Epistle from altar steps could have sounded more sonorously wise.

Miss Lawne now spoke with a freedom rare for her: "Somebody said she kept him waiting on trial a year before she promised to marry him. They said his mother told her to do that. And he never touches a drop now, they said."

"Then perhaps he is her favorite because he has given her more concern than her other children," said Mrs. Ronald.

"You have never seen the mother?" Mrs. Delair asked Gwynedd.

"Oh, often. I said that she keeps to herself now-a-days. She is what the French call a 'great lady.' A great lady, I assure you. Her appearance marks her high race at a glance. Even the gardeners and servants feel it; they style her 'Madam' Hythe. A rare, great lady."

Gwynedd made it impressive. They believed him. Perhaps it was the first thing he had made these ladies believe to-day. Observations now fell from them in quantity:

"Pa and Ma wanted to call when she first came. But that meant knowing her husband. So they couldn't."

"How lonely she must have been!" This from Mrs. Ronald. "How lonely she must be!" she added, thoughtfully and gently.

"If her husband should die——"

"Oh no, Letty. To call then would be an insult. Think!"

"How could she marry such a person?"

"Doesn't she see anybody?"

"This new bride?"

"She sees the bride all the time," said Gwynedd. "She is staying with her now—while the bridegroom is off."

"Goodness, is he off?"

"No scandal, Mrs. Cuthbert," laughed Gwynedd. "They were united in December. Here's June. Honeymoons have to end. Business—it is mines this time—took him to Montana and Idaho in March."

"Three whole months! Couldn't she go with him?"

"The severe and exposing journeys prohibited such a thing."

"Oh—I understand!" This from Mrs. Delair, in a certain tone.

"No, she is not in the least delicate," Gwynedd replied simply, thus disposing of Mrs. Delair's delicate hypothesis. "They had planned to go together and rough it—the mines are quite out of civilization—but word came they would encounter six feet of snow in the mountains."

"And to think of her trusting him in those whiskey-drinking places!" moaned Mrs. Cuthbert.

"Hush!" Mrs. Delair admonished them.

Around them indeed they were sensible of all talk suddenly falling away, of a general fixing of eyes. Except the perfectly trained coachmen, there was none that was not staring. An open carriage was coming up briskly. In glistening freshness and polish, it seemed to outshine those already assembled. It was recognized to be of the latest model, the horses were admirable English hackneys.* The bride sat in it, alone, defence-less amidst the unified scrutiny. It was her first appearance. Evans Gwynedd would have lifted his hat, but she, having from a distance seen him to be with ladies of a social circle that was closed against her, looked the other way as she passed by to the station platform. It was plain to all that she was not "delicate." This was their first curiosity, their first thought. What so interesting as a bride? Moreover, this was a bride of millions. Disappointment was felt that no heir was apparent. Could this marriage, perchance, not be happy? Were mines in Montana his real reason for going away and staying three months? Ten to one, it would presently be known that the marriage was unhappy. They stared hard to discern unhappiness in her face, but none was there. It cannot be known how long they would have kept their staring up; the train rushed in and terminated the interesting scene.

Husbands, brothers and sons got out and began to make their way to the carriages. There was lifting of hats, shaking of hands, interchange of greetings, as people climbed into their vehicles to be driven home. Only two watchful onlook-ers, Evans Gwynedd and his sister Mrs. Ronald, saw what all would have been eager to witness. Out of the last car had stepped a young man of splendid and unusual appearance. He was unknown to Mrs. Ronald, but she did not need her brother's surprised exclamation to tell her that this was the bridegroom, returned from his mines. A few long, quick steps, and he was at his carriage. The bride gave a hand to her

lord, and a long look, and then a smile. Upon seeing that
smile, Mrs. Ronald felt something like tears come to her eyes.
But her word to her brother betrayed nothing of her warm
emotion:

"At any rate they don't kiss in public!"

The gravel had ceased to crunch beneath many wheels,
bride and groom and every one had gone, the muffled trotting of the horses grew distant, and distant the noise of the
puffing train, and there alone on the platform stood a youth,
also entirely unknown to Mrs. Ronald, looking about him
uncertainly.

"I fear it is the Boston guest," whispered Evans Gwynedd,
"and Joe was to meet him in the carriage. Look at his hat.
Look at his shoes, my dear sister."

Mrs. Ronald had already taken note of a round felt hat and
of shoes that needed blacking. "He evidently belongs to the
earnest kind of Boston old family," she said immediately.
"The other kind wear things like ourselves. An established
Boston wit has remarked that the earnest kind dresses like
penwipers and eats alone."

The stranger now raised his hat and seemed about to speak,
when Gwynedd said to him: "Is this Mr. Henry Sumner?"

"That is my name," the young man replied. "I was looking—"

"You were looking for my rude and unpunctual son," said
Evans Gwynedd, as he dismounted to shake hands with the
guest. "This is my sister, Mrs. Ronald. If Joe doesn't come in a
minute, she shall take you to the house."

"Yes, indeed," said Mrs. Ronald. "My mother would much
rather go without the strawberries in that basket than have
you walk to our inhospitable doors."

"Oh, thank you very much," said Henry Sumner, "I should
really enjoy a walk. I have been in trains all day."

"I trust you found the journey on our Railroad a relief after the New York and New Haven?"* Gwynedd inquired, confidently.

"I've travelled by this road before. So I came on by the other one to see the country. It's much prettier country."

"But an inferior road," said Gwynedd.

"I didn't notice that. Are the rails lighter?" asked the statistical Bostonian.

"We never go on it," said Mrs. Ronald.

"I think that I should if I lived here," said the Bostonian. "There's no smoke at all. I should think that your railroad commission would order this road to abate its smoke. I never saw such clouds as it seems to be pouring into the city. If your statutes don't cover it, the Slaughter House Cases* would, I think."

They looked at him and then at each other. They had never heard words like these before. He was treading on holy ground. Order The Railroad to do anything! Order it!

A smile ornamented the lips of Gwynedd. "We—a—think we hardly need a railroad commission here, Mr. Sumner. Do you find that yours works altogether well?"

"It will in time. It already forbids excessive dividends. The Albany in consequence is in good condition. Of course the Old Colony and the Eastern and the Fitchburg and the Maine could learn a good deal from you."

"You are interested, then, in railroads?"

"Merely as a part of our whole municipal problem," explained Sumner. "Just now I'm interested in sparrows."* And he smiled.

"Sparrows!" said Mrs. Ronald.

"I'm hoping to find somebody at your excellent Zoölogical Gardens who can tell me how to destroy them without cruelty. Boston is on the verge of a vendetta on this subject." Again Henry Sumner smiled.

"Well, well, young gentleman!" laughed Evans Gwynedd, as the unpunctual Joe now appeared with the carriage. Greetings and apologies followed, and Henry Sumner with his trunk was driven away. The lawyer and his sister were left the last at Ap Thomas.

The lawyer looked at her. "Sparrows!" It expressed his mind with eloquence complete.

"Evans, do you know I believe I might come to like that serious young man."

For answer she received a groan.

"Yes, I really think I might. His mother should make him black his boots and his father should get him a new hat. But he has a capital face."

"Then I wish he were going for a week to your house instead of to mine, my dear sister."

"I didn't say I could like him in a week, my dear brother."

"A railroad commission!" Evans was scornful. "Municipal problem!" He looked down the road where Joe's carriage had borne Henry Sumner away. "I don't suppose the child is more than twenty-three." The lovely June quietness with its odors from woods and blossoms, filled the gap between the lawyer's remarks. The gentlest rustling came from the trees; so soft it was that their leaves seemed not to move. The perfume of moderation, amplitude, fecundity, hung almost somnolently over the spreading country side. The thoughts of Evans Gwynedd about the young Bostonian reached their oracular climax thus: "Thank God, Monopolis has never produced young men like that!"

If the laughter of the ironic gods were audible to mortal ears, surely the welkin would have shouted now.* But no voice came, except that of Mrs. Ronald: "Well, Evans, I must get on to mother's. So much has happened in the last twenty minutes that I feel as if it were several days since I came here, and as if the strawberries must be much worse than over-ripe by this time."

"One discreet word before you go, Maria, since you're a well of discretion yourself. These clients of mine, these Hythes, have their shortcomings like everybody. I have been at times drawn into the fight this boy, just married, has made against his weakness—and against two brothers. Dug and Mortimer, when he was eighteen, undertook to make a man of him, as they said. I leave you to guess their method. It seems a miracle that his health is clean and that he did not die in some inebriate asylum. I think all this is behind him. I think his fight is over, and is a fight won. Angels should record that I have earned my fee as counsel for the Hythe family! It is nearly three years since his last spree. I want him never to risk another.—And if you would sometime, some-how—a—manage to know them?"

The suggestion was sudden. Mrs. Ronald parried it. "You think of me as a spree-discourager?"

"You know what I mean, Maria."

She wasn't sure that she knew. In silence, in a comprehensive flash, her woman's mind reviewed all possible consequences. Her own children were already too old for any intimacy with children springing from this union. This point came first to the mother's conservative mind, others followed, all weighed within a few seconds, when the lady said: "You tell me nothing of his wife."

"She's from St. Paul, Minnesota. Parents perfectly respectable Army people, stationed at Fort Snelling. Her sisters-in-law don't like her. She is very lonely."

Mrs. Ronald thought it over. "She has a great beauty for a husband."

"Six feet two," said the counsel of the Hythe family.

"His appearance must suffer in a dress-coat," remarked the lady. "The rougher his clothes, the more resplendent he would be."

Evans Gwynedd laughed. "Does that mean you will or you won't?" He mounted his horse.

"I'll think about it, Evans."

Then the brother continued upon his ride, and the sister took the strawberries to their mother.

VI

*In which the hero meets the most important event
of his life and is totally unaware of it.*

As Miss Lawne, Mrs. Cuthbert, Mrs. Delair and all these nice
people drove homeward, they stuck to the topic. Each lady
poured her presentiments into the ear of whatever companion had got into her carriage, whereat the companion also
burst into words; so that nobody heard much of what anybody said—but as everybody knew most of it already, this
occasioned no grave inconvenience. All chickens, even those
who have never seen a hawk, know him at once through the
promptings of nature: this great, fresh *château,* appearing
amongst old, quiet country-places and overtopping them like
a giant—what wonder that Mrs. Delair denounced it as vulgar, and Mrs. Cuthbert declared it was queer, and Miss
Lawne said that Pa and Ma wouldn't call, while all were certain that the marriage would come to no good? Alarm was
stirring in these chickens' hearts; it was at the bottom of their
charitable remarks, though none of them clearly knew this,
any more than the bridegroom thought of his *château* to-day
as being anything but the beautiful nest he had wanted to
build for his bride and his passion. But it was a hawk in the

social sky, heralding more of its kind. Other castles and palaces were to follow, the millions to pay for them were being captured even now in every direction; the chickens who had been cocks of the walk so long that they believed birth, not wealth, to be their patent of nobility, were doomed to have this superstition blasted from underneath them: the new gold would order the old blood, in the words of a song as yet unwritten, to "go away back and sit down."

A revolution was stirring, before which, in time's due course, barriers were to fall, traditions to be mowed as flat as if cannon, instead of dollars, had swept them. To the instinct of the gossipers, obscurely, something of this was brought home. Though their brains were not aware of it, their intuitions told them that this was a portent, an omen, prophesying change. Therefore it was that they had chattered so eagerly, stared so unanimously. But had a shaggy Isaiah come out of the bushes in sackcloth with a scriptural finger pointed at them, and cried loudly and rudely: "You are all for sale, champagne and terrapin and gifts under your luncheon napkins will buy every one of you and your children"—they would merely have stared at the maniac, and regretted the absence of police.

And so they all drove away loquaciously from Ap Thomas—all save two; the bridegroom and his bride drove in happy silence. She had been made uncomfortable and angry by the staring to which she had been subjected by her well-bred neighbors; but now—had not her lord come back to her, tanned by the mountain skies, and with a clear eye that could meet hers? His presence swept everything but himself from her mind and being. Yes, they drove in happy silence between the June fields and woods. She did not want to speak, and she loved his never saying a word. Questions in plenty they had to ask each other. He had seen her parents in St. Paul, whence

they were expecting to be transferred to a more distant post;
she had been putting the great new house in order while he
was away. But nothing of this was said between them as they
passed through the sweet country lanes; their longing to be
alone together did not render less dear to them this lingering
hour of the setting day.

It was in the great house that one sat who found the passing minutes slow, and who looked often at the clock. The
heart of the bridegroom's mother was beating as she waited
for her son. Madam Hythe could not remain quiet in any one
place. Caring nothing if the servants should see her agitation,
unaware indeed of anything about her, she passed from the
drawing-room to the open hall-door, and stood gazing in the
direction where he would come. Then, after watching there,
she went up the stairs and looked from a window. Why did
he not appear? Something must have happened. Again she
sat down, close to the window. She could not see the clock
from this position, and soon got up to consult it. It told her
that he could not possibly be in sight yet, even if the horses
had galloped all the way. She stepped out into the long hall
and walked to its far end and into his dressing-room. The
flowers there had been arranged by herself, not a servant had
been allowed to touch them. She made little light changes in
them, pulling one stem further out of the water, pushing
another a little deeper down into it. She looked at the clothes
laid out for him to dress for dinner, and she smoothed his coat
with her hand. Then she went down to the drawing-room
again and stood a moment by the piano. For the second or
third time that day, an old fear passed like an arrow through
her mind, that when she did see his face she might see in it
that sign she had learned to read with unerring certainty.
While he had been far away, she had been generally free from
this haunting dread. His constant letters proved him to be

keeping straight. But when the news that he was returning reached her, the old apprehension had strangely started alive again. The suspense, as she stood by the piano, caused her to sink into a chair and, for a moment, cover her face. Then she picked up a book and tried to read. Suddenly she sprang up, listened, and ran, as though she were herself a bride, to the hall-door. A distant carriage was passing the gate, but it did not turn in. The clock in the hall told her that certainly now in a few minutes he must be here. Out at the edge of the garden path she saw a rose-bush, and walked to it. It was full of buds and flowers full-blown, an old-fashioned variety, not large but of sweet perfume, which she had chosen and planted herself when the grounds were first laid out, sometime before the sod was broken for the house. One of the buds upon it seemed to her fairer than the bud she had laid upon his dressing-table to wear that evening, and so she picked it. As she turned from the bush, they entered the gate.

At sight of the carriage, all outward agitation vanished from her. It was a calm great lady, standing quietly erect, smiling gently and tenderly, a rose-bud in one of her folded hands, that they saw waiting to welcome them. The bride's eye spoke a proud, swift message to the mother, but the mother had already seen for herself; her fear had been needless.

Little did the three of them say of the many things that were in their hearts, as they walked into the house after the mother had embraced her son. Words they exchanged in plenty, to be sure, words of voluble gaiety and unimportance. The train had been punctual; all the trains had been punctual. Had it been cold there? It had been a beautiful forward season here, as the garden would show. How many miles had he traveled? Fifty-nine hundred! Seventeen hundred in the home stretch! Impossible to realize the extent of such a country. And he had left still unmelted snow behind him out there? How horrible must sleeping-cars be! Not at all. Oh, of course, there had been a private car! No, not this time, but the drawing-room to oneself was comfortable. But the eating? But the washing? Certainly bath and dinner in one's own house would be luxury. The mother put her rose-bud in the traveler's coat.

At dinner he sat glistening in fresh raiment, the rose in his button-hole, telling them some of his adventures. One or two had the strong taste of melodrama, causing a shudder in the bride, and laughter in the mother. On a night between Silver Bow and Pocatello—(What names! the mother interjected)— there had been no drawing-room. Going to the wrong berth at midnight, its enraged occupant had sprung in his face with a revolver. Confusion had ensued for a few crowded seconds, until he had knocked the man senseless with one of the man's own boots. The passengers were for putting him off the train, when the conductor had appeared, and vouched for his good character. Mining involved a miscellaneous life at times. No adventures there were for him to hear, but there was the ordered house for him to see, the tapestry come from Genoa, some Italian cabinets; and they had hung the pictures. He was conducted about by the ladies, until he expressed preference to see the rest by daylight. Then, because he asked for it, his mother sat down at the piano, and played for him the nocturne of Chopin that he had always liked best, even when he was a little boy. He stood beside her, listening, looking down at her until the music was done. They turned and found that the bride had stolen away to leave them to themselves.

"Before you go to her," said Madam Hythe, "come to me in my room to say good-night."

Mother and son shut the piano together, drawing its cover over it, putting in its place the volume of Chopin. As he was bending to the low shelf with the music, she took his face between her two hands, and kissed it with silent gentleness. They walked hand in hand to the stairs, and there he stood watching her as she went up them to the silent upper region of the house. All the house was silent, the servants had been told they need not wait; and through the hall-door and the windows, open to admit the air of the Summer night, perfume of fields entered from the quiet darkness. He strolled out upon the lawn and took a few steps, looking up at the serene stars, and at the lighted windows of his bride. Then he came in and shut the house and put out the lamp that had shone upon his mother's music as she played, and went to her room.

She had put off her more formal dress and was sitting by a window in her low chair, with soft gray folds and lace enwrapping her. A chair stood next her own, waiting for him, but he did not take it. As he had been wont to do always since the days when he had first grown tall, he sat on the floor by her knee, stretching his length out and laying his head among the gray folds and the lace. So, a penitent, had he laid it in times that surely must have come into their remembering thoughts now, so, in those times, had she sat caressing the penitent head. There was no difference in this attitude of mother and son, but every difference in this silent communion that passed between them. Words could not have made it plainer: he had nothing now of which to be ashamed, and she had no forgiving love, but only proud love, to give him. This was what passed between them before she spoke to her favorite and youngest son about the bride he had chosen. Something else there was that filled her mind, but she did not come to it yet. She praised the bride's character, and her ways.

"It has become easy to call her daughter. That is not always easy for a mother to do to the strange woman who marries her boy."

Although he said nothing, he made her know he liked to have her tell him this.

"And I believe I shall be welcome in this house. It is good to find a child's house where one is welcome." Thus much of bitterness did she allow to escape her, but only thus much. Then she recounted to him little things that had brought herself and his bride together while he had been gone. She did not speak of the great thing which had united them—their anxiety for him and his temptation. The mother and daughter-in-law had chosen many objects for the house together, and Madam Hythe was pleased to discover a natural good taste in the bride. She would learn very quickly.

This caused him to speak about the house, and some surprises that had especially pleased him; but she did not attend to his words. She heard them, the sound of his voice was sweet to her, she did not know that she was not listening to what he said. Her hand softly caressed his hair, her eyes seemed to be looking through the open window, but she was seeing visions of what her heart asked from the days to come. The stopping of his voice brought her back from visions: she looked down intently upon him, and her tone as she began slowly to speak what filled her mind, caused him to turn his head and look up at her.

"In my country, which is old," she began, "old with the troubles and the joys of many centuries of mothers and sons, hearts are deep. Deep, also, my son, are the beliefs of the people. *Ach,* how I have missed that depth! American belief—it is not rich, not tender, like that of my old-fashioned land."

Through her utterance swept a wave of longing and recollection, and she paused until she could speak steadily again. Emotion always invested her English more perceptibly with the accent of her foreign tongue. He looked down at the floor again, while she continued in silence to caress his hair.

"The humble folk in our mountains say that before any dwelling-house has known a birth and a death, it is not sanctified; that to make altogether holy any home, a soul from God must come down into it, and a soul must ascend from it to God."

Again she ceased and again resumed. "Dear little boy." From the beginning she had called him so; so would he always be to her, no matter how many were his years.

"I have grandchildren," she now said, very gently. "But am I never to have one to bless in this house, my son? Do you not guess how I long for this gift from you?"

A flush went over his face as he rose to his feet, bent down, and kissed her good-night, whispering: "All the will is here, mother. In both of us."

She sat in her chair, watching him go from the room, watching the door after it had closed behind him. She heard his step pass down the long hall, and the door of his dressing-room shut softly. Her sombre and beautiful eyes glowed while still she sat, seeing nothing but her thoughts. Love's presence in the silent house, the presence of Eros and Hymen,* caused long memories to throb in her breast: she had not forgotten. Eros and Hymen had melted her once in the arms of her buccaneer. For them, for him, she had stolen from her father's roof, renounced her kindred, her rank and her native land. She would have liked on that day to have had more to renounce, more to fling away for his sake as against whom all things else the world held weighed nothing. On that day, and through many days that followed, she had known what comes to few women ever to know, because few women have natures great enough, or because the man they take is not the man who can awaken their nature wholly to its depths. This divinest thing had she known, and if it were a dream—why then nothing in life since had been so real. The poverty of the early years seemed a shadow, the rise in their fortunes, the great riches of to-day—all shadows compared to that time of reality when her lover, a body and a spirit fused into one, made her universe. Even the next thing most real after this Paradise—the losing it—was a pain more like a dream than the joy had been. Affairs first occupied her lover, then engrossed him, then changed him. His pirate spirit, having made her one of his possessions, went after gold. She came to see that this spirit did not even comprehend that it had left her alone, that in giving her everything but itself, it gave her nothing. The women of the chorus that he came to frequent more and more as he grew older, she became able after a time to put out of her thoughts—there were always new ones, shadows. Shadows were the people he brought to the house: brother pirates, senators, railroad presidents, and at times the families of these magnates. She did her duties as a hostess easily, gave to everybody the same faultless welcome. To her foreign race they laid the fact that none of them seemed to know her well. In so far as she ever thought of them at all when they were absent, they were distasteful to her. Sometimes she found the talk of the men interesting, but the women seemed to her intellectually threadbare, barbarians in peacock millinery. She knew there lived people in the city with manners, traditions and knowledge akin to her own, but these had nothing to do with her husband, and she had a pride that conquered the desire to know them. Sometimes she was glad that no visitors to that house (save one) had the perceptions to discern and measure her isolation. Pride was not her sole stay; music and literature she had, and her religion, in which she lived much; but most of all she lived in the remembrance of the supreme happiness that had been hers once, and in a sort of dim belief that beyond this world she would find again the buccaneer of her youth, for whom she should be ever ready.

All these stages of her life she had often reviewed before; tonight she saw them again, clear and successive, as she sat in the low chair by her open window, after her son had gone to his bride. The chimes of the clock down in the hall sounded faintly through the great, silent house. A little breeze blowing in brought more of the perfume from garden and field. The fire in her sombre eyes glowed, died down, and glowed again, following her thoughts. Here, in this house, it was indeed that she wanted grandchildren.

Her own journey was ended. In the lives of others the road before her lay. Son after son and daughter after daughter of the six children she had borne, had understood their father, her they had not understood—save one. The rest had never cared to learn what she would have taught them, they had begun early to draw away from her and near to him. They seemed to be made more of his fibre than of hers, though with little of the compelling power of his nature. But this youngest boy, who had more of the pirate in him than any, yet had remained close to her. In his life she lived forward, and in the lives that must spring from him the rest of her journey should be made. Then, some day, it might be granted her to complete the holiness of this house by departing from it to God.

Once again, as still she sat by her window, looking out with that deep and smouldering gaze, she saw the stretch of years across which she had come; but all that lay between her far-off Paradise and now, was merged in a sort of dusk: the flat landscape of her days showed no features; only at its beginning gleamed that era of happiness, like peaks in the glow of sunrise.

At last she went to bed. For herself she made always the one same prayer—that grace should be given her to do the Heavenly Will, whatever this might be; for the bridegroom and bride she prayed to-night, that when they should reach the inevitable burning out of passion, they might find beneath its ashes that which her spirit had guessed and craved, but never known, that togetherhood for which mankind has found no name sufficiently divine.

VII

Introduces various persons and things, but chiefly an Inn of renown with two who lunched there and laid a wager.

"Dear little Boy" (so ran the note she sent in the morning to their room from hers) "you will be catching the train to hasten to all the work that must have been piling up for you at your office. Don't wait breakfast for me, then, either of you two children. I take mine here. Your old mother shall not spoil your honeymoon any more by thrusting her company into it. She will go home to-day, else your father will begin to think she is lost."

(To all her children, even to her favorite, as to the rest of the world, her domestic life was assumed by her to be without flaw. She laid no stress upon the point, well aware that any unskilful emphasis in such a fiction would produce laughter on the part of people who knew at least the chorus-girl portion of the truth. For the sake of dignity, decorum and her children, surfaces were maintained unruffled. Having taken her husband for better or for worse, and having in the early years had the better, she accepted the worse as belonging to her duty in the late years. Such a view is seen to be old-fashioned, injuriously indulgent to man, not giving woman her just due; and

any argument to the effect that continued sacrifice is apt to
debase the receiver while it ennobles the giver, comes plainly
from the devil. It is the devil who has awkwardly pointed out
the necessity of selfishness in order that unselfishness may
find employment in an imperfect world.)

The old-fashioned mother stopped at the final sentence she
had been about to write. This was: "Come bid me good-bye
before you go." It was not written, the note went without it,
because she was sure that he would come when he learned that
he would not find her on his return from town in the afternoon.

It was only for a minute that he came, with breakfast in his
throat, scant minutes for the train, her rose again in the coat
that he wore this morning. She said the rose was too large
now, she would pick him a fresh bud. There was no time for
it, and he liked this one. He dashed down the stairs, and she,
looking from her window, saw him leap into the dog-cart,*
take the reins himself, and be off. Some words from a psalm
came into her fond fancy: "He cometh forth like a bridegroom out of his chamber, and rejoiceth as a giant to run his
course." She knew by heart the whole of this psalm* in its
English version, which she found more beautiful that that of
her mother-tongue, or even of the Latin. And then, smiling a
little at her admiration of her boy, she resumed the prepara-
tions for her departure.

A bridegroom, though less interesting than a bride, is still
an object much stared at, and such neighbors as knew him by
sight at Ap Thomas, forgot their manners again. The rose in
his coat was not overlooked; some ladies smiled knowingly to
each other, and pictured the bride placing it there. In the
train, young Mrs. Joe Gwynedd seated beside Henry Sumner,
who was setting out for the Zoölogical Gardens to seek a
merciful means of death for the Boston sparrows, told the visitor all that she knew, and more, about the rich owner of the

new *château*. He was curious to see it. It was so very large, then? He did not recall anything of this sort, so far, in Boston, or in Beverly Farms.* That sort of people in Boston seemed not to wish to be conspicuous, but rather to resemble in their external trappings the customary decencies and dimensions set by the regular Boston families. This house was a copy of something in France? Was it beautiful? Mrs. Joe thought that architecturally it might be found so by some people—but consider the shocking taste!

"In what way is it shocking?" Sumner inquired, not in controversy, but seeking information as usual.

"The taste," Mrs. Joe exclaimed.

"But I thought you said it was architecturally beautiful?"

"Don't you think it's bad taste to build a thing five times larger than anybody's private house—large enough to be a hotel?"

"I don't know about that, if it doesn't look like a hotel."

Mrs. Joe found him tiresome; she suddenly remembered she had something important to say to her Aunt, several seats away in the car. She smiled a sweet, deceitful adieu to him. "Don't eat soft-shell crabs for lunch," she advised him.

He had no such plan, he had not thought of lunch at all, but he said, "Why, aren't crabs good here?"

"They're delicious," she exclaimed, "but I am ordered to bring some for to-night."

Her Aunt, Mrs. Ronald, had come to no conclusion about that idea which Evans Gwynedd had suggested to her at Ap Thomas. She occupied a seat with him. "You know, Evans," she said, "I don't quite see your point. You ask me to call on these people, apparently for the young man's moral good."

"Well, hardly that, exactly, Maria."

"But it seems to me exactly that. You hoped he would be prevented from further excesses. I am not apt to call on strangers that have no claim upon me. The claims of charity are often reason enough—provided I can do anything. But if you feel that his perfectly respectable wife and mother may not be sufficient to deter him, I hardly see why you conclude that knowing me would keep him from drink."

Gwynedd began to protest. "You will put things in so ridiculous a light, Maria. Knowing you—knowing us—would bring an entirely new element—a new incentive—"

He could not go on, because at this point the approach of Mrs. Joe necessitated silence.

Mrs. Joe's husband, meanwhile, had taken his place beside their Boston guest. "What a herd of imbeciles you must think we are!" said Joe.

Sumner turned to look at him.

Joe laughed. "Acknowledge it, you serious Puritan!"

"I don't acknowledge it. It isn't true. I've never seen so many pleasant people all at once. Why imbeciles?"

"'This is the house that Jack built,'" returned Joe. "'This is the malt that lay in the house that Jack built. This is the rat that ate the malt,' et cetera, et cetera, and with all our united brains we can't get away from the house that Jack built. Have you heard us discuss any other topic than these new people and their new *château*?"

"Well, if you come to Boston just now, you would find us all talking sparrows. Nothing but sparrows. I confess that I enjoy the change of subject."

Joe now pointed to the bridegroom's back. "He's got a good-looking sister. Some of the fellows—the kind of bucks who run after beauty that's off their social beat—know her. Of course they don't marry her."

Down in the Bostonian's heart these last words produced a slight but displeasing sensation, as of chill. He thought of a certain girl in his town, a maid of beauty, of whom he was

beginning to see much. He had met her at a fancy ball, her
people were to his people unknown, and his conscience,
which was this young man's strongest possession, had of late
been informing him that he ought to speak to his mother
about her. The secret sensation at his heart prompted him,
after a brief silence, to argue a case that might become his
own. "But doesn't a woman, if she's fine and good, take her
husband's position?"

"Fine and good isn't the point," said Joe. "In Europe of
course a duke can make a duchess out of anything. But here—
well, none of us are dukes, and we have to be careful."

This generalization brought no reassuring warmth to
Sumner's heart. "It oughtn't to be so," he said. "I don't believe
it is so. And you tell me this girl's mother is a lady."

"Oh yes, but she took her husband's position here as an
outsider. They're all outsiders. It would never do. And you
know well enough it wouldn't do in Boston either. Just imagine what Beacon Street would say if you married somebody
from the South End!"

"A man's wife is his own business!" asserted Henry Sumner, stoutly, with the shaft quivering in his heart.

"A man's wife is everybody's business," declared Joe, all
innocent of the discomfort he was inflicting.

No excellent arguments could move him; he spoke of facts,
sagely, finding in facts the safest ground for all belief. Rules of
Europe fell away in a Republic, whence the feudal system
was forever banished. To the minds of neither of these young
men occurred the surprising possibilities that lay in money,
because in that day these possibilities still slept, and the young
men were not prophets. The Bostonian held that personal
worth should settle it. The Monopolitan was sure that nothing settled it. He cited cases: such and such a man had married outside, and his name being therefore according to rule

dropped from the list of the Patriarch Balls,* never again was written thereon; such and such a woman, on the other hand, had been socially strong enough to bring her unknown and horrible husband into the fold, he being added to the sacred list. An idea, a principle, shone forth for a moment here: might not our American plan be, perhaps, the opposite of the European plan—the man taking the wife's station? Another exquisite instance of Goethe's eternal-feminine drawing us upward.* And didn't the gender of our Republic show several symptoms of becoming female? They agreed upon nothing, save that the question was evidently clouded. Its remarkable clarification by money both of them were to live to behold: if there be money enough, anybody can marry anybody to-day, receiving the benediction of society and no questions asked about how the money came. But how should these young men foresee that? And so discoursing, they reached Monopolis and parted, one to his office, the other to the Zoölogical Gardens, guest promising to meet host for lunch at the café of the Buena Vista Hotel.*

The renowned naturalist who declared, that from a single bone he could reconstruct the whole animal,* reminds me of something of a kindred nature which I myself can do: show me any town's best hotel, and I will construct the town for you. If I see a plenty of greasy table-cloths, a scarcity of washing arrangements, and a hotel register scrawled with illiterate flourishes by Freds, Als and Eds, I need no more to tell me that the town is a god-forsaken sink, which I must endure until my errand in it is sped, and shall quit without reluctance. If I see long piazzas, hammocks and rocking-chairs, glasses containing cracked ice and straws, and hear an orchestra playing Pagliacci* or some reigning Broadway melody, it is enough; I know where I am, that my bills will be large, and that the hotel-clerk will patronize me from an immeasurable altitude.

On the day when Henry Sumner lunched with Joe Gwynedd, the Buena Vista perfectly expressed Monopolis, both through those whom it entertained, and in its manner of entertaining them. Its snug comfort betokened civilization, its intimacy a sort of provincial but enlightened cosiness. How civil was the manager, how pleasant the waiters Victor and Louis! How well they had learned and remembered what you liked to eat and drink, and the corner where you preferred to sit! The little hostelry was almost like a club. To breakfast there reminded you of your club, you didn't pay, you signed the order, Victor or Louis skilfully serving you. In the ladies' dining-room, almost everybody was likely to know almost everybody else. After the Opera, suppers were the same, gay, snug, intimate, and how good the food was! What pretty women in what pretty dresses went in and out of those doors! What experienced gentlemen were their companions! What unforgettable dinners after the coaching-parade, or when somebody was going to be married, or when—but never mind! I wonder how many thousand corks were popped there in a month? Or how many gallant suggestions rebuked or encouraged? I miss, I shall miss forever, the Buena Vista that we have outgrown, and whose place knoweth it no more. I shall forever remember its homelike brick exterior, where it stood at the corner of Great and Magnolia Streets, its awnings in summer, its flower-boxes, its friendly windows, its late hours, the laughter I have had in it, even the occasional headaches of a morning, with Victor or Louis solicitous for my well-being. Until its advent, Monopolis hotels were gaunt, forbidding caverns of discomfort; the high ceilings, the garish mirrors, the neglected chandeliers, the unanswered bells, the dusty curtains, the shabby carpets, the poor beds, the

bad food, the large bars, the swarming cuspidors—all met
and ministered to the half-civilized taste of senators and rep-
resentatives, convening to be banqueted. Democracy likes
space and spittoons. During its quarter century of existence,
the Buena Vista had more influence in Monopolis than any
one of the hundred churches in the town. These were behind
their age, they at best but held their own in matters of the
soul, they fed the starving spirit with evaporated Christianity;
but the charming, wicked, aristocratic little hostelry made a
new era for the well-nourished body in Monopolis. It wrought
transformations, it educated, it instructed the eye and the
stomach; it also taught drunkards to drink more, and it made
drunkards of some who had never drunk before. Is it not
interesting, deeply interesting, to ponder the fact, that a hotel-
keeper counted for more in the growing-up of Monopolis
than any bishop, priest or deacon within her gates? Boston
had a preacher named Phillips Brooks,* but Boston hotels
were inferior; in Monopolis no preaching equaled that of the
Buena Vista.

When Joe and Henry met for their lunch in the café of the
little hotel, the host's first concern was what they should eat,
and he took the card which Louis handed to him. A glance at
it sufficed him.

"We'll have soft-shell crabs!"

"No," said Henry Sumner.

"Don't you like 'em?"

"Very much indeed. Your wife forbids it. We're to have
them to-night."

"Can't you eat 'em twice?"

"I made no promise to Mrs. Gywnedd."

"Hooray!—Louis, two orders of soft-shell crabs; and Louis
you know the way they do cucumbers here, that way with

cream or something. Two orders, Louis. Now, let me see what next.—Oh, what'll you have to drink?"

"Can't I have water?"

"D'you think because I'm a husband and father I've quit *everything?*" demanded Joe. "Louis, we'll have that Niersteiner cup.* You know. Make it a quart. It's a hot day. And drop in some red curaçoa, the way I showed you. Use egg soda, not siphon.—In my secret heart," he added to Henry Sumner, "I'd love to lap up some champagne with you. But it's vulgar at lunch. Don't you think so?"

"I do think so," said Henry.

"I trusted you wouldn't. I get so tired upholding the traditions. All very well for father. But the Dry Monopole's delicious here."*

"The cup appeals to me," Henry persisted.

"You're a dried codfish.—How about the sparrows?"

Sumner had learned nothing at the Zoölogical Gardens, but since leaving them he had employed his time to advantage; he had visited two historic buildings, and two courts of law, asking questions freely. He had even entered a magistrate's court, but soon come out of it, finding the air bad, the magistrate worse, and the machinery of justice worst of all. Then he had wandered into a big nasty hotel, "dingier than the Parker House," he said, but here he had seen an extraordinary looking man. "He was thin and sallow, with very plain hair and one drooping eyelid," he told Joe. "And two men talked hard to him for five minutes while he sat without any more expression than an idol. Then he tore a page out of a note book, wrote what couldn't have been more than three or four words on it, gave it to them, and they went away. He never spoke or looked at them once."

"That's Mark Beaver, our political leader, and king bird of prey," said Joe.* "Nobody can be governor or judge without him, but he is particularly attentive to the selection of State Treasurer. He—" but here Joe stopped, for his eye had fallen upon two young men who now entered the café, and were taking seats at a table in the bow-window. "Look," he said.

Henry Sumner looked; his look became a stare. "Well, well!" he declared at length.

"The bridegroom's brothers," Joe informed him. "Mortimer Hythe and Douglas Hythe, familiarly known as Mort and Dug."

"Well, well!" repeated Sumner. He had seen nothing like this yet in Boston, except perhaps sometimes on the stage at the Howard Athenaeum.*

Victor and Louis had hastened to attend to the new guests, who proceeded with much deliberation and argument to the ordering of a meal appropriate to a pair of stomachs of such importance. This food began presently to be set in front of them, while a bottle, protruding from ice in a bucket, was placed handily beside their chairs, after some of its contents had been poured into their glasses.

"This is filth," said one of them, after drinking some of his wine.

"That's Dug," whispered Joe.

"Filthy filth," agreed the other.

"That's Mort," said Joe.

"Looee!" called Dug.

"Looee! Looee!" called Mort.

"Yes sir, V'là m'sieur!" said the waiter, running to them.

"Looee, this is filth. Drink it yourself, and bring a quart of Dry Monopole, quick."

"Yes sir, merci m'sieur."

"Monopole for them," whispered Joe to Henry. "Question is, does it pay to uphold the traditions?'

"This cup is good enough for me," replied Henry. He was more and more absorbed in the brothers Dug and Mort.

The pair now sat enjoying life, and gazing out of the window over the tops of their collars. It was plain their tailor had performed his utmost and sent them forth from his shop into the world to show it what he could do. A glazed resplendence seemed to pour from them both. It will be seen that they had something yet to learn in the matter of perfect dressing— how to wear good clothes without its being noticed; give them ten years more, and this also would they master, because they belonged to the sharp breed of Americans-on-the-make. Each would end by acquiring every sign of the gentleman, except the slight trifle of being one. A sporting humor just now possessed both, the simple events of the street providing all they needed.

"Bet y'u five a bay horse passes next."

"Take y'u."

"Ah there, hand it over."

"No bet! You saw the white one comin'."

"Saw nothin'. Fork out the goods."

Currency was accordingly exchanged.

"Bet y'u that woman gets to the corner before that man. Ten."

"Take y'u. Double your ten."

Both jumped up and leaned from the window to follow the course of the pedestrians, while Louis and Victor attentively picked up the two chairs their patrons had toppled over.

"H——! You saw the fello' was goin' to drop his bundle," said Dug.

"Saw nothin'. You cough up the dough again," ordered Mort.

Currency was once more exchanged as the patrons stood in the bow-window.

In a great city, where all the world comes, and no sight is strange, a man may walk at large in a turban and oriental drapery without causing a head to turn, and these two would

likewise have passed unnoticed; but in the café of the little
Buena Vista, Dug and Mort, with their countenances of rosy
opulence, their glowing summer apparel, their glistening varnished boots, radiated like enormous fresh vegetables, they
bloomed and bulged, twin cauliflowers in patent leather.
Who, knowing and revering the conservative traditions of
the old society of Monopolis, could have discerned in Mort
and Dug two of the future purchasers of that society?

"What are you doin' among real money?"

This interesting observation was now made by Dug, who, in
paying his bet, had discovered a two-dollar bill among his roll
of fives, tens, and twenties. He jerked it out from its grander
company, tore it to pieces and dropped it into the spittoon.

"Don't let's go," whispered Henry Sumner to Joe over at
their table, where their simpler lunch was finished. "Let's
wait. I'm spell-bound."

"I'm a bit hypnotized myself," whispered Joe. "They're better than usual to-day. We'll order some more coffee—Or—"
(here his eye wandered to a fresh pint of Monopole which
Victor was about to open for the sporting brothers) "it's not
too late yet, y'know, to let the old traditions drop."

"Sot!" said Henry.

"Cod-fish!" said Joe.

So they only had coffee.

"Do you suppose they're showing off for our benefit?"
Henry now asked.

Joe shook his head. "They'd play to the gallery if it was
empty."

The power to compel attention is very various and often
unwitting. By their clothes and their voices, Dug and Mort
were the overweening centre of the café; but whether they
desired an audience, or were not so much as aware they had
one, I cannot be sure; I can merely give you Joe's opinion.

"There *he* goes," observed Mort, looking out of the window.

Dug perceived that it was their brother the bridegroom, and he made a half-jump. "Hi! Come in here!" But the passer had gone out of hearing.

"He'd not come where a cold bott was, anyway," remarked Mort with scorn.

"Unless it was milk," said Dug. "He got back yesterday. Three months away."

Mort leaned to whisper some words in Dug's ear, at which Dug gave a loud animal laugh. "Right you are!" he said hoarsely, "if he's the boy he used to be."

"Bet y'u I can get him drunk."

"Bet y'u don't."

Now here was something in the betting line worth while, a wager with a spark of imagination in it, brilliantly struck off by their joint brains: to break down their younger brother's three years of reform, and make a sot of him once more! They found a strong appeal in it. In laying a plan for their campaign, they not only neglected the wine in their glasses, but even lost sight of their opposing interests; the bet grew into a plot with a convivial aim—if the plot failed, Mort was to give Dug a dinner of ten at twenty dollars a plate; if it succeeded, Dug was to give the dinner to Mort.

Their plotting was interrupted. The sound of a voice filled with laughter of the ho-ho, ha-ha kind, approached from the hall, where the voice was greeting everybody in general and nobody in particular; and a slim citizen entered the café.

"Watch him!" Joe eagerly snapped.

Henry Sumner obliged, but asked, why?

"Bet y'u," pursued Joe, adopting the language of the brothers Mort and Dug, "he'll shake hands with that man first." And Joe indicated an elderly person who was lunching quietly in a distant corner.

Sure enough, the slim citizen made his way straight to the elderly person.

"Always shakes hands first with the biggest income present," explained Joe.

"He's not an actor?" inquired Henry.

"Ha ha!" went Joe, almost as merrily as the new-comer. "Ha ha! Well, Timothy Tingle's seven generations of eminent ancestors must be all turning in their ivied graves to hear you say that. And his wife's related to all the people he isn't. He married her for her prospective fortune, which her father immediately lost in Texas Pacific. But Timothy'll never do such a thing again. He's my cousin in five ways, I think."

"Well—" stammered Henry Sumner.

Joe put a grateful hand on Henry's shoulder. "Don't apologize! Actor! Why did it never strike any of us before?"

Meanwhile, Joe's cousin in five ways had been deferentially conferring with the biggest income present. These respects being properly paid, he now hailed the brothers Mort and Dug, but with a far greater familiarity.

"Hello, you flesh-pots!" he called out. "Hello. At it again, I see. Champagne in the middle of the day. Ho ho!"

"Take a chair and have some, Tim," they invited him.

"Thank you, no. I'm a working man. How d'ye do, Joe! You're a working man. What are you doing here?" Joe introduced him to Sumner. "From Boston, eh? Great town. Just been there. Glad to see you. How long are you staying? Joe, have you put Mr. Sumner down at the Club? Let me do it. Just going there. Delighted to. Can't stay now, thank you, I'm a working man. Ha ha."

Persons difficult to please would have found one point for doubt in the gaiety of Mr. Timothy Tingle's laugh; during even its heartiest explosions, his eye was watching you; it was a dark, strong eye.

"Mr. Sumner stopping with you, Joe? I'll have the card sent to your care. Good-bye. Got an engagement. I'm a working man. Seen your brother, Mort? He only got back from Montana last night, and he's got to go South this afternoon. Telegraphed for from Birmingham—more trouble with the titles of those coal lands he and your father have gone into. But he'll pull 'em through. He's a working man. Ho ho!" And Mr. Timothy Tingle departed with his nods and his laughs for everybody in general and nobody in particular.

"That busts our game," said Dug.

"Busts nothing. Are you trying to crawl out of your bet already?"

A thump with his fist on the table made the plates jump, and signified that Dug never crawled. Birmingham merely postponed the working out of the plot; ample time was to be allowed for this wager.

"How much time?" demanded Mort.

Dug drew out his watch and consulted it, as if that large gold time-piece could determine the question. "How about a month?"

"A month goes."

"Well, I want more."

"Take more, d—n it. Take two, take twelve."

"Done. It's only fair after he's been three years on the water-wagon. If I've not made a boiled owl of him by this day year, I pay for the dinner." And on this they drank the rest of their wine. And each recorded the bet in his notebook.

"Match y'u who pays for the lunch."

"Oh, call dates."

This final sporting event decided, the brothers Mort and Dug went out to walk up and down Oak Street, where the shop girls were.

"A charming couple," said Henry Sumner. "Married, you say?"

"Both. Fathers also, several times."

"I pity the mothers."

"Spare your pity. They knew what they were getting, and they got exactly what they wanted. You should meet them. Mrs. Dug looks like an indigo bird, and Mrs. Mort looks like a wild wax-doll."

"Why, where do *you* meet them?"

"Charity Ball: Place where you meet folks your sisters don't know."

"Oh!"

"Place where you meet all sorts of folks you ought to speak charitably about—only you don't."

"Oh!"

Once again Joe's words had brought a chill to the heart of Henry Sumner. His thoughts flew to Boston, flew to that bewildering girl whom he had met at a fancy ball and whom his sister wouldn't have known—if he had possessed a sister. Yes; but his Priscilla was no indigo bird or wild wax-doll; she was a lady whose appearance and qualities Boston society ought to be glad of the privilege to admire. He would see to it that she became known and accepted. Individual worth should always determine a woman's position. And then, Priscilla's family was really a good one when you came to learn about it. To be sure, you did have to explain to people who she was; but wouldn't his mother—? Poor Henry's thoughts could only lead him to the same unanswered question, they couldn't warm that chill! He became aware that Joe was narrating anecdotes of interest about the Charity Ball, and he listened. Presently Joe was telling Henry more about Douglas and Mortimer Hythe; but into these somewhat intimate confidences between two young men there is no need to enter.

I, however, will tell a bit more; because in following the history of Romney Hythe we shall be obliged to meet these relations of his again, greatly as Aunt Carola objects to them and to hearing a single word concerning such people.—Mort was the first person I ever saw to sit whistling with cheerful loudness in a Pullman car for about eighty miles, quite regardless of the unfortunate passengers whom he was subjecting to this concert. And Dug's wife—the indigo bird—was the first person I ever saw in a railroad car to take out a powder-puff and dab her long nose with it. But who says free-born Americans haven't the right to whistle or dab their noses whenever and wherever they please? If a lady can't make her toilet in public without being criticized, what is become of our boasted liberty?

"Well, old man," said Joe to Henry, after entertaining him with a number of tales which very fortunately needn't be told here because they couldn't be told here, "I've got to get back to my office. I'm a working man, as our great weather-cock observed."

"Oh, that's what he is?"

"My cousin Timothy? He's an attorney-at-law. He's a coming man. He's the comingest man in Monopolis. The Railroad has already marked him for its own. Even father has to pretend he likes him. I divide people into three classes: those whom you can trust round the corner, those whom you can't trust round the corner, and those whom you can't trust as far as the corner. Oh, Timothy's grand! And the women find him fascinating—among others, his really charming wife. Aren't women extraordinary? Good-bye, old man. Don't miss the five-fifteen."

The lively Joe and his guest now parted company for a while; and when, after a couple of hours they met again in the train, the guest had spent his time profitably, like the serious Bostonian that he was, in seeing and hearing as much as he could of this city that was in many ways so different from his own.

VIII

Is very short, but contains much that is not said.

The customary gathering at Ap Thomas was a gathering of many disappointed people this afternoon. How should these excellent and inquisitive ladies not feel, even though the train punctually and safely brought their husbands, fathers, brothers and sons to them, that they had nevertheless been cheated? No little bride was here to-day to meet her tall, straight, exciting bridegroom. News of him and of her, and of how she looked and of how he looked, had spread at once after his arrival yesterday, and had gathered momentum as it spread. Gossip does not behave itself like the rolling-stone; romantic details abounded. Kisses had been exchanged as he got into the carriage, the number of these being a mooted question, and rising as high as six. On the other hand, somebody was sure Mrs. Cuthbert had said there had been but one embrace—a very long one. But somebody else was perfectly positive he hadn't kissed her in the carriage at all, because she had jumped out of it as the train came; they had met at the very steps of his car, and there the kissing was done. Still a third version had it that nothing of the sort had occurred anywhere; warmth being quite absent; a constraint between the two had been plainly discerned. The sum of it was, that more of them than yesterday had driven to Ap Thomas to-day, and behold! there was nothing to see. This was quickly accounted for after the first blank drop of expectancy. They spoke busily, like an orchestra tuning up, all odds and ends.

"My dear, it has just leaked out."

"Good gracious, what?"

"He's gone off again. Straight back to Montana."

"Idaho, my dear."

"No Lizzie, it's South now."

"Idaho, my dear."

"Lizzie, it comes straight from Mr. Tingle. The four o'clock train."

"Earlier, Gertrude. Twelve-thirty."

"Well, I always said it would happen."

"But what did happen?"

"His awful habits, Ethel. How is your poor Aunt Sophy?"

"Miserable. She hasn't slept for three months and she eats nothing but ice-cream. Has he run away or was he taken for his health?"

"I'm perfectly certain it's Idaho."

"Mr. Tingle must know, Lizzie. He does business for them, and he told Laetitia Lawne himself. Of course I may have got the train wrong. It may have been twelve-thirty, but I certainly understood it was four."

"Well it's a mercy she hasn't any expectations!"

"Yes indeed! Oh, yes indeed!"

Three or four of them murmured Yes Indeed, seeming to derive much comfort from this expression. One lady whispered to another, while she mournfully shook her head, that with such an inheritance nothing but the worst could be expected. In short they all experienced that pleasurable sensation in contemplating the misfortunes of others which has been pointed out by an eminent Frenchman.* And while they were doing this, a sorrowful and yearning bridegroom was journeying southward away from a sorrowful and yearning bride.

Is it not wonderful and forever wonderful, how people get a thing a quarter or a third right? The only greater wonder is when they get it right entirely. The bridegroom had been advised to start for Birmingham by the first train that he could catch, but this he utterly declined to do; he would not go without bidding good-bye to his wife. So it happened that he sent a telegram to the country, bidding her meet him at Ap Thomas with his valise, and so it happened that he took the four o'clock train instead of the twelve-thirty. Well versed in railroad time-tables, moreover, he proved to others, as well as to himself, that this delay at the beginning of his journey would make no difference at its end; that south of Washington he would take precisely the same train by the Piedmont Air Line.* This was the simple origin of the ladies' dispute over the hour of his departure. What they knew nothing about whatever, was the meeting and the parting at Ap Thomas. This had been at a time after the morning travel into town had stopped and before the return afternoon travel had begun, and it had been witnessed by nobody, because the ticket-agent who lived in the station was eating his dinner with his wife and children.

He stepped out of his train, she was there alone; she had sent the carriage back. He asked for his mother. His mother had been unwilling to share in their good-byes, she had remained at the house; but she had put off going back to her own when his telegram came with the news that some more inexorable loneliness was now in store for the bride. Must he be away long this time? Oh, no. It might be a week, it might be ten days at the worst, but if the titles by then should still be unsettled, he would arrange matters somehow so as to permit him to return to her, and this Birmingham business could be resumed later. Letters could come every day from where he would be; he wrote his address for her. And then, as it had fallen yesterday, silence now fell again between them. They walked slowly together up and down the platform. Now and then face turned toward face, and they smiled, but said nothing, because they needed to say nothing. The warm June odors filled the quiet air of the mid-day, and from somewhere far across the fields came the voice of a crow: voice of wildness, voice of sylvan eloquence, voice that calls to those who know how to hear, and speaks of the primal and brooding mystery which enwraps our world. Then, in the distance, they heard the train leaving some station on its way hither. They were to be separated only for ten days: but in every parting trembles the shadow of that final good-bye which, be it far away or near, is coming for all lovers. She took from her belt a rose; his mother's was in his coat still, drooping now, but not to be thrown away for that. He folded it flat in a letter, and so placed it in his pocket book to become pressed; and thus, when the train came in, the fresh rose was in his button-hole and their good-bye, save to themselves, had been invisible; it was made and ended before the witnesses in the car-windows were there to see. All they saw was a girl on the platform, watching a man as he got into the car, and watching him like the cheerful soldier's daughter that she was. Hadn't she since earliest childhood been seeing her mother bid her father good-bye, as he rode out of their various posts at the head of his troop over the plains?

She strolled homeward slowly from the station; slowly away from that platform where he had been walking close by her side but a moment ago; once or twice she turned back to look at the now silent, empty place, as if something of him still hovered there. As she walked along the summer lanes she had only one thought—that it was here they had driven together from the station through the setting day. When she reached the great house, his mother stood there to meet her, his mother, whose own life had taught her such wise, tender and saddened understanding. Upstairs, the elder woman took the younger in her shielding arms, and comforted her tears.

IX

Contains a glimpse of the Safe Side and a letter to Boston.

"No, Evans; I don't really see why you expect me to be a temperance pledge for that young man."

This was what Mrs. Ronald said to her brother by way of final decision. It was the night of what he had termed his house-warming, and the lady had arrived somewhat in advance of the hour he had named—enough in advance to find her nephew Joe and his guest Henry Sumner in flannels on the lawn, violently playing tennis, the new game which was leading all people to desert croquet.

"Boys!" called Gwynedd. "I beg your pardons—young men is what I mean: stop that at once, and go take your baths and dress."

The boys obeyed, and brother and sister sat alone upon his piazza.

Mrs. Ronald reviewed the question. "I'll not fall back like a coward upon Charles, whom the flies are still biting in Maine. I know he would agree with me, because I know what he thinks about the whole Hythe family. You asked me to call on this young couple for what cannot be considered anything but a charitable reason. But they are not objects of charity. Indeed, in comparison to what their wealth must be, I am much nearer destitution myself."

Gwynedd rejoined testily, "Well, Maria, you choose to quibble, and I say no more."

"But I will say more, Evans. It isn't the first time you've asked me to be civil to people whom I didn't wish to know—generally new Railroad people, and always very rich people. I can't recall a single pauper in whom you've ever invited me to take the slightest interest."

"Maria! I—"

"Don't be angry, Evans. I didn't mean it disagreeably. And you know, dear Evans, this is the first time I haven't done what you asked. The very first. I will confess that the bridegroom's appearance made me feel that I could easily fall in love with him if I was perfectly crazy and not already happily married to Charles."

The pacified brother laughed. "Well, your morals would be entirely safe if you called now. You'd find no one but his lonely bride."

"He's gone off again?" The lady sat straight up in her chair.

"You didn't know it? Then you're the only woman in forty square miles who didn't!"

"No, there have been two of us. I've been staying with mother. Gone off again! Goodness!"

"Yes, you all use the same words! 'Hoping for the worst!'"

"I seem to make you angry to-day, Evans."

"Gone off drunk again! Everybody instantly has to assume that!"

Mrs. Ronald turned a wondering face upon her brother. "I didn't say it, nor did I think it. I'm merely sorry for a bride whose husband is obliged to leave her so often."

But Evans still took it hard. "None of you will know him, not a neighbor desires to be neighborly, he's to be nothing to any of you—except that you'll all help each other to remember the bad habits and the youthful excesses that he's struggling to forget."

"Evans, what's the matter with you?"

He waved her off. "The best thing in that family is the fight this fellow has made, and his mother's love for him is the most beautiful thing I have ever seen. Can you not understand that he has shown a genius already in great affairs which may exceed his father's, and that his absorption in conducting all these enterprises and in pulling them off is his best safeguard, even if it compels him to be away sometimes? I wish you could take the right view of these people, Maria." (At this point the ring of nature in Gwynedd's voice changed in a singular and subtle manner to the tones of art—and his sister heard it.) "Mr. Jacob Hythe is a man worthy of—a—the highest esteem. His faults are the faults of—a—his powerful temperament. A very interesting man. A great reader. Our city will remember him long for his large ideas. His—"

"Is it the old scamp you're talking about now, Evans?"

The lawyer smiled. "A woman convinced against her will," he repeated in his indulgent voice. "Of course, Maria, I should be the last to defend—a—certain things that he—a—may have done at one time and another. They say he has done them. Well, admit this. No man is perfect; and a great man—"

Mrs. Ronald ceased to hear him, her attention waned. She was aware that he had begun to explain the nature of the imperative business reasons which had compelled the bridegroom's departure to the South. But what were the titles to some coal lands in Alabama to her? And why did her brother protest so much? When he talked of the old scamp's boy she believed him, she felt he spoke from his heart, that the boy's well-fare was truly dear to him; but when he invited her to admire the original old scamp himself, became the old scamp's apologist and champion, began to wave his hand and speak in that forensic tone she knew so well, then she felt ill at ease. In old days her brother never dragged up the Hythes, either to justify or to condemn them. Had they all become so interesting to him on account of one boy and his mother? Was it wholly for the boy's sake that Evans had urged her to take the very marked step of calling upon the young couple? Mrs. Ronald, while her lawyer brother of whom she was so proud continued to explain to her the "right view" of the Hythes, looked at him with something in her eyes that was well-nigh a dawning doubt, something that had stolen into her thoughts unbidden, that she would have kept out of them if she could have been warned of its invidious approach. So dim it was, so hazy, so vague, that it did not even shape itself in words;—yet she blushed with shame at herself.

Then her quick and able mind ran to the rescue with suggestions. "He's in love with the Austrian great lady." "Nonsense!" answered the same quick and able mind. "Can he possibly owe money to Jacob Hythe?" "Nonsense again!"

With an impulsive, affectionate, almost sheltering movement, Mrs. Ronald laid her hand upon her brother's arm. She could not have said why. "Evans, what's the matter with you?" she had asked him a few minutes ago. Nothing was the matter with him. He was rich, distinguished, influential, at the head of his profession, in the full power of his mental and bodily health, with larger plans and prospects of ambition. His soul wasn't his own: that was all; a mere trifle, and he didn't know it yet. She had laid a sheltering hand upon his arm. Did something deep within her know (though she did not know) how often in the coming years her loyalty to her brother and her blood was destined to eat into her heart with pain, and bring to her eyes the bitter tears that she would have died to keep the world from seeing?

A carriage drove into sight from the gate, and presently Mrs. Cuthbert stepped upon the porch, all delicate in cool gauze hues of lilac. She made her greetings at a gallop, she came at once to her point:

"How long is poor Sally Tingle to be away?"

The host replied: "Her husband will inform us. We expect Timothy here." He abstained from comment on the lady's compassionate adjective; comment from herself was known invariably to follow.

"I know she's been gone a week," pursued the lilac one, dropping the note of drama into her voice. "I met her driving to the ferry. I don't know a woman whom I would rather help, if only I knew how."

"Dear me, Mary!" said Mrs. Ronald, cheerfully. "Is she so ill—or he so destitute?"

Mrs. Cuthbert looked cavernously at them. "There is such a thing as having too much confidence."

"Out with it, Mary. Upon whom is the lonely Timothy casting his false black eye?"

Another carriage spared the lilac one her answer; the ponies were trotting up with Mrs. Delair; her groom held the reins, Timothy Tingle sat in the rumble.

"He calls me his consolation," said the adequate lady, crossing the porch. She too was a cool vision of Summer, in *crêpe de barège*.

Scarce less adequate was Timothy. "I offered to get out at the gate, but was told such a move would confirm the worst."

Mrs. Joe Gwynedd had now just come down stairs, and to her Mrs. Cuthbert whispered ominously: "He would have got out at the gate, but they saw I saw them."

"Dear Mrs. Cuthbert, the groom sees them all the time."

"Oh, the groom! She understands his use, and he knows his place."

"Well, Gwynedd. Well, Maria. How d'ye do everybody."

An erect, slim, high-bred, dangerous-looking old lady sat speaking from her carriage. Her eyebrows and nose were to be seen first, then the wicked sparkle of her eyes. Some sort of white shawl was tied round her neck, but instead of making her look dowdy, it increased her rakishness. Her voice croaked, rakish and vigorous.

"Tingle, you come and get me out of this thing. I haven't a joint in my legs to-night."

The host and Tingle both hastened forward.

"Don't touch me, Gwynedd, we'd both fall. I'm a broken umbrella. Here Tingle, I'll lean on your shoulder. How handsome you are! Gracious! If there was nobody looking I'd kiss you. How you'd hate that! Gwynedd, I'll kiss you anyhow. You don't look forty in this light. But I know the year you were born, my boy. I hope you've got something very good to eat. I'm not hungry, but I'm greedy. Well, Mary Cuthbert, how are you? You didn't know you were to have the pleasure of seeing me to-night? Then you haven't had a chance to take away my character. Let me sit down. I'm a broken umbrella. Seventy next month. Well Joe, how d'ye do? If you're a true son of your father you're not good enough for your wife. Who's that young man? I don't know that young man."

Henry Sumner was presented to the formidable and frisky old lady. She had told the truth about her age. Truth was an old habit with her; nobody remembered when she hadn't told it; she would appear to have begun life as a privileged character, and she sustained the part to her latest breath; happily this was not destined to be drawn yet for more than twenty years. She may have suffered somewhat from rheumatism; but I think it likely that she was pleased to put on a good many extra touches of infirmity for the fun of it; old people are fairly prone to this amusement. I have seen her hop across a crowded street as lively as a bird. She was Mrs. James Poyntell—an Aunt of Uncle Andrew's; and she was Aunt, or cousin, or something through blood, or through marriage, to almost everybody assembled on the porch of Evans Gwynedd, as well as to a great many more people than that. Henry Sumner had never before heard any lady address men by their last names. The effect of a stranger upon her was immediate, though of short duration.

"Mr. Sumner, you mustn't mind me. I hope that you're having a pleasant visit?"

Henry assured her that he was indeed.

"You come as a friend of Joe's. Joe, are you doing anything for Mr. Sumner?"

"He's doing so much," said Henry, "that he has made me promise to stay three days over my time."

"I like young people. I'm having some to tea on Thursday. Joe, can't you bring Mr. Sumner? You'll not have to talk to me, for there'll be at least three very pretty girls." This invitation being gratefully accepted, the old lady began to question the Bostonian amiably. He was telling her what people and what things he had seen, when high-tea was announced upon the arrival of the final guest, who said that he feared he was late.

"You are late, Johnnie Adair," said Mrs. Poyntell, "and I can say so because it's not my own house. Is the United States safe for the night? Have you tucked it up in bed? I suppose that's what delayed you. Gwynedd, come and help me up. Ouch! Walk slowly, or I'll break."

At the old lady's question about the safety of the country, Henry Sumner looked hopefully at Johnnie Adair. Was this a reformer at last, a brother spirit in Monopolis, concerned

with public problems and Democracy, and not exclusively
devoted to his own private well-fare and to dining out with
the right people? Then he and the brother spirit would confer
over the cigars, and he would learn more about the strange
state of municipal affairs in Monopolis.

When they were seated at the excellent and skilfully devised
meal, Henry Sumner could not help the sense of pleasure that
invaded him. The mahogany table, without a cloth, shone
with a mellow lustre; the family silver shone; the glasses were
bright; so were the decanters upon the handsome side-board.
How very good the food was Henry didn't know, but he
knew how good-looking were those who ate it. He appreci-
ated the distinguished nose, the strong face, the delightful
smile of his host; and not a woman sat there who did not in a
way remind him of the people whom he had always admired
in Boston. The resemblance was by no means complete; these
Monopolitans had something which he could not describe,
but which he knew that his friends and relations at home had
not. On the other hand, his own people possessed something
which these people seemed to lack; and this thought gave him
a new pride in his own people. With impressions of this kind,
young puritan Henry Sumner looked at the laughing, lively
company.

Old Mrs. Poyntell had her impression too, announced at
once in her own particular manner:

"Upon my word!" She surveyed them all, and then
addressed Sumner. "You shall be treated better in my house,
young man."

Gwynedd laughed. "Now look out, everybody! Something's
coming."

The frisky lady beat upon his shoulder with a clenched fist.
"Why have you collected us old girls for this Boston boy?"

The lawyer looked at his very pretty and young daughter-
in-law. "What have you to say to that, Nellie?"

There was some malice in her reply. "We're quite young enough for Mr. Sumner."

Mrs. Poyntell grew alert. "Now what does the child mean by that?"

"She means," explained Henry Sumner, "that I'm made of wood."

"But are you?" asked Mrs. Delair, softly.

"Please, won't you test me?" said Henry, to his own amazement.

"Why Henry, you're developing!" shouted Joe.

"He's never said a thing like that to me," said Nellie; "and we've often been alone for hours."

"He's not all things to all women," Mrs. Ronald remarked.

A little quick mischief came into Nellie's eyes. "I wonder if he isn't all things to one woman—somewhere!"

Poor Henry Sumner! Scarlet instantly mantled in his young cheeks and forehead.

"Look at him!" cried Nellie.

But Henry was game. "Well, Mrs. Joe, you'd make a horse blush!"

General laughter gave him the victory, Tingle's ho-ho! ha-ha! sounding for the first time. It recalled the Buena Vista to Henry Sumner. He now perceived that the ho-ho's hadn't come out in this house so blithely as at the hotel. Tingle's mirth was apparently tempered, diluted, for the present company. In fact, as Henry now watched him conversing to right and left, he saw an exquisitely adjusted Tingle, a Tingle finer and quieter, from head to foot, inside and out. To be sure, Timothy couldn't change his eyes:—and the women liked him; this was plain; even Mrs. Cuthbert liked him when he was beside her.

"Sally writes to-day," he was saying to Mrs. Cuthbert; "here's her letter." It came out of his pocket, and sentences were read from it.

(Mrs. Cuthbert said later to Nellie when the ladies had left the gentlemen: "I doubt if it was her letter at all. I couldn't see the writing.")

But how did Timothy Tingle manage to be a sort of opera-glass, screwing himself to suit all eyes? "Not that they see through him," thought Henry Sumner. "But Joe's right about him." And he watched Timothy the adroit.

Sundry fish, animals and other living creatures there are (we know this from science) that take on whatever at the moment is the safest color for their well-being. Are these fish and so forth aware they do it? Henry Sumner looked at Timothy again; did this promising Tingle calculate his effects, or did they manage themselves, like the circulation of his blood? Possibly the young man's eyes gave the answer. From them it might be fair to conclude that their adjustable owner never for one unqualified instant forgot that whoever he was talking to, banker or boot-black, might in some urgent hour turn out to be useful to him.

Mrs. Poyntell now fixed her merry, merciless eyes upon him. "Tell us about yourself, Tingle."

"Oh, I'm not interesting! I wish I was."

"But we all know better. How many rungs have you climbed this week?"

It took away Henry Sumner's breath: so they did see through him, then! But this appeared not to disturb him, he lost no breath. His answer—a modulated ho-ho!—was perfection.

Mrs. Poyntell stuck to it. "I've not seen you for a month of Sundays, Tingle. Don't tell me you've not been climbing!"

"Not a rung. I'm on the ground. Fame's only visible through a telescope in the clearest weather." Another diluted ho-ho! rounded it off.

"I'll live to see you at the top, Tingle. I'm not sure—yet—what your genius is—but you have it. How's your partner?"

"Sally? Coming home from the shore to-morrow."

"No, child, not Sally. Your partner, Mr. What's-his-name. The nice ugly man who doesn't brush his hair."

"Tom McNary? Oh! He's very well, thank you. As well as you can be down on the ground!"

"Ah, he's more likely to stay there," remarked the terrible old lady. "They tell me he is criticizing the politicians. Can't you stop him?"

"Never!" laughed Tingle the unperturbed. "He's my most respectable asset!" But a slight dampness now shone on Tingle's forehead; it was the only symptom that he showed.

During this assault, Mrs. Cuthbert had been watching Mrs. Delair's face closely, but that lady was in animated talk with Evans Gwynedd; thus Mrs. Cuthbert suffered disappointment.

Johnnie Adair spoke to the stranger. "What have you seen that interested you most, Mr. Sumner?"

"It won't be a girl!" Nellie Gwynedd interposed.

Henry gave her that smile which Mrs. Ronald liked. "Second to all the girls, I'll name one man."

"He means you, Tingle," said Mrs. Poyntell.

"I don't know him, and I've forgotten his name," said Sumner. He looked at Joe. "That man at the Hemisphere Hotel. You called him your king bird of prey."

Evans Gwynedd caught the phrase, and stopped in the middle of a sentence.

Henry explained further: "He always chooses your State treasurer."

"Why Joe," said his father, "what on earth have you been saying to Mr. Sumner?"

Joe looked a bit dogged, and a bit like somebody caught at something.

Evans Gwynedd now quickly laughed it off. "Mr. Sumner has been to the Zoölogical Gardens, where of course he saw birds of prey." The lawyer was vexed with himself for taking Joe up at such a public moment. He glanced round his table and was relieved to find the surface rippling with light conversation. There were times when he regretted having sent Joe to Harvard; that New England atmosphere seemed to give a warp to young minds.

But once more Mrs. Ronald had glanced at her lawyer brother as he spoke. She saw that same expression of face, she caught that same tone of voice which had caused her the vague bewilderment when he had spoken of the Hythes. Surely this was new in him! She couldn't remember anything like it when she had been a little girl and he a college boy of twenty, her splendid elder brother. She couldn't remember anything like it, until—how far did it go back? She could fix no date. Perhaps the change was in herself; perhaps life had tarnished something in her; how could this brother ever be anything but right? She rose, and the ladies left the gentlemen to their cigars.

"That man has a remarkable face," said Henry to Johnnie Adair. Now was the time at last to discuss municipal problems with the brother reformer who had tucked the United States safe in bed for the night. "A face once seen," continued Henry, "not to be forgotten."

The tucker-in was at a loss; he looked it.

"He means Mark Beaver," said Joe.*

"Joe," said his father, "it isn't well, my boy, to speak recklessly of people, even when they are—a—public character. Our second statesman—in a few years he will be our first statesman—is a man of parts, Mr. Sumner. He falls in the class with Webster, Clay, and those great figures, and it is merely because he happens to be our contemporary that we don't do him justice."

"Well, father, when the last election came, everybody knows he owed—"

"Nobody knows it, sir! Do you believe what some black-guard paper happens to say for the purpose of making sensation? Mark Beaver is a man I esteem. A remarkably well read man, Mr. Sumner, by the way. Our commonwealth should be thankful that she has such a statesman to make her interest identical with his own."

"And some of her capital too," muttered Joe, unheard by his father, but suspected of further treason.

"What's that, Joe? Mr. Sumner, you must remember that our Joe resembles Gratiano,* in that he talks an infinite deal of nothing. You know Mark Beaver, Mr. Adair?"

"I know his cigars, sir."

"Your father knows him well. A great reader. A broad mind. With sentiment, too. His feeling for the Delaware Indians is deeply touching."

"My father's?" asked Johnnie, astonished.

"No, no, Mark Beaver's!" And Gwynedd engaged Tingle in particular conversation.

Mrs. Ronald was not present to hear her brother upon Mark Beaver, to note the waving of his hand, the forensic cadence, and that look in his face expressing tolerant wisdom, wisdom that would be annoyed were it not so wise. At that moment the ladies were discussing Timothy Tingle (whose ears might have burned—one ear at least) and Mrs. Ronald had said prophetically: "Time will get even with the successful Timothy. In ten years he will be fat."

"Mr. Adair," said Joe in the Library, whither they had withdrawn to smoke, "there seems to be a conflict of opinion about your great man: is he a Webster or a bird of prey?"

"All I know about him is the black cigars he smokes."

"Oh, let him have all the private vices!" said Joe. "I only ask for purity in his public life."

"The American people prefer it the other way round," said Henry to Adair.

"Do they?" said Johnnie.

"Don't you think so? Doesn't it generally seem to satisfy them if a public thief is faithful to his wife?"

"Well, very likely. I'm not in the way of hearing much of that."

"Oh!" Henry looked interrogatively at his brother reformer. "Then perhaps your line is the school system? Or is it charities? Or immigration?"

"He's in the navy," said Joe; and mirth doubled him up for a while.

Henry Sumner abandoned all hope of meeting brother reformers in Monopolis after this. There were some in the city, but his path was not likely to cross theirs. The warp which New England atmosphere had given to Joe's lively mind was enough to inspire him with remarks that grated upon his father's ears, but more than this is required to make a reformer. Other topics were therefore now chosen by the young men, until Evans Gwynedd and Tingle came to the end of their particular conversation, and their cigars.

"Shall we join the ladies?" said Gwynedd.

All rose.

"As to that matter," said Tingle, "keep in touch with the old man."

Gwynedd nodded. "I understand."

"He can see you through," Tingle finished. "And anything I can do——."

Gwynedd nodded again. He looked like a wise man who has had a talk satisfactory to him.

The ladies soon began to exclaim that they had no idea it was so late; good-byes and good-nights followed, and the putting on of wraps, and the calling of carriages. Mrs. Cuthbert hoped for something more to occur between Mrs. Delair and Tingle; it did—in her opinion.

"If you're going home by the upper road," said Mrs. Adair, "I'll take you as far as the corners."

Timothy thanked her; he was going by the lower road, and needed the walk after a day's office work.

Mrs. Cuthbert felt this to be full of significance, and said so to Mrs. Joe. "Cool impudence" was her phrase.

Mrs. Joe thought Mrs. Cuthbert tiresome, but kept that to herself.

For Henry Sumner old Mrs. Poyntell had a parting word. "You're coming to me Thursday, remember. And I'll let you teach me to suck eggs. They never will in this house." She was assisted into her carriage, warning everybody to lift her carefully, because she was a broken umbrella.

To his mother in Boston Henry wrote that night, sitting up in his bed-room. His mother was a widow of the Civil War, one of those who live their lives in the sanctification of their sacrifice. The sword of their dead husband had drawn a magic circle around them, as a poetic orator has said.

"Dear Mother: This ought not to be my first letter since I left you, but my hosts keep me going all the time in their kind, hospitable way, so that I have had little chance for anything beyond enjoyment, and some study of this place, which I ought to study more. I've learned nothing about the sparrows. I am enjoying myself extremely. These people have something I wish we had more of. I miss something in them that we certainly have. Professor Lovejoy used to say in English Five* that if Browning and Swinburne had been rolled into one, we should have had a really great poet. Boston and Monopolis are somewhat analogous to Browning and Swinburne. Of course I would never exchange our quality for theirs. The other day when I was talking to a perfectly charming girl about the Australian ballot* (there are lots of

pretty girls here) what do you suppose she said. "Oh, jigger!
As long as we're all so nice and have such a nice time, why
worry about the horrid politicians?" I never heard a Boston
girl say anything so irresponsible. You haven't an idea how
cordial these people are. They pass you on to more and more
friends, who ask you to do something pleasant with them.
You find they know more than they seem to. They have an
ease and a way of talking that seldom suggests books. But
many of them read the same books we do. They're very like
us in having been here a long while, and caring about this,
and everybody seems to be related to everybody, which is like
us. It makes a sort of rich close-knit social texture that no
cities but old ones can have. They value their old things, side-
boards, pictures, libraries, just as we do. But their family portraits seem different from ours, which I find rather stiff and
cold. Their family portraits are apt to look as if they had been
dining together rather convivially. Did you ever read *Tom
Jones?* Monopolis reminds me of Fielding, somehow. I wish I
could explain myself better. These people are the most personal people I ever saw. I don't mean they are rude. Their
manners are far better than ours. But it's always persons, and
not things, with them. One old lady here to-night would
seem rude if I wrote what she said. She said quite awful
things; but nobody minded, and everybody swears by her—
not at her; she said something to me that I actually liked, but
would not like usually at all. I have said the girls are very
pretty. I am quite sunburned from rowing. We had a river-
party. That was like Fielding. The girls carried off a situation
with one of the men who had supped too well that would
have floored any girl in Boston.

"But the city is a shame. They're proud of it, yet take no
care of it. They don't seem to feel it's their business. The bad
gas, the bad water, the nasty street-cars that tinkle torpidly

through streets paved with big cobble-stones all seem to them quite right. It surprises them if you mention it. Their new city-hall, not a quarter finished yet, though it's been going on I forget how many years,* has a fence around it covered with nothing but advertisements of whiskey. Their school buildings are filthy. I heard a teacher who spoke ungrammatically and pronounced like a gutter-snipe teaching the children English. As for their magistrate courts, you can go into them and tell any lie you choose about anybody, and have them arrested, and yet not be liable for perjury. Swearing to these lies is a profitable profession here. Could any despotism have a neater trick to choke off its enemies? I mentioned this to several people, but they never had heard of it! But if I once start on Monopolis's politics I shall write till morning. But isn't it strange that such nice people should tolerate such a nasty state of things? Good-night. Your affectionate Henry.

"P.S. They are even more absurd than we are about society. They think no girl or man, no matter how worthy, should be let in simply on personal merit. I shall never hold such an opinion."

Mrs. Sumner, in Boston, read this letter with interest, and no portion of it interested her more than the final sentence. It is a great and common error to suppose that only female correspondents reserve their heart for the postscript.

When Henry Sumner returned to his home, he had much to say of his visit to Monopolis; and his mother found him intelligent, as she always did. His cousin Chauncey Chippendale, a youth patterned more on the Monopolis plan, found him entertaining also. For in summing up Monopolitans, Henry said:

"They are at their best at table, and at their worst when confronted with an abstract idea."

"Well, old man," said Chauncey, "while they had you, they were confronted with an abstract idea all the time!"

Before we again meet Henry Sumner, he will have been married, and happily, to the girl he saw at the fancy ball. He stuck to his opinion, and he proved a lover more ardent than might be predicted from the chilly qualms he had felt in Monopolis. His union proved acceptable to his family—this was helped, possibly, by the very large fortune which the lady unexpectedly brought him. I think he was too good for her; but if you want to know more about her, you must read the admirable chronicle of the Chippendale family, written by my friend Robert Grant.*

X

Shows an old-fashioned grandmother
in advance of her generation.

Society was disappointed again! There wasn't any scandal, after all. The bridegroom hadn't lapsed into what the lady at Ap Thomas was pleased to term his awful habits. He wasn't in Idaho or Paris or Brazil or sailing his yacht in the Mediterranean with an unmentionable person whom everybody had mentioned. No; he was just simply at home again from Birmingham, Alabama; sober, too. His sobriety was a daily sight. No clock was more regular than this uninteresting young man. Business held him attentive to work, going into town and coming out like anybody else—even more often than many at this season of the year—in short without a rag of disrepute on his back to stimulate conversation for the neighbors. So they dropped him from their conversation, after shaking their heads ominously: very likely it would turn out yet that there was something behind it all. Had they been asked, Behind what all? lucid explanation might have been found difficult. Had they been told, Dear ladies, you are merely displeased with this young man because he hasn't fulfilled your expectations by doing something bad—they would not have been comforted.

Yes; the bridegroom was home from the South, and four-teen letters from him to his bride during his absence, lay bound with ribbon and treasured among her tokens. These had not come every day, he had been prevented from keeping his promise so punctually; emergencies arising in the business in Alabama had several times obliged him to take horse and visit some rough hills that were out of the beaten way. She had found the separation long, very long toward the end. June being passed and July becoming well established, this mere change in the calendar added imaginary lengths to her suspense—for it had proved more than passive solitude. She even spoke a few words of reproach. How could he stay away so long? He was puzzled by her. In his very last letter had he not written that though the business was unconcluded, he would leave it so? So had he left it; necessary witnesses were still not to the fore, still had to be found, the Southern courts were—to say the least—not expediting matters; he would have to go back and put it through himself sometime, but not soon. He had so arranged as to tie up everything down there, that he might come to her up here. Surely all this was plain in his letter? And was it not plain in all the letters how he had chafed at each new delay? Didn't she know how he had hated to leave her? All these truths—for truths they were, and as such she knew them—left clouds in her face; she gazed at him through tears, holding his coat, and looking up at him silently. If man could fully comprehend woman, or she him, where would romance fly to? Let us give thanks for the eter-nal misunderstanding.

Their talk left him still puzzled. He could not see in what he had failed. She repeated that she had missed him so. Then did she think that he had not missed her? Whatever either of them said left it unsolved for him, though there was so little to be said, and this so simple. Silence at length seemed to him a better plan—silence with much tenderness. It was a better plan, it would have been so from the first, his words did no good; they were all true, but what had truth to do with this? His excuse—if he needs one—must be that he was young, and a husband of but brief experience. She hid her head in his coat and wept, while he sat holding her most wretchedly.

It was not until many hours after this first one of arrival, that the puzzle was solved. At her blush and her whisper he caught her in a new embrace.

Not until next morning did it come into his slow mind to ask, did his mother know their news. Then, indeed, was he reproached. Did he suppose that anybody should hear this before himself? Even her own mother in the West knew nothing of it. If Birmingham had kept him away for twice as long, why then—why then, she would have come to Birmingham. But these were cloudless reproaches, these he could understand; with happy laughter he acknowledged his dullness. The new bright July day beamed upon a couple in bliss. No office should take him into town, work could wait, what was Summer for? They spent such a holiday as could be forgotten never. Even among the memories of later holidays that they took, this one bloomed an everlasting rose in a radiance unchanging. Now and then Art closes her eyes and walks more surely in the right road than when she keeps them open. The poetry, the music, the painting, she makes then are like the happiness these two lovers were knowing now; beyond thought, unaccountable, a part of the planet's breath. August found them keeping their secret; how much more it was while no one knew it! It was she, not he, who presently began to say that his mother and hers must not wait longer in ignorance. It was she, because she was a woman; his love for his mother did not give him this deeper understanding. But now he remembered those solemn words: "It is in this house that I

must have grandchildren. Do not let me be disappointed."
Once a woman had made him see it, he could see it: of course
they must tell their mothers. They waited until Madam
Hythe came to pay them a two days' visit; she was spending
her Summer as usual at the sea-shore, in Jacob Hythe's staring varnished palace, that seemed to be built of wafers and
lady-fingers.

After her first joy over the news, joy for them and joy for
herself, she spoke with serious authority. "I should have been
told of this before."

They remonstrated, they begged her pardon, they even attempted to explain. No one else knew, save the bride's mother.

"Hush!" she bade them. And then, with smiles, to her son:
"Go out of this room. What do you know about being a husband or a father? I have things to say to this daughter of mine."

She drew the bride close and kissed her, and then made her
sit down to listen. The bride had learned to love this great
lady who was like no woman she had ever seen; but the great
lady, looking into the girl's eyes, read some timidity there.

"Don't be afraid of me!" she begged in her deep voice.

The answer reached the great lady's heart: the bride didn't
want to be afraid of her; somehow she couldn't seem to help
it! It was a happy, natural answer and it made them both
laugh, which was a good preparation for less timidity.

"But you should have sent for me at once," declared
Madam Hythe.

Even though she understood why they hadn't, she said that
it was an insufficient reason. Weightier considerations were
here at stake: a grandchild's well-fare. She scouted the bride's
next remark, that everybody's well-fare had received the best
professional attention.

"Doctors? Pooh!" said Madam Hythe. "What do they
know?"

But the very best in Monopolis had been consulted, the bride assured her.

And now the great lady expressed herself:

"My child, we are nine months old already when we come into the world."

The bride had not heard this so expressed before.

The great lady took her hand. "It is now that we must have care of character and temperament for the new soul and body, When we are born it is sometimes—many times—too late."

Then she fell to asking questions, listening intently to the answers, and nodding her head. What she heard was mostly of a sort to win her approval. "So far it has been right, though by accident only," she said. "These doctors seldom remember that their medicines are the smallest part of it." Very sage she now grew as she began to lay out the life which the bride must lead. Alarm faded away from her listener; she was to be doomed to nothing. The prescriptions for the well-fare of the new soul and body were easy and natural to such a bride as this. "Have one thought always," said the great lady: "that you are now a mother, and you are already preparing your son for life." The bride smiled at this, unseen; the joke should be kept for her husband. The many counsels made really but one—to be wholesome alike in spirit and in occupation. Simple counsels indeed for such a bride as this to follow; most helpful to the brides of our yellow-rich—but this was before the day of cock-tails, bridge, and female nicotine. The great lady must have detained her daughter-in-law with her during nearly an hour. Advice did not consume the whole of this time, though it must be said that age did most of the talking while youth kept respectful silence. Advice was changed to reminiscence at times; motherhood that looked back opened its heart to motherhood that looked forward; these two women had never drawn so close together before; after reminiscences, advice would come back, and so the hour went. Finally the older woman dismissed the younger one with a word that reached her heart indeed: "Tell your mother from me, my child, that I know how you must want each other. Best go and lie down after all this. But send him to me at once; I have several things to say to him also."

The bride found her husband in their room, expectant. "You're to go to her now."

"What did she say all this time?"

Mirth and blushes filled the bride's face. "She orders a grandson of us."

He threw up his hands. "If the poor baby disobeys her the first thing!"

To him also his mother had much to say; his conduct was now only second in moment to the bride's. Upon him and his solicitude depended entirely the bride's state of mind, he could give serenity to her or destroy this for her by what he did. Let him not be too much absent. Was he affectionate to her in small things? He must remember to bring her little presents—not great rich overwhelming ones, but trifles to show that he had been thinking of her while he was out of her sight. He thought that perhaps he had already performed some of the acts which his mother so earnestly and wisely mentioned, but this son did not tell her so. Since knowledge of paternity had been given him, he had grown in spiritual stature and thus divined something of his mother's heart. With his new light he saw that she was happy, and, perceiving this, had also a clearer revelation than ever before that her happiness was—himself. But then, was he all, and how long had he been all? He put away so dark a question and rose and suddenly kissed her while she was in the midst of a grave recommendation. She sat erect, full of advice-giving and stately responsibility. One unused to her countenance might have

been misled to thinking it severe, and that here was a son
receiving reprimands. The son knew better; his mother was
merely earnest and interested with her whole soul. Those
lines which seemed severe had been drawn by the years of
repression and sacrifice that she had lived. He was not impa-
tient beneath all these counsels, being moulded large by
nature and loving her dearly as well; he silently revelled in
the way that she was telling him what to do, as if he knew
nothing whatever and the whole of experience lay still before
him. He had stretched himself on the floor by her chair in the
old way, and rested his head in the folds of her soft gray dress.
She was talking from sheer happiness, she impressed details
upon him with a lovely importance. And at length, still
stately, and as if a duty had been performed (as had it not?)
she dismissed him with a certain imposing affection.

He stole back to his bride, who craved to hear the latest
orders from their Commander-in-Chief.

The bridegroom laughed joyously. "I felt about eight years
old."

"I felt about six."

And so these two came down to dinner with the Commander-
in-Chief like a pair of children—nay, like a pair of culprits; they
had been lectured separately for their good; after dinner, in
the drawing-room, they were lectured jointly for the same
end; but in no way to embarrass the modesty of either; the
great lady chose her words with tact, aware that intimacy
between three can not trespass upon the confidences that
have been between two. Lecture by no means filled the entire
evening, there was talk upon subjects less personal, and there
was music. The child culprits listened to Chopin and Bee-
thoven, played by the Commander-in-Chief. Such playing
exists no more in our over-fed country—over-fed with operas,
orchestras, singers, players, performers of all sorts, who swarm

in, doing it all for us as we sit stupefied with digestions
impaired. The great lady belonged to the era when many private persons could play with taste in their private houses, and
give pleasure. Thus they listened to a short sonata, and to a
polonaise, and lost themselves in listening: the son watched
his mother's fair white hands; her fifty-eight years had left
them as smooth as a girl's.

Commander-in-Chief she remained, repeating quite often
that they must not allow her to oppress them; they saw her
handsomely leaving them to themselves. They guessed sometimes that she was staying away through fear of oppressing
them. This helped the bride over certain hard moments when
she felt that the great lady's surveillance ran close to the danger
line of oppressiveness. But these moments were lived through
without a petulant word to her husband—without any word
at all; she never forgot how light a burden—compared to
some she had witnessed—her husband's mother made herself. This happy young man had no mother-in-law at hand to
poke her nose into his domesticity and treat him to surveillance. The parents of his bride were stationed at present in
New Mexico, at Fort Bayard, to which no railroad had come
yet; it was a safe, epic distance away from his front-door, a
journey full of sands and shores and desert wildernesses, with
a sprinkling of hostile Indians and cactus. In such circumstances the most inveterate mother-in-law wouldn't be likely
to drop in at any hour of the day and be met walking upstairs
unannounced. This one never did; she consoled herself as
best she could with such news as the mail brought her—by
no means daily. Let us wish for her sake that she had not been
so far away from her child at this time; let us wish it for the
child's sake too; the army daughter seldom betrayed to her
husband those moments when she longed to put her arms
round the neck of her army mother in New Mexico. She

wrote fully and faithfully to Fort Bayard, dwelling often upon the affection of Madam Hythe; but we can hardly be sure how far a commendation of one mother-in-law gives comfort to the other. So, like Madam Hythe, we should be sorry for the absent one: and nobody seems ever to have said that if a mother-in-law were not more than inquiring she would be less than human. For all these good meddlesome ladies I feel deep sympathy, but I shall try to marry an orphan.

The bride and bridegroom went so far once, during a visit,—each venturing this alone—as to ask the Commander-in-Chief what the name should be, supposing—well, just supposing—it was a girl.

The great lady's countenance became august to a point that caused her son to add hastily, "Of course it won't!"

"We will wait until such a thing has occurred." This was the mother's ruling. "He will be named after you, as arranged," she added.

"But if—." The son's words stuck in his throat. He was trying to tease his mother—but courage ebbed suddenly.

"There will be plenty of time for girls," said the Commander-in-Chief, bringing their interview to a conclusion. With the bride she would seem to have been less formidable, although she declined to admit the possibility suggested.

The bridegroom grew jocular over it. "Whose fault will she consider it?" he asked his bride. He thought they had better have a choice of names ready. He grew very jocular; his mother was quite right about there being plenty of time for girls. "Twins, too," he remarked. He computed their future with its offspring; she was not yet twenty-four and he not yet twenty-nine. The bride turned her face away from the amorous hilarity of his talk; and he and she were happy indeed.

From Mort and Dug he had to endure some well-meant and fraternal congratulations that brought the color to his own face. They found him inexorable, however, about health-drinking; not a toast!

Mort expressed reprobation. "What! Not even one to coming events?"

Reprobation failed to move this prospective father. Even when he was seeing his brothers off to Europe, whither they and their wives were going for six weeks among the tailors, he would pledge them in nothing stronger than apollinaris.*

"He's afraid of himself," they told each other. Perhaps they were right.

Madam Hythe did not tell the bride and bridegroom everything that she had in her mind concerning them; there was a step now which she could not take without being advised first. Her pride, as we have seen, held the general world, even those who often visited her house, far off from any knowledge or suspicion of her opinions about family matters; but, as has also been said, there was one visitor to whom a more intimate glimpse was opened. She wrote a note, she made an appointment, and one morning Evans Gwynedd stood at his office-door to admit her.

Tingle was coming out of this same private door; and to see the lady there caused him wonder. Her name had not been mentioned to him by Gwynedd during the confidential talk they had just completed. Gwynedd expected a "client on business"; this was the extent of his reticent remark. His way was apt to be more explicit, he would say "so and so is coming in a few minutes, when you will have to excuse me." Madam Hythe a client? Tingle had been in consultation with Gwynedd, during which he was careful to say several times how rejoiced he felt over Gwynedd's prospects. If more men like Gwynedd took such a view of their public duties (declared Timothy) the public would be better off. Now Gwynedd, although knowing that words from Tingle were never worth their weight in more than brass, yet was pleased to hear this. He had smiled and waved it aside as undeserved, and the consultation about the prospects had gone on until the client was announced. It was a pleased Tingle who went away; he was being useful to Gwynedd in this matter of prospects and of public duty. What is sweeter than service to those who may possibly some day serve you? Tingle's guesses about what could have brought Madam Hythe to the office of Evans Gwynedd were busy for a while, and also quite wide of the mark, and did neither harm nor good to himself or any one else: Tingle did much ingenious guessing about other people's business—but he never allowed this pastime to make him forget his own.

Mrs. Ronald had wondered if her brother were in love with Madam Hythe; this had appeared to her, immediately, a nonsensical surmise, to be dismissed. But—has anybody counted how many states of love there are? Love, we may be sure, is a bargain that two are needed to make in most cases; yet it is to be doubted if we have discovered any scales delicate enough to weigh every quantity of this passion. A bargain may be struck: the man's eyes, the whole man except his spoken words, may betray what he would hide. And the woman, reading this, may not reply at all, yet give him his answer. Then, she being honest, the bargain hangs upon his fibre. He may stay and serve, not only expecting no more, but knowing her to be far above granting more. To call this platonic would be error, for somewhere in it there is sacrifice. There is to be no way of learning what sentiment Evans Gwynedd felt for this great lady, unless it appear through his course during these later years of his life.

"You are going to think me superstitious," she began in her deep voice, but smiling.

"Aren't you going to sit down?" he asked.

She gave her cloak to him, beautiful and gray (she always dressed in white or gray, and always in her own fashion) and she took the chair that he placed for her.

"How shall I begin?" she said, with her eyes fixed thoughtfully upon him. He watched the fire smouldering in their depths, and waited.

"I do not like round about ways," she pursued. "You will tell me if I have no right to ask you this: Has my son made his will?"

She had several sons, but Gwynedd did not need to ask which one she meant. "You have a perfect right. I might not feel that I had the right to answer you, but in this case I can with entire propriety. He has not—at least, I have drawn none for him."

"Do you think that he may have gone to someone else?"

"It would be the first time in his life that he hasn't consulted me in a matter of business."

"Then I don't believe he has gone to anyone else.—I wish that he had sometimes consulted you in matters that were not business."

The lawyer bowed. "I am too old," said he. "Not even my own sons consult me much." His smile was more like a sigh.

"Will your country never learn to listen to experience?" demanded Madam Hythe.

"Never until it has had some," returned Evans, still with the same smile.

"And that will be too late," said she. "But people do not care about consequences until they have felt them.—Mr. Gwynedd, I am extraordinarily alone." No complaint was in her voice, merely a profound recognition.

Once again he bowed, but in silence. Who was there that understood her exile and isolation so well as he?

"If my son has made no will he—must make one." She spoke very slowly, each word full and quiet, with a power stronger than emphasis.

"In his journeys to these wild regions, he runs danger. Perhaps he has not told you of a man in a sleeping-car who would have shot him if he had not knocked him down first? Oh, he knocked him senseless." The mother smiled as she thought of it. "But if he were some day—not to come home—there is much money and property. Some of this I think is all his own—he has been very energetic since he became steady—he is steady, you know, now—but some things I think he must own with his brothers, possibly, and with his father. I do not want to ask you any questions that I should not. But the care and management of his fortune—ought it to be left to what others might arrange if he—were not here?"

"I will think this over," said Gwynedd. Jacob Hythe was in his mind; he must beware of offending that great man.

Madam Hythe smiled again. "No, my friend, you and I will think it over now, together, if you please. In March the child will arrive. Everything must be secure for him."

Evans Gwynedd smiled also. "I don't think I have heard his name yet."

"It is Romney, of course," said the grandmother. "We will think it over together, now. I will tell you what should be done, and you will tell me how it can be done. That fortune must be in hands that must never touch it except for its own benefit, until the boy is old enough to take care of it himself. My husband might wish to use it—honestly—in something that he was doing on his own account. Mortimer and Douglas might wish to do the same, and that would be even less good. There must be no risk, Mr. Gwynedd."

The lawyer thought gravely for some moments. Then: "Must this advice be volunteered by me? Can you not give it yourself?"

"I shall do so when I can say that you approve the step; and I see already that you do approve it. You have—are they not called trustees? So! There would be much complication if—

my son did not knock the next man down first." She leaned forward and laid a hand upon his arm. "My friend, I am extraordinarily alone. Let my son make his will before he sets out on another journey. And I desire that you shall be trustee. His fortune must be in hands that never shall touch it, except for its own benefit." The repeated words deepened in tone and urgency.

She rose, and over Gwynedd's face swept a look which softened and ennobled it. Let Jacob Hythe take offense if he so chose; this woman was right. "Tell your son that I do approve it," he said, "and tell him to come and see me."

They both forgot that he had explained nothing to her about the law, that they had not thought it over together, since she had thought of the needful thing by herself. The mere technicalities of the will could now be left to those who had lacked the prudence to see that such a will should be made. As he was showing her out to her carriage, she turned to him on his door-step:

"I am sure that you don't believe in dreams, Mr. Gwynedd."

"Perhaps not, perhaps not!"

"Has no dream ever frightened you?"

"In childhood, yes, I can remember—"

"But not in age? Then I will not tell you mine, for you will think me superstitious.—Yes, I will!" she exclaimed, suddenly and unaccountably. "Twice I have seen a train rushing through the night. There were lights in the windows of all the cars except the last one, and that was black. A body was stretched out in it. I could not see the face, but I knew who it was. I have told this to no one else."

He tried to make a light answer. "But you know that you would have consulted me without the help of any dream." More he would have said; he could not; some torrent of awe had come from her, and his words as he handed her into the carriage were a mere formal good-bye. He stood looking at the vehicle as it drove away over the cobble-stones and around the corner of the square upon which his office fronted; and in his brain the words were repeated:

"His fortune must be in hands that never shall touch it, except for its own benefit."

The bell, tolling noon in the old tower that looked over the square, recalled him from his revery. He looked up at the tower and then at the branches of the quiet trees; then he wheeled round and re-entered his office.

XI

*Contains sundry wise reflections and
tells how Tingle climbed a rung.*

No young devils of law students ever observed their precep-
tor with more affection and less reverence than the sprightly
lads in the office of Evans Gwynedd observed him. Impertinent they were not; there was a tradition that he could be ter-
rific if he chose—but nobody now in the office had seen him
so. This place was almost the last of its kind in Monopolis;
boys were beginning to go to law-schools. Hitherto, the manufacture of Monopolis lawyers had been conducted more per-
sonally, by the eminent elders of the bar, to whose care it was
esteemed a great chance for a youth to be entrusted. What such
a lucky youth did was (usually) to sit reading his Blackstone,*
learning by heart what that author had to say in his excellent English about Law and Equity, Persons and Things, the
Statute of Quia Emptores and the Rule in Shelley's Case. Upon
these and cognate matters the eminent elder would from
time to time "quizz" the boy, who thus ripened gradually into
something or other, went up for the oral examinations and
having passed these duly entered upon his professional career.
Many admirable lawyers were thus made in Monopolis dur-

ing several generations; but there were moments when you wouldn't have thought it. Evans Gwynedd came in so suddenly from his revery on the door-step, that it is a mercy his nose wasn't struck off by the bevelled-edged ebony ruler which Dicky Lawne just then hurled at Bob Adair. Aleck Croxton was seated on the mantle-piece, playing a jew's-harp accompaniment for Billy Cheswold, who was singing a lightly turned set of rhymes, most improper, to the tune of *Voici le sabre de mon père,* while he danced upon some volumes of Meeson and Welsby* that were arranged like dominoes upon the floor. No dissembling could be improvised; there they were.

But Evans merely smiled at them while he stood surveying this legal arena. "I don't go to lunch quite so early, boys," he remarked. Then he picked up the missile that had so nearly disfeatured him. "If this had hit me, Dicky, would the action have lain in Tort or Assumpsit? Remember you are *deins age,* an infant."

"I'm afraid I am an infant, sir," remarked Dicky, truthfully.

"Well, well, young gentlemen! You must cut up, of course; but I wish you'd manage to do it before you arrive, or after you go. What do you think?"

"Yes, sir," they severally murmured, and Evans went back into his private room.

A brief silence attended his exit, broken at length thus:

"He's always such a regular brick."

"Do you know who the lady was?"

"Never saw her before."

"Evidently foreign."

"It's something important. Lepidus Senex* never looks like that unless it's important."

It will be seen that these lads knew their Latin comedies. In those pre-historic days it was not yet generally understood that to force a free-born American boy to know anything, was an insult to his manhood. Lepidus Senex may, for the benefit of such readers as have not been insulted by obligatory classics, be translated "gay old cock." Had Evans Gwynedd been aware that it was thus his irreverent boys described him, I am not sure how well he would have liked it.

He could not have been described so now, during this noon hour, while he sat at his desk jotting notes. That softened and ennobled look which Madam Hythe's appeal had brought to his face, came back again two or three times. She had begged him to assume a great responsibility, she had spoken to him as he knew she spoke to no one else in the world, he was all the friend she had to turn to. He had been absolutely trusted by a proud, sad, reserved woman, and his spirit rose to accept the challenge, rose to its full height, the level which his sister knew and loved and below which he had begun to live almost habitually. Treat a man as if he were better than himself and you will often make him better than himself—for a while, at least. Evans turned his back on the Safe Side; if what he was going to do should make Jacob Hythe angry, he could stand such anger. Was he not the bridegroom's legal adviser?

He jotted his notes between intervals of thinking, at which times he leaned back, striking his pencil against his handsome teeth. Twice or thrice he rose and pulled out boxes to read certain papers that were in them. There was, indeed, property of all sorts to be cared for, nursed, managed, possibly to be sold at some right moment, or held during years for the right moment to come; personalty and realty, some of this last owned jointly and even severally. No one in Monopolis knew better how to provide for and against everything than Evans Gwynedd. At that time trust companies were not common; even had they been so, such a complicated estate as this required persons, not corporations, to see to it. The lawyer drew a long breath and jotted down two or three final memoranda, as the bell in the tower tolled one. Its vibrations passed quietly through the quiet branches of the trees, and Evans listened to them.

"His fortune must be in hands that never shall touch it, except for its own benefit."

With the sound of the bell these words returned to his brain once more, so clearly that he heard the solemn voice which had spoken them first.

As chief counsel for The Railroad (these capitals are not big enough to fit the importance of that great institution, but bigger ones would deface my page)—as chief counsel for The Railroad, Evans Gwynedd was expected at a Safe Side lunch in thirty minutes. Jupiter and Pluto and the other gods of Monopolis would confer pleasantly over plates and glasses at half-after one, and Evans, desiring to arrive a little in advance of the hour, locked his notes up, and came out upon the beautiful old square.*

Several passers-by touched their hats to the leader of the bar. It was pleasant and natural to greet with respect any man of appearance so eminent and reassuring. His handsome brow wore the air of carrying the town and all its fortunes gallantly to a safe and prosperous future; nothing could possibly go wrong while such a sharp eye was always watching out; could anything be more reliable than the crispness of those clean, short, silvered side-whiskers? The ruddy cheeks were hardened with horse-back exercise in all weathers, the nose had a dozen successful grandfathers in its chiselled bridge, the pepper and salt clothes so good, the feet so well-shaped, their boots polished so bright, the lean height of the man and his carriage and step as he walked—how excellent was it all, how perfectly it matched the very square itself! The small buildings with great lawyers inside them have been replaced to-day by great buildings with small lawyers inside them, lawyers without any special identity, all crated like eggs in tiers twenty stories high. No lawyer such as Gwynedd walks along the old square any more. He was a part of it. It was a part of him. His ancestors, his dear town, had made it, and over his childhood its serene and lovely influence had flowed like a baptism. Upon its acres illustrious feet had trod, feet historic, feet revolutionary; no worthy stranger could behold this place and its renowned adjacent halls without knowing in his heart that here remained not merely the site of great deeds by-gone, but a voice, that, night and day, still breathed the message of those deeds to mankind. Nothing like the square could be made to-day, nor any lawyer like Gwynedd, and Dicky Lawne, Bob Adair, Aleck Croxton and Billy Cheswold will always remember and boast that they were once his students. Among others who saluted the lawyer as he passed along the square, were Mrs. Delair and Timothy Tingle. They were descending together the easy steps of the library, quaint with its Greek pilasters and old-time simplicity.*

"He orders me to read this," said Mrs. Delair, holding out a volume to Gwynedd.

The lawyer saw the title. "A very clever writer. You had best be obedient." Smiling, he passed on. "Now I wonder about those two," he thought. "Poor Sally should have married a less—a less—." He didn't finish; and he strolled onward down-town to the offices of Jupiter, Pluto, and the rest of the gods.

The same lady who compared the grass at Ap Thomas to the lawn of an English vicarage, had once remarked that Evans Gwynedd looked like an English duke. I can't say that she was mistaken, although the two or three dukes I have seen did not remind me of him; I believe that I have seen pictures of Englishmen with authoritative noses and supercilious eyes, who evidently bathed, showered, and put on a clean shirt every morning, which bore a sort of general likeness to Gwynedd—but I'm not sure that any of them were dukes. Be that as it may, Jupiter, President of The Railroad,* certainly looked like an English coachman of the veteran, mid-Victorian type. Short white hair, very short white whiskers—shorter than Gwynedd's—thick wide body, big mouth and chin, eyes that were at once cold and bold: he needed only livery and a cockade in his hat and a seat on the box of a brougham in Hyde Park to give him a perfect setting. In his black frock coat, though he was undoubtedly Jupiter, he was also undoubtedly vulgar.

As the name of the lawyer was sent in to his private office, he was winding up what must have been a conversation of great interest. He stood up by his broad office table, and on the other side of it was standing Mark Beaver.

"Then it's understood," said Jupiter.

The bird of prey nodded an imperceptible yes.*

"You're sure the Snyder gang will vote right?"

The nod was even more imperceptible. The eye-lid drooped a hair's breadth, the black cigar took a quarter of a twist between the closed lips.

"We mustn't appear in any way," pursued Jupiter.

"Nobody appears." You might have supposed the cigar said it.

"Well, then, there's the price."

"I'm afraid that'll cost fifty thousand dollars. I could place some more free passes to advantage."

"I'll write to you."

"Don't write. Send."

"You'll not stay to lunch with us?"

"Thank you, I'm too busy to-day." It was the visitor's final remark. He went out by a private door. Would you know what

this bird of prey's business was this afternoon? I could tell
you—indeed I did describe him and his doings in the haunt of
relaxation whither he now repaired; but Aunt Carola handed a
pen full of ink to me, saying: "Strike all that out, Augustus.
Everybody knows that the man's life was vile without your
telling us." So I obeyed her.

Jupiter rang a bell. "Show Mr. Gwynedd in." The man in
livery obeyed.

There was cordial greeting between the two, but prelimi-
naries with Jupiter were apt to be short. "Mark Beaver has
just gone out," he said. "That'll be put through the legislature
next week. The riparian owners* won't be able to hold us up
after this.—Well?"

"Tingle reports progress," answered Gwynedd.

Jupiter appeared not to notice it. "Mark Beaver is a great
character," said he, laughing. "Had a book with him. What
do you suppose it was? An account of Semiramis." Jupiter
laughed again. "He's better read than most college presidents.
To-day he talked freely—not always a habit with him. He
said: 'In a Democracy, if you don't drive the people like a
flock of sheep they'll turn to a pack of wolves.'"

"There's a good deal in that," said Gwynedd.

"It's God's own truth," said Jupiter. "You're sure Tingle's
up to the job?"

"Tingle's sure he is," Gwynedd answered.

"Well, we'll call that certainty enough for the present. I
don't want to build a parallel road if I can help it.—* If
Tingle brings it off, we'll make him a director. Old Cheswold
Lawne is getting very shaky.* He'll not last till Spring."

"How far can Tingle go with Boston?" Gwynedd now
inquired.

"Is he sure those people are going to make a bid?"
demanded Jupiter; "they're laying very low."

"Well, he suspects so from the way Baxter Chippendale acted."

"Then he can go as far as five points higher—for a start. I don't want to build a parallel road."

"Lunch is ready, sir," announced the man in livery.

Talk to me, my Muse, I ask not that you sing, you are seldom equal to lyric strains; merely talk, and tell me of these gods at their mid-day meal; how Jupiter with Gwynedd came out of his office, how Mars and Mercury came out of their offices, how Pluto came out (or up) from his office, how every god came out from somewhere, except those who came in from somewhere—the lesser deities, arriving from the outside, like Gwynedd; how these directors and vice-presidents shook hands and spoke of the weather, of the stock market, of the English cricket-match some weeks ago, of the approach of the canvas-back duck season, of freight prospects east of the Missouri, of the foolish game the Erie people were playing, of the deep game the New York Central people* were playing, and of old Suydam and his whiskers and his horses during the Summer at Saratoga; how they sat down and chatted over good soup, some game birds and salad, with cheese and coffee to finish. None took wine, many drank water, whiskey was preferred by some few—the doctors at that time were beginning to recommend Scotch for the venerable and the dilapidated. Upon the features of all, save one, sat the Safe Side visibly, in spite of their good appetites and occasionally good jokes. Poor old Cheswold Lawne had an attendant to bring him along the street—he had been keeping on the Safe Side for nearly four-score years; Spencer Adair had been cautious for some sixty-eight; Atbury Jones, Wilfred Harris, David Pike, Thomas McGee Secane, Frederic Wallingford, Chester Chadd, Edward Brandywine and the rest*—each had begun early to be cautious and had been cautious for twenty-five years at least, and most of them for considerably longer. It was Jupiter alone upon whose daring brow no Safe Side sat, and this was because at the right instant he could always cast caution to the winds; he was a creator, a poet; instead of Pegasus he bestrode locomotives.*

"By the way," said he to Gwynedd, who sat on his right, "how about that woman who lost her legs?"

"They'll compromise," returned Gwynedd, easily. "We can prove contributory negligence."

"I don't like that accident getting into the papers," Jupiter remarked.

"It's lamentable that the public should read these sensational stories," Gwynedd agreed.

"Yes. The papers usually treat The Road right.—Did she die?"

"Two weeks ago."

"Children?"

"Six. Her husband deserted her two years ago, you may remember."

"No, I don't remember. Six children? Well, in the circumstances—the unfortunate publicity which has been given to the matter—fight the suit to the end—get all the delays you can—tire them out—tire their witnesses out—and then when they name their compromise figure, why, double it. Double what they ask. Do you take me? Let The Road pay them of its own free will twice as much as they ask. Then see *that* gets into the papers. All the papers. Do you take me?"

Gwynedd bowed. Jupiter's power had suddenly wakened for a moment to fill his voice with humming vibrations. In spite of his white tie and his black coat, he was unquestionably Olympian.

"How came the thing to get into the papers?" he pursued, chewing on a tooth-pick.

"From the outside, I believe. From a county paper some-where. They had to give it space after that."

"Do you suspect any particular quarter as its source?"

"I only suspect," said Gwynedd.

"Is it that McNary feller, Tingle's partner?"

"I am not certain, you understand," replied the lawyer.

"I'll not have that feller around, bothering me," declared Jupiter. He sat still for a moment, and a frown gathered upon his brow. "That's a bad kind of partner for a rising man to be tied to," he continued. "Better let Tingle know that somehow."

Gwynedd bowed for the third time. He had received an order. He would take it. Jupiter's frown went far. It came into his mind, since Jupiter was being confidential in a way, to speak of his own private ambitions over which he and Tingle had recently conferred. But this inclination was now swept aside by a sudden change in the thoughts of the great man. A story had occurred to him, he burst out laughing, and told it to Gwynedd. To be sure, the slender wit that it contained was smothered altogether by its coarseness—but what could the chief counsel of The Railroad do, except laugh heartily when Jupiter was pleased to jest? He had hardly recovered from this enjoyable mirth when the man in livery brought him a note; the telephone was not yet established, the world stood on the verge of this momentous change, and notes were still sent by hand from office to office.

"May I read this?" asked Gwynedd.

"Surely," answered Jupiter.

The lawyer did so, then handed it to the president, who cried, "O-ho!" with satisfaction. It was from Timothy Tingle, and it announced that he was going away for a week's shooting in the neighborhood of the Bayside Air Line. More it did not say, perhaps Timothy had no more to say yet, and might return without being able to report progress; but the two men understood quite well that Tingle was somehow in active pursuit of that Bayside Air Line so much needed by The Railroad, because its possession would save the heavy expense of constructing a parallel line. Jupiter nodded his approval over Tingle's adroit sounding of Baxter Chippendale.*

"Now why does a man like Tingle want to stick to a man like McNary, when he might become so useful to us?" The threat in these words may not be clear to the innocent; but to Evans Gwynedd it was as plain as if Jupiter had spelled each syllable aloud. The lawyer felt that he would indeed fail in friendliness if he did not convey a warning to young Tingle.

"It's premature to speak to 'em of this," said Jupiter, returning the note to Gwynedd, "but they may as well know about the bill.—Gentlemen," he continued, raising his voice, whereat all the lesser gods down the table became silent and attentive, "Mr. Beaver has informed me to-day that no further anxiety need be entertained by us regarding the riparian owners." There was some clapping of hands. "I'll ask your assent to a trifling special expenditure." The assent was given with alacrity, accompanied with gaiety; Jupiter's asking for their consent, even for the consent of committees, always stirred such sense of humor as was among them. In the management of The Railroad, it was generally the trifles that filled solemn hours of routine and evoked grave discussions among the gods; the great steps were taken imperceptibly, lightly, with a word or two and a nod or two, as if nothing in particular were happening. This was because it had already happened behind the brow of Jupiter, in which invisible spot The Railroad eternally and prosperously resided. Don't pity the riparian owners whom the bill was going to settle. No unrighteous hardship thereby fell upon them. It so happens that they were in the wrong, a set of greedy unthinking rustics, whose single idea was to worry this rich corporation, to bleed it, to make it pay them four prices for the sake of peace from their obstructions. This particular bill would really usher in a public benefit, like many another of The Railroad's measures— and unlike many of them as well. But whether they were good or whether they were bad, Mark Beaver capably saw to it that the legislature "voted right" upon them all. His question never was: Is this a just measure? The bird of prey had a simpler method of doing business. "It will cost you fifty thousand dollars." That was his method invariably; the price— only the price—varied. Why did Jupiter submit to this blackmail? Why did The Railroad pay heavily for justice as well as for injustice? Why was it willing to pour its dollars into the pockets of the scoundrels whom the people elected to serve them? And why did the people elect scoundrels? Don't ask me these questions—I'm asking you. Perhaps we had better both of us ask Democracy what she thinks of her glorious institutions. All I know is, that Jupiter and his Railroad were sowing the wind and that you and I, or our children, shall reap this whirlwind.*

"Yes," said Jupiter to Gwynedd, "we must have Tingle with us. Poor old Cheswold Lawne's breakin' up fast. Wonderful the way he can eat and drink, though. That's his third apple."

He gazed down the table at the little gods, his directors, and jovial laughter shook him quietly.

"What is it?" said Gwynedd.

"David Pike's got that same button off his weskitt he had off last meetin'! Don't he ever spend a *cent* on *any*thing?"

The little gods were now sipping their coffee and puffing their smoke. Here a god helped himself to fruit, there a god was using his finger-bowl, and in sooth they made a representative company. David Pike's shining pate wagged as he chatted to Frederic Wallingford, whose snapping-turtle lips and immovable eye showed him plainly to be a pillar of the state. Chester Chadd, opposite, was ruddy, and his red hair curled—he wasn't old enough to be a pillar quite yet; but next him sat Wilfred Harris, with a face of firm financial importance and a mouth like a slot into which the widow and the orphan could drop their pennies with absolute security; while the appearance of Thomas McGee Secane would have adorned any severe, dissenting pulpit. Nothing on earth would have been the matter with any of these respectable citizens, if only they hadn't all believed quite so hard in keeping on the Safe Side. This creed gave something stale to them; in spite of their various natures and attainments, and their many good and useful qualities, something certainly stale in their voices and their manners made them, as they sat there, like cards belonging to the same pack—a pack which a good many dealers had handled.

Jupiter once again addressed them all: "Gentlemen."

The table's instant attention was upon him, they listened for something further in the way of business news, good or bad; but their president had a joke ready for them this time.

"I've a motion to read," he said. "'Resolved, that the treasurer be authorized to expend a sum not exceeding twenty-five cents for the restoration of the missing button on Brother Pike's waistcoat.' Is it seconded? Those approving will signify—"

How the gods laughed! It wasn't in good taste—but why talk of taste when you come to Jupiter? They leaned back in their seats. But what sound was that? It caught Jupiter's sharp ear through the laughter. Was it a groan?

"Catch him!" shouted Jupiter.

A commotion, a shuffling of chairs, a heavy crash, a general springing up—and a silence, as several now lifted the body of Cheswold Lawne to a sofa. Somebody undid his collar, some one else leaned over him, a second came to bend and look, and a few of them whispered to their neighbors. Still more shook their heads. This and that and the other was hurriedly brought by servants.

"Don't wait, gentlemen," said Jupiter. "The doctor has been sent for."

"Anything I can do—" said one.

"There's nothing, I think," Jupiter answered. "His brother should be here in a minute." He looked at his watch; it set several of them looking at their watches. One opened a window. They hesitated, standing, or moving a little, speaking in low tones. A bright bar of sun-light came through the window, slanting down to the red carpet, and the dust danced in it silently. One stooped carefully and picked a napkin from the floor and laid it on the table with great precision. Another set an overturned glass upright again with equal care.

Chadd looked down on the figure. "Poor fellow," said he, shaking his head. "A fine man."

"That's the way I want to go," said Harris.

"Yes, yes; it's the best way," murmured Brandywine.

Their voices were coming back from the whispering stage a little, as they began to take their leave. They departed mostly in twos, walking soberly along the street toward their various offices, and speaking as they went:

"He was eighty, wasn't he?"

"More."

"Wasn't he in the Mexican War?"

"I've heard so—Navy, I think."

"Well, well. He ate too much always."

"Yes, he did. Wonder who'll get his money?"

"Worth a lot, wasn't he?"

"Very close, always. It'll be two millions anyhow. Very close man."

"Well, well. We've got a vacancy to fill."

Yes; they had a vacancy to fill. Directors die, vice-presidents die, even Jupiters die—but The Railroad never died. Every man jack of them who had eaten that lunch would make room in his due turn for some other man to eat lunch, the faces round the table would change and change, the office itself would move away from down-town, might make many moves in the course of time; but the wheels of the heavy cars loaded with human beings and human possessions would go on turning and rumbling, as they rolled westward and eastward along The Railroad's many thousand miles.

Gwynedd waited for the doctor's coming, and his verdict; he stayed to shake hands silently with the brother of the dead man, and to offer his services. Then, as he was walking away slowly up the street, alone, he was hailed by a deep and cheery voice from a cellar-door.

"Good afternoon, Mr. Gwynedd. A fine day, sir."

"How are you, Atco?* How's your boy?"

"Pretty well, the both of us, sir. The boy's getting to be a fine shot, sir. Don't you want some nice birds to-day, Mr. Gwynedd?"

"Let me look at them." Gwynedd descended the cellar-steps into a room where game of several sorts was hung or heaped. The lawyer sat down on a box, and wiped his forehead.

"You're not looking very stout, Mr. Gwynedd. I've a bottle of good brandy—"

"Thank you, thank you, Atco. It's nothing. I'm all right. Atco, Mr. Cheswold Lawne is dead."

"Indeed, sir! Isn't that very sudden?"

"Very sudden."

"I can see him like yesterday, sir."

"Yes, yes. Like yesterday."

"He was very fond of wood-cock, sir. And I can see him talking to my father about the best place for reed-birds."

Gwynedd gazed about at the feathered game, small birds and larger birds, lying in soft heaps, or hanging in bunches from nails.

Atco watched him in kindly massive silence, as he wiped his forehead. "He'd often walk down-town with your own father, sir," he said presently. "Many's the dozen of terrapin he has bought of me, though he never bought so free as his father. A nice family, sir."

"Oh, yes. I can remember him all my life." And then, sitting on the box in the cellar, with Atco seated on a neighboring box, among the birds and the fish (for there were fish here, too) Gwynedd told Atco how it had all been, what the doctor had said; he talked quietly, on and on, while the big Atco sat nodding his wholesome face. Why did the lawyer wish to stay with this rustic and unburden himself? Why did he speak confidential words to sportsman and fisherman in coarse rough clothes without a collar, finding in this company something that he had missed in the company at lunch? "The old faces are going, Atco," he said. "There used to be so many."

"I'm not so young myself, sir."

"Nonsense. Where should we buy our game?"

"I'm training my boy to it, sir—Tim, not Allen. Allen's smart at ciphering."

"Well, Atco, good-bye. And don't you die for a long while."

And so, after almost an hour of chat, Gwynedd climbed out of the cellar, carrying away with him some birds, wrapped in a brown-paper parcel. As he proceeded along the street, Jupiter passed him driving his own pair of thorough-bred trotters. This was a familiar sight in Monopolis, the president of The Road seldom came to his office in any other way. The two men nodded to each other gravely, as Jupiter drew up to the curb.

"Will you come for a drive in the park?"

"Thank you. Somehow I want just to walk about a little."

"Yes. Sudden thing. A man with a weak heart must look out what he eats. You'll remember about Tingle?"

Gwynedd nodded.

XII

In which Tingle climbs a rung.

Of course it is exceedingly audacious in any author, exceedingly audacious, obnoxious, impertinent and otherwise unsuitable, to say at the beginning of a chapter, as I did at the beginning of the last one, that it contains three superfluous remarks*; for thereby he invites from the reader the very natural criticism that the author grossly flatters himself in imagining that there are only three observations of this character, whereas the reader could easily show him forty or fifty, indeed the whole chapter might have been omitted to advantage. But I don't care. I have been through all that sort of thing. Once I wrote a book wherein a dozen critics discovered superfluity, the only trouble being that, as each of these self-erected Solomons picked out a different chapter which should have been omitted, nothing at all except the covers would have been left of the book. Ever since the writing of volumes began, readers and critics have shown an intelligence so greatly superior to that of authors, that it is plain the only person in the world who is unfitted to write any work is the man who did write it, and so I beg you clearly to understand that, while I sincerely trust

some at least of these pages may interest you, I write to please
one person only—myself. (Aunt Carola tried her best to induce
me to obliterate every word of the above; but I would not do
it.)—I hope that you are still anxious to know which are the
three remarks? They were all made by Jupiter, whose knowledge of Timothy Tingle was as yet comparatively slight. It was
not in the least necessary to warn this astute young man that
Tom McNary was a partner to get rid of—honest, headlong
Tom McNary, who didn't brush his hair, and who spoke out
his mind about the politicians, about The Railroad, about
Mark Beaver, and about everything and everybody in Monopolis, whether his mind happened to be complimentary or not.
There was no Safe Side about Tom at all—and do you suppose that Timothy needed Jupiter or Evans Gwynedd to tell
him that? Or to intimate in words delicately arranged that if he
continued in his association with a man so rash in his speech,
his promising law-practice would mysteriously, steadily, and
undoubtedly dry up? We have said that Tingle had eyes, and
that he used them by no means exclusively upon the fair sex.
He had looked at Monopolis closely, and if he had not, perhaps, seen the city through and through (for to see anything
through and through needs a good heart as well as good eye-
sight) he had perceived that success generally attended those
who loved The Railroad and Mark Beaver, and that failure
was apt to be the lot of those who didn't. It was not to the
Law alone that this interesting rule applied; medicine, bank-
ing, broking, almost every profession and career was subject
to it; even hospitals, churches, and seats of learning had to toe
this Monopolis mark, because the State, by means of appro-
priations and subsidies, took care of its own, and Mark Beaver
and The Railroad were of course The State every whit as
much as Louis Fourteenth was France.

When Tingle decided that he was going to love The Railroad and Mark Beaver (and he had come to this decision sometime ago) he was compelled to think his situation out pretty sharply. Tingle had begun by enrolling himself with "Reform." Reform, at the particular moment when the young man was entering upon his career, had seemed to be the coming thing*; and Timothy dearly loved the crest of any wave. But here was one of Timothy's rare mistakes in judgment—these grew fewer and fewer as he ripened to his perfection—the wave broke in spray upon the hard sand beach of the Safe Side, and there was poor Timothy rolling over in the receding flood with Tom McNary, a brother in reform to whom he had tied himself. Yes; Timothy had to think pretty hard then. Tom was useful to him still, almost indispensable. Tom had come from Kentucky to try his fortunes in Monopolis, where his vigor and sagacity had brought him clients. Success in uncommon measure had been won by the fiery stranger. McNary was in need, however, of a partner with Monopolis connexions, if he could get the right one, and anybody might have supposed that Timothy Tingle would be exactly the right one, to look at him as he had been then, in the day when Reform was fermenting. The dark eyes could blaze with a perfect imitation of sincerity, and the handsome mouth could utter eloquence that rang with the tones of independence. McNary took the young man in with him, and the young man was very glad so to be taken. He was McNary's junior by some twelve years, the combination promised well, each bringing his own contributing strength to the joint business. And then—well, there's no need to narrate how, in the years which followed that particular defeat of Reform, the widening process of estrangement began and continued between the partners. Neither ever said a word. Business went on not

so ill; they consulted, collaborated, apportioned, as if nothing
were the matter—but both were really waiting. McNary, the
elder man, had foreseen it first, not because he had a better
head than Timothy, but because he had a heart, and this happened to be one of the cases where the heart, rather than the
head, is the foreseeing organ. For at least a year Tom McNary
had been waiting for the day when Tingle would come out
with it. He knew quite well what he should do then, but he
had determined, very wisely, that the person to come out with
it should be Timothy, and not himself; if Timothy intended
to break the connexion between them, he must say so and do
so of his own accord. This was what Tom waited for, while
Timothy waited for the right, the tactful, the easy, obvious
moment, when he could point to circumstances as not merely
justifying himself, but also as making a separation plainly the
best thing for McNary. Nay, this was the ground he would
try to put it on, if it could be managed: Tingle in a graceful
pose, self-forgetful, all consideration, thinking only of his
brother's well-fare. He was aware that it wouldn't be quite
the easiest thing in the world to manage, this attitude of
grace; and that was why his forehead grew damp when old
Mrs. Poyntell at Gwynedd's tea-table had poked her words
into the small, secret places of his mind, like a dentist.

He couldn't forget the probe of her remark. "They tell me
he criticizes the politicians. Can't you stop him?" That was
what the sharp, dreadful old lady had said to him about his
partner; and although he had replied gallantly, preserving
appearances, the dampness had come out on his forehead. If
anybody saw his predicament well enough to joke about it to
his face, why then the time for his long-meditated step must
be closer at hand than he had imagined. Timothy, with the
thing so filling his own mind, didn't guess that the old lady's
shot had been accidental, a piece of random sport on her part,

striking in much deeper than she knew. He would have hated her—but Timothy didn't hate anybody; for hate, just as much as for love, a heart is needed; and furthermore, the clever young man had formed existing attachments early in life, to which he was forever constant, and which used up all the real passion there was in him: Timothy loved himself very dearly.

He sat in his office. Through one of its windows there was to be seen a slice-glimpse of the square. Tom McNary, as senior partner, quite properly had the front and best room, whence he could look out on the square from three of his windows. Both partners were busy writing. Like the telephone, stenographers and type-writers had not yet entered into the life of the world, but stood at its threshold; therefore correspondence still lagged behind the age of machinery, and lawyers, doctors and all men still wrote important letters with their own hands. In the silence of Timothy's office, his rapid pen made a sound that was not unpleasant. It was enough to see him hold his pen; enough to see the quick firm writing flow from it, line after line down to the bottom of the page; the look of his fingers and knuckles was enough—you didn't have to read the words, or spy into the thoughts behind them, to know that this was a coming young man, a young man who would be heard from, as they say. He hummed as he wrote; it wasn't a tune, Timothy couldn't tell Yankee Doodle from Old Hundred, no musician would have called it anything—but it was something. Young Timothy often hummed it, or something like it, when he was vigorous, and busy, and happy, and delighted with his past and his future. It was like the strong beating of his—well, of whatever organ pumped the blood so lustily through his veins. If it could have been translated into words, it would have sung: "I'm a cork, I'm a cork, I'll float, I'll float!" Yes, Timothy was humming as he wrote his letters this afternoon before taking the train in pursuit of the Bayside Air Line; and I don't know how he managed to make those letters so coherent. For all the while that he sat writing them, his thoughts were balancing the great question of Tom McNary. Was the hour come, was it time now for the graceful pose and the brotherly consideration? When he lifted his eyes from the paper, he could see through the open doors into Tom's office, he could watch Tom's broad back and unbrushed hair, as he sat bending over his desk. Was the hour come? The balance between yes and no was so nice, that it broke off the humming two or three times. "Um-de-dum, um-de-dum, di-do, di-do, hoping you will be able to see the situation in this light, I remain Yours very um-de-dum, di-do, Timothy Tingle"—he threw aside the letter he had just signed. There was only one more to be written. He consulted his watch, and once again his eye contemplated his partner's back through the open doors. What a pity nobody could see that eye then—especially a painter! It wasn't a sinister eye, there was nothing in it of threat or of bad feeling, it was rather good-natured, almost merry in a way—unless you looked into it very deep indeed, and then you saw—Timothy Tingle. He got up and stretched himself. He took a turn to that window whence the slice-glimpse of the square could be seen. His fingers drummed for a moment on the glass. Then he came back and sat down with a fresh sheet of letter-paper ready for the last note. But his pen paused, and for a third time he looked at Tom McNary's back. Then the pen began slowly (of itself, perhaps—pens can be very queer) to draw lines through some words at the top of the paper. These words were engraved, and ran: "McNary and Tingle, Attorneys at Law," with the address. The pen made quite an important alteration, taking its own queer, slow time to do so. Tingle looked at the paper, and noticed what the pen had done. He gazed at the sheet contemplatively, with his head a little to one side (why is it that you can judge so many things better if you tilt your head slightly?) and then, like the prudent Timothy that he was, he tore the paper into very small pieces indeed, threw them into the basket, slid a new sheet in front of him and began his last letter. "Dear Sir, referring to yours of the um-de-dum I should be inclined to di-do," and so forth, and so forth. Timothy was humming again all through to his signature, which he wrote with a particularly fine specimen of that flourish with which he always concluded his name. Better wait. Oh yes, decidedly. Hullo! Time to start.

"Well, old man, good-bye till Thursday or Friday." Thus, Timothy, jovially, to his senior partner.

Tom of the broad back and the hair unbrushed swung round in his office chair. "Off, are you?" He was jovial too.

The junior partner was standing in the open door, his face buoyant with good humor. "Off. Yes. I'm a working man. Quail this time. Ho ho!"

"Well, good-luck! My regards to any fellows I know at the club."

They exchanged the frankest of nods and smiles.

"Some letters in there," said Timothy, with a backward head-jerk toward his office. "Wish you'd just run your eye over what I've said to that Pierson concern, and see if it's right."

"About their contract, you mean?"

"Yes. Don't let Samuel mail it before you see it." (Samuel was their office boy.)

"All right."

More frantic nods and smiles, with another glance at his watch by sportsman Timothy.

"Hullo, I'll miss the train. Good-bye, Tom."

"Good luck, Tim."

Thus parted Tom and Tim until Thursday or Friday. You wouldn't have supposed there was a secret that they didn't share. You wouldn't have supposed, from their heartiness and from the slap-on-the-back way they had with each other, that Tom, sitting at his desk to resume his work, was saying inwardly:

"It can't possibly be shame that makes him put it off?"

While Tim, rushing down stairs with a valise and gun, was thinking:

"Not till I'm director."

And so, while the carriage was rattling and jolting him over the cobble-stones to the train, and so, while the train was more smoothly conveying him toward the quail, he would take up his humming from time to time. "I'm a cork, I'm a cork, I'll float, I'll float!" Several passengers admired sportsman Timothy's appearance—ladies mostly. Such a pleasant, fascinating face! Strong, too.

No; not until they made him a director. Better hold on to what you've got. Bird in the hand. Mustn't drop Tom before thing was certain. But they would make him a director at the very first vacancy, if he secured Baxter Chippendale's stock for 'em. That would give 'em controlling interest in the Bayside Air Line. Then they could sit down and laugh at the other fellows. Then it would be the other fellows who would have to build a parallel line, if they wanted a through connexion for their railroad. "I'm a cork, I'll float." He was so happy and hopeful as he turned his thoughts over and over and found that never a single troubling thought came to light amongst them, that the miles and the hours passed as nothing, time vanished like a conjuror's trick. He looked out of the window at the fields and woods, benignantly, at the villages and horses and cows, benignantly, as if they were all doing something just right, something that had been arranged exclusively for his benefit and entertainment. A flagman stood at a crossing and waved his flag as the train went by; and the flagman was doing it just right, and he had been arranged for Timothy's benefit and entertainment too. Bless me, it was dark! Who'd have thought it? And here was the junction, where you got your supper and changed cars. A conspicuously attractive lady dropped her handkerchief and sportsman Timothy picked it up and gave it to her, which was what she had dropped it for. She wanted his company at supper, and no doubt after supper; there was a hotel here, and she thought that they made an agreeable pair of travelers. Timothy went with her plan as far as taking supper together, but drew the line there; this was a place where people might know you, and besides, Timothy had to get on to the quail. He had really come for quail. It was a real gun he had in his case. But another sportsman, a member of the club, was coming for quail too— the president of that other railroad suspected to be flirting with Baxter Chippendale in regard to the large block of Bayside Air Line stock. Timothy had learned this, quite by chance, from Mort and Dug Hythe that very day, lunching at the Buena Vista. The brothers had just come up from the club, where the president was expected. Mort and Dug belonged to several clubs of this kind—clubs that couldn't get on without some pretty rich members. Timothy himself wasn't rich enough (yet) to be a member, but he had various good friends who took care of him during the season. His eye, open forever to opportunity as we know, saw one instantly. "Get any birds?" he inquired. "Bet your life," said Dug; and he named their several bags. "They're thick this year," he said—"Hm," said Timothy; "don't one of you fellows want to give me a card? I'd like to get a few before Ben Staples kills 'em all off." "He won't. He can't," said Dug. "Yes he can," declared Mort. "He knows how to shoot when he isn't drunk." Timothy affected to see a difficulty. "I haven't any dog," he said. "Dogs nothing!" cried Mort. It appeared that there were several down at the club, and at Timothy's disposal. "Make Simon give you what you like," urged Mort. "Make yourself at home. If there's anything you don't see, ask for it." "Tell him you're our guest," Dug added, with a slight touch of grandeur. "D'y'u play écarté?" "Yes," said Timothy; "Why?" "Staples plays. It's his game. He'll make y'u play all night, if y'u let him." "Ho ho! Did he make you?" "He ain't there yet. Expected there to-day or to-morrow. Hope you'll not be held up by the wash-out. We had to drive thirty miles. Well, be good to yourself." Thus the brothers Dug and Mort, heartily. And Timothy's spirit had bounded as his course opened in his imagination, clear and prompt. Oh, yes! He would be good to himself! When wasn't he? But this time he meant if possible to be very good to himself indeed; better than he often had the chance to be. It was an opportunity such as mightn't come again. He thanked his stars because he knew écarté and because Ben Staples didn't know him; wouldn't associate him with Jupiter, or Air Lines, or Baxter Chippendale. The Railroad wouldn't "appear in it" at all. Timothy couldn't see yet what would happen, he only saw that something should happen, if he could make it. Écarté! What an opening that might prove! Ben Staples, president of the Chesapeake, Cumberland and Western, almost certainly wanted Baxter Chippendale's stock in the Bayside Air Line, almost certainly was, even in these very days, making up his mind what Baxter Chippendale would take for his stock. If Timothy should now play his cards well (not merely in écarté, but in the much more impor-tant game of life) the number of things he might "learn to his advantage" almost made the brilliant, handsome young man's head swim—almost, but not quite. The head of the brilliant, handsome young man very seldom swam entirely; I can foresee only one occasion coming when it will perform that feat. Before his lunch at the Buena Vista was ended, a card for the club was in his pocket, and that note to Evans Gwynedd announcing that Timothy was going to shoot quail—the note which had elicited such marked approval from Jupiter when it arrived among the gods seated at their lunch—had been written and dispatched down-town by private messenger. Of Jupiter's nod and smile Tingle knew nothing and could guess nothing; nor could he guess Jupiter's opinion that the firm of McNary and Tingle wasn't just the best arrangement for a young man of promise; still less could Timothy dream that, even as the gods sat at lunch, a vacancy had been suddenly created among them; he had left town before any news of that meeting had begun to spread. But to all of us come times when the current of our blood seems at one with the favoring universe, when each thought that we think, each act that we do, seems part of a happy scheme making for our furtherance in well-fare. Timothy even took away more money with him than he needed, more money than he could afford—except to lose to Ben Staples at écarté. Such a loss as that might pay better than most winnings!

Do you wonder that Timothy hummed as he journeyed, that he looked out of the window benignantly upon all passing objects? And do you wonder that the conspicuously attractive lady found his company delightful as the train sat eating their supper together in the dining-room of the junction hotel? By the end of this meal she was more than ready for any suggestion from him that she modify her plans of travel and prolong a meeting so agreeably begun.

But what is that train arriving now? Through the stationary windows of the dining-room its moving windows are seen to pass slowly and come to a halt. It is the branch train that Timothy must take, and neither he nor the fair one has been aware how swiftly time was speeding. He rises, she rises; gallant nothings are smiled from the gentleman's lips, from her lips come arch replies which are tinged with just a suspicion of mockery, because the fair one is not accustomed to having her signals for trumps ignored. He has failed to make those masculine advances that she had the right to look for. He gathers his effects and emerges upon the platform, bowing a last farewell to his companion, who has come as far as the door herself, in spite of his neglect of her promising charms. He knows well enough what she is thinking; and by way of retort he is thinking, "She's thirty-five, anyhow, in this light. Wonder how old she is in the morning?" For he resents her resentment, being but man, and young withal, and no better adjusted to the institution of monogamy than many others of his kind; and if things didn't happen to be as they were, he would give her quite a different account of himself. But what palatial car is this at the rear of the branch train? It has six-wheeled trucks, windows of a wide pattern, a glassy and well varnished aspect, and it doesn't belong to this road. Chesapeake, Cumberland and Western are the words painted along above its windows, it is the president's private car, and there, sitting inside, in full view, is a heavy man finishing his dinner. The negro steward waits upon him skilfully and assiduously, pouring his glass full to the top again from a bottle wrapped in a napkin, opening for his selection several boxes of cigars, setting a little cup of coffee beside his plate, pushing a bowl piled with fruit a little nearer to his reach. It is not the simple life by any means, it is very obviously the sumptuous life, that surrounds Ben Staples as he finishes his dinner in his private car. Now the assiduous steward is asking him some question, bending respectfully as he stands by the magnate's chair; and in consequence of what the magnate answers, a bottle and a little glass are brought, and the little glass is filled nicely to its brim with green stuff from the bottle.

"That cert'nly ain't no whiskey," says a slow, Southern voice on the platform, in tones of serious interest.

"Shrub, I reckon, some kind o' fancy shrub,"* says another, equally serious and attentive.

For outside on the platform, there are employees and others with the rustic mind of the region, staring in at the sumptuous life. They stare with admiring respect—too much respect, exaggerated respect; for those were still the days when the spectacle of power and wealth raised emotions of worship in the American breast, just as to-day the same spectacle rouses emotions of hate: the American breast dealing only in superlatives and extremes, between which it goes swinging extravagantly on to the day of reckoning ahead.

Sitting in the radiant midst of the sumptuous life, and admired from the darkness outside by travelers with bags and fellows in overalls with oil cans and hammers, who tap on the wheels and grease the journals,* Ben Staples is blowing slow rings of smoke upward to the gorgeous roof of his car; and Tingle on the platform is watching him; watching him with nothing so mild as admiration or so poisonous as hate: there, inside the bright car, sits Tingle's Opportunity. Opportunity is doomed presently to play the mouse for the handsome young cat on the platform. Heavy, swarthy, thick-lipped, thick eye-browed Ben Staples doesn't look like a mouse at all—but it's not a good thing to be the son of a Napoleon of any kind; Waterloo is apt to be waiting somewhere along the path to glory. Ben Staples Senior, Napoleonic creator of the Chesapeake, Cumberland and Western, had never met his Waterloo, dying at the zenith of his powers and his success; but they shouldn't have let the son step into his father's large

shoes; he wobbled about in them, wobbled to the undoing of
his father's work, never went anywhere unless accompanied by
the sumptuous life, conducted his road with what he imagined
was the true Napoleonic dash—campaigns taken in at a
glance, quick moves, offhand decisions that involved millions
sometimes—because he had the American breast (which his
great sire hadn't in the least) and believed that you can invent
short-cuts to solidity, stability and thoroughness; whereas there
is no short-cut in this world, except to perdition. And now he
thinks he will take a breath of air before the train starts. Tingle
sees him rise heavily, walk heavily along inside his car, disap-
pear into the passage between private state-rooms, re-appear
on the steps and heavily descend into the common world. The
handsome cat has managed somehow meanwhile to look
merely like a kitten, it isn't the junior partner of McNary and
Tingle on the platform, it's just a boyish fellow with a gun-case
and a gay sporting appearance, evidently come for quail, evidently no member of the shrewd, hard, business, railroad
world, quite ignorant of those subtle and mature games, but
quite likely to play écarté and be a good shot, and a good judge
of whiskey, and help Napoleon pass a holiday. Napoleon does-
n't look like a mouse, but you can hear it in the voice that he
thinks he always succeeds in making sound masterful, and in
which he now addresses the apparent kitten.

"Bound for the club, I take it?"

"Yes, sir."

That "sir" is a triumph of art. Timothy has never done
anything better. In it Napoleon hears recognition of his greatness, not from the lips of servility, but by a social equal.

He coughs, and speaks foolishly. "Then I must introduce
myself."

"No need of that, sir." Timothy's smile completes the
approval of the great man. When you know you are great,

but sometimes suspect that it isn't known by others, such confirmations go to the right spot. A divine gift of tact now holds Timothy back from mentioning his own name until it is demanded. "May I ask what you've heard about the birds this year?" he inquired in the accents of modesty.

"It's good this year. Good, I'm told." Napoleon still keeps up the grand but indulgent manner as a matter of principle.

"Douglas and Mortimer Hythe told me they had luck," says Timothy. "That's what brought me."

"Oh. You know those boys? Then perhaps you're from Monopolis?" Napoleon has unbent a hair's breadth, perhaps.

"Yes, sir. I'm from Monopolis." Timothy's modest tone doesn't give a notion of how hard he's watching Opportunity now.

Napoleon looks at him. "Do you know Evans Gwynedd?" Timothy hears something new in the great man's voice, and answers most judiciously:

"I know his name very well. He's the leader of the Monopolis bar."

"Yes, I know, I know." The voice has lost the something. Its owner ruminates briefly. Timothy can almost see the Napoleonic thoughts: "Here's a young man not in touch with those railroad people up there in Monopolis, he's not worth pumping, though if he did know anything I could easily get it out of him." But Timothy mustn't let Napoleon's interest in him die out. He perceives that the great man's brain, by what he has been drinking before, at, and after dinner, has been started toward a state that may become most useful.

"I'm a lawyer myself," says he. "But I'm afraid Mort and Dug are more in my line than any leader of the bar is likely to be for several years yet."

"Well," says Napoleon, remembering that he has lapsed from the grand manner and suddenly resuming it, "the sons of Jacob Hythe are bound to have a future. Bound to get into the big game. I happen to know that they're in it now. Jacob Hythe is a Rothschild. Jacob Hythe has guts."

"Oh, yes, sir! Guts indeed!" And Timothy looks at Napoleon, and sees that he may wink safely.

"Haw! Haw!" goes Napoleon.

"Ho ho!" goes Timothy. Then he affects to shiver slightly and puts down his gun case, which all this while he has been most deferentially holding. "Do you mind, sir?" he asks, and he pulls out a flask. "These nights are getting a bit sharp." He is about to offer it to the great man, who stops him with a gesture as of the paw of a bear, imperiously hospitable.

"None of that while you're on my line—or mine that will be! Come inside and sample my stuff."

"Isn't this road yours? I thought you owned everything round here."

"It'll be mine next week. D'you think I'd let a road be in the state this is in? That ain't Ben Staples's style! I'll have dinner back. Come in."

"Oh, don't think of it, sir! I've had supper."

"You're coming in, anyway. And you'll drink my stuff while you're on my—while you're in my car. What's your name?"

Timothy tells him, but he doesn't listen, because he has caught sight of the conspicuously attractive lady, to whom he lifts his hat, as he speaks in pleasurable surprise. "Why there's Eliz—good evening Mrs. Brielle." It is thus that he amends his familiar beginning and lowers his voice at the same time; for the lady has approached him somewhat rapidly, and her movement causes him to collect himself. But even had he begun with the discretion that he now heavily puts on, wits less sharp than Timothy's could have read the situation easily, and would have known that Mrs. Brielle was a part of the sumptuous life and of Napoleon's holiday with the quail: their meeting has merely occurred prematurely, or at any rate not quite as it had been planned. And now Timothy is making his bow, as Ben Staples says to the lady:

"Mrs. Brielle, let me present—what did you say your name was?"

So Tingle tells him again, and admires the manner in which the lady goes through with it, giving him her hand most graciously, and indicating with light and perfect skill that he and she have never set eyes upon each other before. By this superfluous warning she fails to pay an agreeable compliment to Timothy's *esprit de conduite*. He thinks that decidedly she lays it on beyond necessity when she says to Ben Staples:

"If you, by any chance, have a sandwich in your palace?" And she sighs, as if weak from long fasting.

"I've had supper, you know," repeats Timothy, giving an exquisite imitation of a young man who knows his place and isn't important enough to be invited to sandwiches or anything else in the palace. And of course Ben Staples will not hear of it, for Ben Staples likes to shed the sumptuous life upon all those that are plainly fit for boon companions: it ministers to his Napoleonic sensations.

No sooner is this very interesting company of three inside the palace, and the shades of the windows drawn down by a steward who is well-trained in discreet precautions, than a toot from an asthmatic locomotive, followed by successive jerks between car and car, announces that the branch train has started.

"Feel that?" growls Ben Staples. "I'll have the Miller coupling* all over this system."

And as they jerk and joggle along, many a criticism falls from him regarding the poor condition of the road which is to become his by next week. Even this piece of news is worth

Timothy's journey, will throw his resource and alertness into a fine light in Jupiter's eye; but he must have more, and he knows that more is sure to come, very likely without any further help from him. Napoleon's mind is becoming more and more like a Spanish omelet, hospitality, railroading, quail and self importance being all stirred and beaten together in it. Dainties, decanters and bottles are set upon the table; Mrs. Brielle, after a sparing repast, revives and adds much to the charm of the occasion. Nay; she accomplishes more than this; for, hanging as she does upon the words of the great man, opening her pretty eyes and mouth at his vast plans, which she now and again begs to have more clearly explained to her, she draws the great man out by this flattery and entirely relieves Tingle from making any efforts himself to this end that he so much desires. He says very little, plays his part of modest boon companion, swallows and compliments the drink, smokes and compliments the cigars (for he has discerned that Ben Staples has a taste for all sorts of praise) and all the while the great man talks, and the lady exclaims, to the accompaniment of much creaking from the car. Its joints complain, its springs groan; for rains, if recent and copious, can make a road-bed that is stone-ballasted very much like a cradle. And now they learn there's to be no further progress this night. A long stop wakes Ben Staples to the fact of some emergency outside, and not even his Napoleonic mind can surmount it. Nothing can cure it but several hours of hard work by carpenters and other people of the sort, for it is a wash-out which is almost, but not quite, repaired. They may get away by ten in the morning. They are ten miles from anywhere; nothing here but a way-side station with one bed, occupied at present by the wife and two children of the agent. Ben Staples breaks into fury, but at once forgets it to show hospitable care for Eliz—Mrs. Brielle, I mean. What does the wash-out matter? They're all better off here than they would be in the hotel at the end of the branch. This car has three state-rooms. "Oh, no!" says the lady. She can't think of it, really—and what's he thinking about? She laughs delightfully, but is quite firm in having herself and her bag conducted into the common car, where she will be perfectly comfortable, thank you. She hadn't an idea it was so late. No, indeed, thank you, nothing more, and good night!

Ben Staples doesn't play his part nearly so well, plays it rather grossly, in fact; has a fit of sulks after the lady's departure, is very nearly rude to Tingle, but recovers from this, and makes the young man at home. "You're a good fello'," he says, filling himself another glass. "You'll stay here, anyhow. Plenty room. She could a shtayed puffictly. What's th' harm? You're a good fello' anyway. What'd y'u say y'r name—oh yes, Tingle. Beg pardon. See so many people all the time. Not so many like you, though. You come with me on a trip on my road and I'll show you what's what. Play écarté? Steward! Bring cards. Ain't this a God damned road? Get away!" This remark is addressed to the cards, over which he places both his paws and shovels and slides them off the table to the floor, where they are picked up by the steward. "You go bed, steward. Don't wait for me." He is obliged to replenish his empty glass before continuing: "What's any game of cards to this? Steward! Bring map! Oh, he's gone bed. Get map myself." But Tingle, following the point of his thick finger, gets it out of a drawer. "There! See?" He drags the thick finger heavily here and there, drags it over some blue veins in the map, over some red veins ("that's Chespeake Cumben and Wessn," he explains to Timothy, who nods intelligently), drags the finger over some black veins ("that's this one, Bayside Air Line, here we are"), the finger stops at a point. "What's cards to that? Tell y'u, I've got 'em euchred. You go home and tell 'em from me I've euchred 'em. Here!" He drags a newspaper out of his pocket, and rips it open at the page of the stock quotations. "Bayside Air Line. No sales. See? Last sale there. See? But I know where I can get all I want, and it'll only cost me two points better'n market. Whash cards to that?"

The small hours are come, and a fool sits sleeping in his chair; a vain, sensual fool, whose place in the world, whatever and wherever it be, is not at the head of a great railroad. The big drunken face of the president of the Chesapeake, Cumberland and Western is down on the table, and his snores break out in spurts of hoarse sound amid the silence of his palace. One of his paws rests upon the crumpled newspaper, its stubs of fingers pointing stupidly every way, like some thick star-fish; the other paw is beneath his jowl. Beyond his head, and spread out flat and gleaming on the table, lies the map with the blue and the red and the black veins.

XIII

Decoration of Tingle.

Had Timothy been a great man, he would have gone to sleep as soon as his head touched the pillow. Jupiter would certainly have gone to sleep; so would Jacob Hythe; and it is true that Timothy seldom failed to find slumber quickly when he sought it. Not many agitations were able to render wakeful this perfectly healthy and vigorous young man. The pangs of love had never disturbed him to such severe extent, nor had any grief or misfortune or anxiety caused him to toss feverishly until the dawn: when he lost sleep, it was because he was engaged in some one of the several agreeable occupations which properly belong to the night. But when Tingle rose from his chair beside the drunken, snoring president, and stole noiselessly away to his state-room in the presidential car, he was very wide awake. The thought of what he had accomplished set his brain in a blaze of light; the whole of his life, the past he had made and the future he intended to make, came together in a sort of flash, and it was with nerves strung as tight as fiddle-strings that he saw himself at a turning-point in his career. It might prove the greatest turning-point in store for him, if he could make the end of the adventure as successful as the beginning.

Why had he stepped away so noiselessly from sleeping Ben Staples? Thieves do that when they rob a house. Was this the reason? I don't know. But if it was, Timothy didn't know it either. If he walked through the car like a thief, it was his feet that grew stealthy of their own accord: his conscience said nothing to him. He had accepted of a man's hospitality in what was virtually the man's own house, and being thus his guest, had played the spy and the cheat. But his conscience said nothing to him—because he hadn't any. And had someone asked him if he considered himself a man of honor, he would have laughed one of his merriest ho-ho's. He would have said that it was "all in the way of business," or, "merely playing the game": for Tingle, in his way, was as much a herald of things to come as was the new *château* at Ap Thomas; to-day it is the accepted custom for the sons of gentlemen bearing honorable old names, to lie and cheat "in the way of business"; and for dealings which would have brought ostracism upon their grandfathers, the grandsons win the flattering reputation of being "smart" and "smooth"; and we are all delighted to dine with them and swallow their stolen meat and drink into our complaisant stomachs. So Timothy was among those pioneers of the New Code who discovered that Decency is a ridiculously heavy ballast in the race for Success, that there is no success except money, and that to get it you are justified in throwing everything overboard. I am glad that the duel is gone; but it took some good manners and standards away with it out of the world—and not a drop of shame entered into Tingle's vivid and racing thoughts, as he sat in his clothes on the edge of his bed, without beginning to unbutton his waistcoat.

Hadn't he better go back and put his host to bed? He had often paid this delicate attention to hosts; and a few years ago, before he had set his eye so hard on Opportunity, the attention had been occasionally paid to himself. But he didn't know Staples. How would the man act? Suppose, while he was pulling Staples's boots off, this host should rouse up and not remember his guest, begin to fight and to roar and alarm the train, and in general behave himself inconveniently? That would never do. Timothy could see two or three horrid consequences which might follow from such a disturbance. No; he must leave the man snoring where he sprawled, and take the risk of what suspicions might enter that drunken brain when it should revive and be met with the sight of the map and the crumpled newspaper. At this point in Timothy's meditations, while he continued to sit on the edge of his bed, the very simple and useful thought came to him that this car had certainly been the scene of other revelry before to-night; that this could be by no means the first time the head of Ben Staples had sunk torpid on the table after an evening of pleasure; and that Gabriel the *chef,* so skilled in cookery and in serving plenteous meat and drink, must be without any question as thoroughly trained in caring for those who were overtaken by the results of his ministrations. Gabriel would be sure to attend to his dilapidated master in the proper way at the proper time.

With that, Timothy tossed this particular concern lightly from his mind, and began to unbutton his waistcoat. He wound his watch (it had been his grandfather's), slid it beneath his pillow, hung up his coat, folded his trousers smooth and flat, quite unconscious of these habitual steps; he even looked at himself in the glass without knowing it, so deeply engrossed in his thoughts was he. Once he gave a short chuckle. This was when he was taking things out of his valise, and came upon the money, that extra large sum, which he had brought with him to lose (if need be) to the President of the Chesapeake, Cumberland and Western at the President's favorite game of écarté. No wonder the sight of the fat fold of bills made him chuckle! There they all were, safe and sound, and here was he with the secret he had come for, equally safe and sound in his possession, and not a penny paid for it: safe and sound, that is, so far; the adventure wasn't over; he wasn't out of the woods; he couldn't crow yet.

I have said that Timothy was not a great man; but he was undoubtedly performing one of the acts of greatness just now, though you couldn't have seen him doing it:—I fancy greatness, when it's at work, is generally invisible, and that's why we're so apt to deny it to our friends and contemporaries until they're dead and buried and comfortably out of our way:— what is there so very remarkable in the sight of a man in his shirt and drawers, brushing his teeth and otherwise going leisurely and methodically to bed in a sleeping-car? That is what Timothy was doing. You and I can do that too. But it isn't everybody by any means who, in Timothy's circumstances, can *think* as Timothy was thinking. When something really prodigious happens to us—to most of us—either our brains are numbed by it, or else our thoughts pour over us by the dozen at once, like a huge discord of simultaneous notes, instead of one after another, and so we sit mentally self-drowned, and can't emerge to any action. Timothy didn't allow himself to be thus overwhelmed. He seized his thronging thoughts with his will and held them, separated them, set them in order, made them follow one after another as words and sentences do, and so dealt with them: for to-morrow was coming, and to-morrow must be laid out now. Perhaps, after all, Jupiter and Jacob Hythe, when they were still young men like Timothy, had sometimes lain awake in the dark too, thinking urgently about the morrow. Timothy would have been much nearer to greatness (or at any rate much further from little-ness) had his nature contained a single passion which could ever make him forget himself. Like a wary chess-player he now planned the various possible moves that he might have to make on the morrow to meet the various possible actions of Staples; and the mere pleasure of exercising his brains so cleverly, lulled his nerves and caressed his self-esteem. He thought of his host as of an adversary. It never once crossed his mind that he was shooting an unguarded and friendly man in the back. That was just like Timothy! And it was just like him to forget how much of his success he owed to the lucky presence of Mrs. Brielle, and to lay his score in the game entirely to his own cunning. Drowsiness crept over him as his task drew to a close, and Timothy Tingle, while con-templating himself with affectionate content, fell asleep.

Coffee woke him—or rather its delicious perfume, stealing into his compartment. He sat up quickly, lifted the window-shade and saw that the train had not yet budged, and also thought instantly of the map and the newspaper. He went out in slippers, as he was, to the saloon, and knew at a glance that all was well so far. Not a sign was left of last night's doings, bright silver and china were set on a cloth spread white and chaste where the bottles had been; while further agreeable odors came from Gabriel's end of the car, where the *chef* could be heard over his kettles and saucepans. From the total silence in the president's room, Timothy concluded that Staples was finishing in bed the night's rest which he had begun in a chair. This conclusion was strengthened by the sight of the presi-dent's boots, newly polished and standing neatly outside his door. Yet Timothy saw fit to proceed in his bluff, hearty way to the kitchen, wish Gabriel a bluff, hearty good-morning, and hope that he wasn't too late to breakfast with Mr. Staples. By this little dodge he learned that Mr. Staples was more likely to be too late to breakfast with him, and that he mustn't think of waiting. But Timothy wouldn't think of not waiting. He couldn't desert his host like that. Bless your heart, he wasn't in a hurry, he was on a holiday! So he dressed himself carefully and gaily, came forth from his toilet like a genial breeze, and gave Gabriel five dollars. How should the surprised and delighted darkey ever know that this munificence was not really his reward for blacking the nice gentleman's boots? That Timothy's own large gratification with himself was at the bottom of the large tip? Gabriel hoped that the nice gentleman would often sleep in that car; and he poked his head out from the platform and admiringly gazed after the guest, as he walked forward beside the track, "just to see how they were getting on with that wash-out," as he explained. You might have supposed from his robust, capable walk and the efficient look of his back, that he was going to mend the wash-out himself, and that it would be mended five minutes after he began to take hold of the work. But you would never have guessed from his manner when he returned that he had met with a slight set-back. "They're getting on famously," he reported; "we'll be starting inside an hour." And he inquired whether Mrs. Brielle wouldn't be expected to breakfast? and mightn't she be more comfortable here in the car? and he would go forward and see about her.

Of course Timothy had been to look at the wash-out, and it was quite true that the track was nearly repaired; but when he had slipped into the little station to take an important step that he had planned in the dark hours, the set-back met him. Telegrams couldn't be sent from here. So it was a baffled and somewhat anxious Timothy who talked with Gabriel so cheerily and went forward to inquire for the well-fare of Mrs. Brielle.

But he didn't go to the lady until he had talked with the conductor and given him a present, too, for being so obliging. The conductor would send the telegram over the company's wires; and Timothy made him read the message aloud to be sure he had it right.

Mrs. Brielle wasn't quite as beautiful in the morning before breakfast as she had been in the evening after supper; but too much should not be expected of a lady who has passed her night sitting up in a railroad car;—and indeed Timothy didn't expect anything more than her company itself when Ben Staples should come out of his room. He wanted her to be present then, so that her gay talk might distract the mind of Staples and keep him from any effort to recall what had happened last night. Before the president's entrance, Gabriel showed Mrs. Brielle to a room whence she presently re-appeared with looks greatly freshened and improved; and so the sight of a pretty woman was ready for the president's eye, just as a cup of hot and fragrant coffee was ready for his palate, when at last he did come. And Tingle was right to have Mrs. Brielle there. Coffee wouldn't have been enough, nor anything else that Gabriel could provide. Ben Staples had a bad ache in his head and a bad taste in his mouth, and he looked round his saloon with a slow and sullen eye. Was he trying to remember? A grunt was the good-morning he gave Timothy, and not much more to the lady. But she had known this spoiled brute for a long while and now employed all her tact to revive good humor in him. His eye rested upon Timothy more than once during this well-cooked but uncomfortable breakfast, and Timothy bore the scrutiny well, thanking his stars for Mrs. Brielle's presence and conversation.

"We're going on at last!" she cried, as the train jerked once more into motion.

"Huh!" said Staples.

"Come sir!" she ventured. "I've sat up all night; and all's well that ends well."

Timothy talked exclusively about dogs and birds and guns as he played the part of an enthusiastic sportsman, innocent of railroads and the great games of magnates. Gradually the president's manner changed from rude and sulky inattention to something a little better; and by the time that the train had picked its cautious way through the wash-out district and reached the journey's end, Ben Staples was exhibiting his own expensive English weapons to his guests, and boasting of them, sober, even as he had boasted of his railroad strategy, drunk.

And next, while they were partaking of a light lunch at the club, a telegram was brought to Timothy. Although he knew quite well what it would contain, he opened it with an air of surprise and apprehension, and then dramatically dashed it down beside him on the table. Mrs. Brielle hoped that it was no bad news; upon which he handed it to her.

"They're sending for you to go back already?" she exclaimed.

Timothy mutely nodded. His silence and the look of his countenance excellently expressed the feeling of a crestfallen young sportsman, torn away from his holiday just as he was stepping across its threshold. "Well," said he, with an admirable effect of assumed cheerfulness, "after all, I'm a working man!— But I did think I had everything arranged until Friday."

"Don't go, Mr. Tingle!" urged the president, heartily. "I'm counting on your using one of my guns this afternoon."

Timothy sat back, his eyes fixed upon the telegram.

"Don't go," echoed Mrs. Brielle, sweetly.

Timothy sat a moment longer. "Let me have the time-tables," he said to the servant; and they were brought. He consulted them. "Hang it!" he burst out, "they can just wait for me." And he called for a telegraph blank and dashed off a message. After this, he turned to Ben Staples. "We'll make an afternoon of it, anyhow!" he declared. "And a morning of it to-morrow, if you say so. Then I'll have to get back, worse luck."

They made an afternoon of it; during which the tactful Tingle missed some shots, and the president got a few of the birds which his young friend thus missed; and the young friend noticed what a good humor this put the president in. He hadn't liked his host's bad humor, or his host's eye which he could see still resting dubiously upon him from time to time. That questioning gaze betokened only too plainly that Napoleon was trying to remember if he had forgotten himself in his cups. So presently, judging by Napoleon's increasing affability that he might venture to be a trifle more familiar than he had dared to be thus far to-day, he missed a particularly easy shot (the bird rose right in front of him and flew straight ahead over an open field) and he cried out to Ben Staples, who was laughing at him across a fence:

"Hang it! You mustn't expect a fellow to drink your whiskey all night and shoot your gun all day."

Now this was the first reference to last night which had been made by either of them; and that Timothy should be the first to make it—so easily and naturally as he did—was what the young man considered a very pretty "play for position."

"I hope I didn't bore you last night," said Staples;—and Timothy knew immediately what to answer: not in vain had he lain awake thinking, and his night meditations had provided more carefully for what he felt was coming now than for any of the various delicate moments which he had foreseen might be in store for him: he must come out of this encounter with innocence proven—or last night's triumph might turn barren in his grasp. He looked across the fence at Staples with a making-a-clean-breast-of-it smile:

"So you did catch me!" he said.

"Catch you?"

Ben Staples said those words rather quickly, and he was looking at Timothy across the fence rather hard.

"Tell me honestly," said Timothy (and he broadened his clean-breast smile to a grin and his steady eye grew more sincere than ever) "how much did I drink? When did we go to bed?"

"Only God knows, if you don't," responded the president with a big laugh.

"Look out for the poison-vine!" cried Timothy; for the president's thick hand had closed over some red leaves that were twined over the top of a fence-post.

"I'm not susceptible to it," said Staples. He was still looking at Timothy, and he kept his hand on the post.

"So you never caught on!" the young man exclaimed.

"Caught on to what?"

"Me! Me pretending to understand all that railroad stuff you were telling me! Me going to sleep in the middle of it! When I waked up you'd gone to sleep yourself. Ho ho!"

"But what railroad stuff was I telling you?"

"Only God knows if you don't!" cried Timothy joyously. And these boon companions joined in boisterous laughter. Is there anything makes two male hearts beat as one more confidentially than comparing notes after a night-of-it?

"When I waked up," Timothy continued, frankly, "all sorts of things were scattered about. You must have got 'em—or Gabriel—after Mrs. Brielle went. Maps. Newspapers. Cards. Cards all over the floor. You evidently played solitaire."

"Why evidently?" inquired Napoleon.

"Because I had all my money this morning—and not a cent of yours."

"Ha ha!" went Napoleon.

"Ho ho!" said Timothy. And he climbed over the fence to join Napoleon on their homeward way. And so in brotherly

bond after their confessions, they strolled through the twi-
light together toward the club; and as they went, Napoleon
nudged his young friend in the ribs with his elbow: "Good
whiskey all the same," he said.

"Where do you get it?" Timothy asked.

"It can't be bought in this country," replied Napoleon, with
a shade of importance. "I'll send you a dozen if you'll give me
your address."

"A dozen! Oh no!"

"I insist," said Napoleon.

Now this dozen of fine whiskey was just as exaggerated a
gift to Tingle as Tingle's gift of five dollars to Gabriel had
been excessive; and both presents were caused by the same
emotion—each giver being hugely satisfied with himself. As
they walked along, the president of the Chesapeake, Cumberland and Western was thinking: "I'm all right. He doesn't
know what I told him—if I did tell him"; and Timothy,
keeping step by his side, was thinking: "I've proved a mental
alibi. He believes I'm harmless."

But Timothy by no means felt himself to be yet out of the
woods; he drew a breath, to be sure, over the outcome of this
particular talk; might nothing mar its bright promise! What
if Mrs. Brielle should make some reference to her share in last
night's conversation that should start Napoleon's suspicions
awake again? Timothy was rejoiced to find a new arrival at
the club; the presence of his cousin Charles Ronald would
divert Napoleon's mind from the dangerous subject. Timothy's gratification made his greeting to his cousin Charles ring
with unwonted sincerity; and when the hand-shaking was
over, his worldly-wise relative looked upon him with an eye
that had seen life, and remarked:

"L-let me know the w-worst."

"Oh, I'm not asking for a loan!" cried Timothy, with one
of his best-humored ho-ho's. Good humor was one of his

adroitest methods both of defense and attack. "I don't want anything!"

"You were so d-devlish g-glad to see me," said his cousin, "it w-worried me."

The very few people who disliked Charles Ronald (they were those whose weak spots had felt his wit more sharply than they could enjoy, and Timothy was one of them) declared that his remarks would be pointless if he didn't stammer. There's no doubt the stammering helped, but Monopolis possessed in those days no master of pithy syllables equal to Charles Ronald. He was what is known as a man's man—but yet an affectionate and perfectly correct husband. No Mrs. Brielle hovered round his holidays; he had come here for bird alone. But fishing and shooting took him continually away from his hearth: a few days with the trout in Maine, a fortnight with the tarpon at Aransas Pass, a month with the salmon on the Grand Cascapedia, six weeks with the elk among the Big Horn, prairie chickens in Minnesota, quail in North Carolina, duck at Curry Tuck—thus were his years composed: with cards at the Boeotia Club* rather regularly between whiles. So that Mrs. Ronald had been heard to say:

"If Charles would only be unfaithful to me in the neighborhood instead of true so far off, I should feel more distinctly like a wife."

"That makes me f-feel just like a husband, anyhow, my dear," retorted Charles.

Yes; Timothy Tingle disliked his cousin Charles Ronald and was afraid of him: every sham dislikes the real thing. And Charles knew his cousin Timothy better than to believe there had been nothing behind all that hand-shaking. "I wonder what he's up to?" thought Charles, several times during that evening at the club; and he still expected Timothy would try to make use of him somehow. A penetration more than earthly would have been needed to divine that Timothy was indeed making just the use of him that he wanted, for the entertainment and distraction of Napoleon. His good company was skilfully served up to the great man, even as Gabriel served delicacies for the great man's table. Timothy relished no moments of his adventure more than these in which his cousin Charles (whose formidable powers of repartee always left him second best) was the clay while he, Timothy, was the potter.

And so the next afternoon found him on his journey homeward with the enormous secret that he had bagged. Not a mischance had befallen him. From those cryptic words, "Wire me back at once," which the conductor had telegraphed for him to his office, and which had elicited his telegraphic and spectacular recall to business, up to the latest moment of his stay, he had played his scurvy game admirably. He had seen during his night meditations that he could not possibly telegraph the secret itself, but must carry it with him as quickly as he could get away without risk of

*   *   *   *   *

After completing the thirteen surviving chapters of *Romney,*
readers may be forgiven if their first question is, "Where's
Romney?" Wister's novel, splendid as it is in portraying both
Romney's heritage and late-nineteenth-century Philadelphia,
is certainly slow to introduce the character himself. Few novels—Laurence Sterne's *The Life and Opinions of Tristram Shandy*
(1760–67) is one that comes to mind—have the hero *in utero*
for such a large part of the story. When George Brett read the
first seven chapters of *Romney,* he noted the stately movement
of the narrative, as is suggested by Wister's account of his editor's reaction: "he says if I can keep up the pace I have set I'll
write *3 volumes*!!!" (OWP, Box 101, journal entry of 2 May
1914). Whether or not Wister could have ever produced the
equivalent of a Victorian triple-decker novel on the life of
Romney, it is clear that he planned a vast social tapestry placing Romney (from conception on) into the context of Philadelphia and its people. That we have fewer than nine months
of this ambitious story is indeed frustrating. But Wister's
extended treatment of a concentrated time period does give a
comprehensive view of a particular moment in the city's history. Monopolis/Philadelphia, not Romney, is the protagonist
of this novel in the fragmentary state in which it survives.

At least we do get one "Romney" in the novel, even if he is
not the man planned to be the hero of the story. As we find out
when Madam Hythe insists that her unborn grandchild must
be christened for his father, that father's given name is "Romney." Wister's narrator Augustus refers to the father throughout as "the bridegroom," no doubt to prevent confusion with
the unborn son Romney poised to make his appearance. What

would have next happened in the novel to Romney the father? Wister is a meticulous writer who foreshadows his plot, so some guesses can be made. Omens for the bridegroom are not favorable: Madam Hythe in Chapter X asks Evans Gwynedd to convince her son to make a will, and she tells Gwynedd of dreaming that she saw her son's dead body stretched out in a railway car. Furthermore, the bridegroom's brothers, the despicable Mort and Dug, have a sporting wager that within a year he can be reduced from straight-arrow entrepreneur to dissolute drunkard. But as part of the description in Chapter X of that luminous holiday taken by the bridegroom and his pregnant wife, we do discover that "even among the memories of later holidays that they took, this one bloomed an everlasting rose in a radiance unchanging" (page 107 above). Those "later holidays" hold out the welcome promise for failure by Mort and Dug, but it is hard to imagine that Wister would devote so many words to the will-making if he were not foreshadowing that Romney the son would inherit the family fortune sooner rather than later. The money will presumably come to Romney while he is still young; the will should guarantee, Madam Hythe insists, that the "fortune must be in hands that must never touch it except for its own benefit, until the boy is old enough to take care of it himself" (page 117 above).

In *Romney,* Wister deliberately obscures the exact dates, thus giving himself the artistic freedom to deal as he wishes with the historical background. Scholarly editors, no doubt, are overly concerned with tracking chronologies in fiction, but, before speculating further about what might have been planned for the plot, it does seem worthwhile to consider the dates of the novel's two time periods. When Augustus first appears in Chapter I, we learn that he understated his age in *Lady Baltimore* (1906), claiming to be twenty-eight when he was actually thirty-five. At the time Augustus is writing *Romney,* he is five years older. Since the events of *Lady Baltimore* seem to take place in

1902 (when Augustus was thirty-five),[1] the later time sequence in Romney is perhaps five years afterward in 1907 or, at the latest, in 1911—five years later than the publication of *Lady Baltimore*. That latter date, 1911, has the advantage of being close to the year in which Wister began *Romney*. In the flashback that begins Chapter V, and continues throughout what survives of the novel, Wister again masks the date ("What year it was by the calendar needs not be too precisely told," page 36 above) but sets the events a generation earlier. Datable events in these flashback chapters all cluster about the mid-1880s (see the various notes to *Romney,* below). Wister also refers in his novel to his friend Robert Grant's parallel story of *The Chippendales,* and Grant tells us that Henry Sumner first met his future bride at a masked ball, an event also mentioned in *Romney,* in the "early eighties" (*Chippendales,* 7).

Given that early-to-mid-1880s date for the initial events in Chapters V–XIII of *Romney,* our then literally embryonic hero would therefore be in his mid-to-late twenties in the later time sequence (1907–11) of Chapters I–IV. With the clues provided in those opening four chapters, and with information from elsewhere in the book and from Wister's other writings, we can see at least part of how the story would have developed. Romney, considered "that odd young man" by Aunt Carola, has been to college, where he acquired his nickname "Rummy." Despite that nickname, he did not drink excessively in college, perhaps warned by his father's sad example. Romney married a Bostonian, Alix Sumner, the daughter of Henry Sumner, whom we meet in his early twenties in the 1880s time sequence, and granddaughter of a Boston Chippendale. (Wister seems to have forgotten that, according to Grant's novel, Henry did not marry

---

1. In *Lady Baltimore,* the characters discuss the appointment of an African American as Collector of the Port; Roosevelt made this appointment of Dr. William Crum in 1902 (see *Roosevelt,* 114–18).

until 1898 [see *Chippendales,* 532, 583–84]; if Wister was using Grant's time sequence, Henry's daughter would thus be too young to be Romney's bride.) Wister planned a forlorn honeymoon for Romney and Alix, judging from journal entries written in Germany:

> *27 June 1914:*
> There is a honeymoon being passed at our Hotel Schwarzwold—not very successfully. . . . The bride looks and dresses like a servant. And seems sulky rather often. The groom dresses very well and has a pleasant face—he looks perplexed most of the time—but always amiable. . . . But the couple is very unenterprising—They walk & drive nowhere—but pass their days sitting reading in front of the hotel—
> *28 June 1914:*
> The bride and groom have given me a valuable suggestion for Romney. Lame honeymoons have been done in novels ere this but I will do another and make Uncle Andrew talk to Romney out of sympathy. (OWP, Box 101)

Not having Uncle Andrew's chat with Romney about sex is certainly a loss to comic literature; that Uncle Andrew spoke directly to Romney perhaps further suggests that the young man's father is dead. It is unclear whether this or some other conversation is the source of Aunt Carola's vague comment in Chapter I ("I hadn't known before about your Uncle and Romney and the Madeira. He tells me that he has always liked that young man," page 18 above). In the novel as a whole, Augustus threatens or promises, "There's not one of the Ten Commandments that isn't broken" (page 10 above)—not surprisingly, since the list of broken commandments is pretty well exhausted, except for murder, in the thirteen surviving chapters.

When Wister outlined *Romney,* then called *Dividends in Democracy,* to Theodore Roosevelt, he described it as "a picture of Philadelphia, and its passing from the old to the new order; the hero of no social position, married to a wife of good social position elsewhere, and turning out superior to his wife" (*Roosevelt,* 319). It thus remains to speculate, and it can be no more than speculation, how *Romney* would have shown this superiority and demonstrated the "dividends in democracy." In his account of the 1880s, Wister gives so much space to the railroad's power and to municipal corruption that corresponding sections in the novel's later time sequence (1907–11) seem inevitable. In the period between the publication of *Lady Baltimore* and the abandonment of *Romney* (1906 to 1915), progressive Philadelphians fought for honest and efficient government. Scattered early victories culminated in the election in 1911 of Rudolph Blankenburg ("Old Dutch Cleanser"), producing what was seen as a mandate for reform. Owen Wister and especially his wife, Mary Channing Wister, fought hard for Blankenburg, and their seven-year-old son remembered for eight decades how joyful his mother had been after that election.[2] Certainly *Romney's* participation in the municipal reform politics of Monopolis/ Philadelphia would bind together the two time sequences of the novel, would carry into the twentieth century the idealistic hopes of Henry Sumner, whose daughter Romney married, and would offer the possibility of defeating the Mark Beavers and Timothy Tingles of the world.

In the "Re-dedication" to Theodore Roosevelt in the 1911 edition of *The Virginian,* Wister recorded sentiments that would probably have become the major themes of *Romney. The Virginian,*

2. Taped interview with William Rotch Wister II (1904–93) by James Butler, 23 October 1993, La Salle University Connelly Library Wister Family Special Collection, PS3345.V536 1997rc.

Wister wrote in the year before he began *Romney,* "is an expression of American faith." True, the big-money interests and the labor unions threatened the nation, and "if the pillars of our house fall, it is they who will have been the cause thereof." Owen Wister, however, professed optimistic (and "Progressive") hopes about the nation's future: "But I believe the pillars will not fall, and that, with mistakes at times, but with wisdom in the main, we people will prove ourselves equal to the severest test to which political man has yet subjected himself—the test of Democracy" (*Virginian,* vii).

page 6 *"I liked nothing in that whole book so little, Augustus, as your not being candid about your age."*

The book Aunt Carola refers to is Wister's novel *Lady Baltimore* (1906), also narrated by Augustus and framed by opening and closing discussions with his Aunt. This novel of manners is set in fictional Kings Port (actual Charleston, South Carolina). Its title refers not to a person but to a kind of cake, thus explaining Aunt Carola's comment in *Romney* that the "very nice girl who made the cake" might have been the right woman for Augustus; Augustus is undeniably smitten with that "very nice girl," Eliza La Heu, but she marries his friend John Mayrant.

There is a technical problem in using the Augustus of *Lady Baltimore* (set in 1902) as the narrator of *Romney,* because Augustus is not really old enough to remember the Monopolis/Philadelphia described in the latter work, set in the mid-1880s. Wister's solution is simple: Augustus lied about his age in *Lady Baltimore.* If Augustus had been thirty-five in 1902, it moves his birth date back to about 1867, making him more nearly the contemporary of Wister (who was born in 1860).

page 8 *". . . to rival* Hugh Wynne?*"

S. Weir Mitchell's *Hugh Wynne, Free Quaker,* a historical novel set among Philadelphia Quakers during the Revolutionary War, was America's second best-selling novel of 1897 (see Frank Luther Mott, *Golden Multitudes: The Story of Best Sellers in the United States* [New

York: Macmillan, 1947], 211). It was physician-novelist
Mitchell (1829–1914) who in 1885 prescribed the "travel
cure" for his distant cousin Owen Wister, sending him
West and to eventual fame as a Western storyteller (see
Payne, 75–76). Wister's novel *Lady Baltimore* is dedi-
cated to Mitchell.

page 9 *"George Washington . . . the strong language he used to
General Lee upon that occasion."*
Major General Charles Lee ordered a retreat at Monmouth in defiance of George Washington's orders, pro-
voking the Commander-in-Chief's wrath and possibly
his profanity. Wister may have been thinking of such
accounts as the one by General Charles Scott, who,
asked if Washington ever swore, replied: "Once. It was
at Monmouth. . . . he swore till the leaves shook on the
trees, charming, delightful. Never have I enjoyed such
swearing before or since. . . . he swore like an angel from
Heaven." Unfortunately, the documentary evidence for
this scene and for the words then spoken is conflicting
(see Rupert Hughes, *George Washington: The Saviour of
the States, 1777–1781* [New York: William Morrow,
1930], 362–81). Owen Wister begins his biography, *The
Seven Ages of Washington,* by objecting to early writers'
censoring of Washington's language; "to-day we can see
the live and human Washington, full length . . . and we
gain a progenitor of flesh and blood" (New York:
Macmillan, 1907, 4). Wister's grandfather, Charles Jones
Wister (alive when Owen was a boy), had talked with
George Washington (see Payne, 9).

page 9 . . . *"like the famous marsh instead of like the famous
painter."*
Romney Marsh, a seventy-square-mile region in Kent in
southeast England, extends inland between the coastal

towns of Hythe and New Romney. The name "Romney Hythe" also pays tribute to Wister's novelist friend
Henry James, who lived at Rye—about ten miles from
New Romney. Augustus is, at least in part, modeled
upon Henry James.

English painter George Romney (1734–1802) is particularly known for his upper-class portraits.

page 13 *". . . Chateaubriand . . ."*
French Romantic writer François-Auguste-René,
Vicomte de Chateaubriand (1768–1848), in very popular works such as *Atala* (1801), *René* (1802, 1805), and
Voyage en Amérique (1827), presented glorious descrip-
tions of American scenery that fired the imaginations
of Europeans for the new world. Chateaubriand's
mixture of poetical religion, sublime nature, and fer-
vent romance had understandable appeal.

page 15 *"My friend Robert Grant has written a delightful account
of that family."*
Wister must have savored having the fictional Augustus refer to the fictional Chippendales in his friend
Robert Grant's novel *The Chippendales* (1909). Like
Romney, The Chippendales portrays the values of an old
and established social order giving way before com-
merce. Wister's and Grant's most intensive contacts
date from the time of their joint service on the Harvard overseers' English Department Committee; during the early part of that period Wister was at work on
Romney (see Payne, 283, 308).

As *The Chippendales* makes clear, Henry Sumner's
daughter Alix is indeed a great-niece of Georgiana Chippendale; in Grant's novel, Henry Sumner married in
1898 and his first child was a daughter. In *Romney,* Henry
first appears in the mid-1880s flashback with which

Augustus begins Chapter v. The St. Michaels of Kings Port/Charleston appear in Wister's *Lady Baltimore*.

page 17 *". . . than to wish to see that terrible play again."*

Aunt Carola's distaste for *Othello* echoes that of Wister's cousin and mentor, the Shakespeare scholar Horace Howard Furness, who had a hard time returning to his work on the play after his wife Kate died in 1883. Furness wrote on 1 October 1884 that "'Othello' is pure, unalleviated, black tragedy, too bitter bad to be read twice" (Furness to H. Corson, quoted in James M. Gibson, "Horace Howard Furness: Book Collector and Library Builder," *Shakespeare Study Today: The Horace Howard Furness Memorial Lectures* [New York: AMS Press, 1986], 178). The Virginian also disliked the work: "I have read that play Othello. No man should write down such a thing. Do you know if it is true? I have seen one worse affair down in Arizona. He killed his little child as well as his wife but such things should not be put down in fine language for the public" (*Virginian,* 278).

page 17 *"The victoria was there . . . "*

"A light low, four wheeled carriage having a collapsible hood, with seats (usually) for two persons and an elevated seat in front for the driver" (*Oxford English Dictionary,* also citing an 1876 passage: "A victoria is the prettiest carriage a lady can possibly drive in").

page 18 *"Imagine dear Sir Walter!"*

Both in his youth and in his maturity, Wister much admired Scottish novelist and poet Sir Walter Scott (1771–1832), and his *Kenilworth* is a favorite novel of the hero of *The Virginian* (see Payne, 19, 163). Wister's grandmother Fanny Kemble, upon whom Aunt Carola may be partially based, had met Sir Walter Scott.

page 20 *"'Change and decay . . . abide with me.'"*
Aunt Carola quotes from the second verse of the hymn
"Abide with Me: Fast Falls the Eventide," with lyrics
by Henry F. Lyte (1793–1847) and music by William
H. Monk.

page 21 *"I speak like Lucio, 'according to the trick. . .'"*
Shakespeare in *Measure for Measure* (V.i.506–8) has
Lucio explain that he was joking: "'Faith, my lord, I
spoke it but according to the trick. If you will hang me
for it, you may; but I had rather it would please you, I
might be whipt."

page 21 *"They flowed in the two rivers . . ."*
The two rivers are, of course, the Schuylkill and the
Delaware, between which William Penn laid out
Philadelphia in 1682.

page 22 *". . . quaker-lady . . ."*
Owen Wister's brother-in-law, John Caspar Wister,
writes as follows in his *Collier's Encyclopedia* entry for
"Bluet": "*Houstonia caerulea,* a tiny perennial of the
madder family, also called Quaker Lady, or innocence" (1st ed., 1950).

page 25 *"Two wars we had in the next fifty years . . ."*
Wister's reference is to the War of 1812 and the Mexican War (1846–48). In Chapter xi, the characters discuss whether Cheswold Lawne had served in the
Mexican War.

page 25 *"From England . . . And lastly . . . a phlegmatic foreign
race . . ."*
Wister's own heritage combined these English and
Germanic stocks. For his further thoughts about how
those nationalities combined to produce Philadelphia's

"moderation" and resistance to change, see "The Keystone Crime" in Appendix II, below.

page 26 *"Where there is no vision, the people perish."*
Proverbs 29:18.

page 31 *". . . San Domingo . . ."*
Inspired in part by the French Revolution, a slave revolt, quickly to be led by Toussaint L'Ouverture, broke out in 1791 in Saint Domingue (the French colonial name for the entire island of Hispaniola, now divided into Haiti and the Dominican Republic) and lasted thirteen bloody years. As Wister describes in *Romney,* many of the French fled the island, and some of those refugees ended up in Monopolis/Philadelphia.

page 33 *"The tradition of our chicken soup and croquettes still haunts the palate."*
Compare the following passage from Chapter XVI of *The Virginian:* "There was a man named Saynt Augustine got run out of Domingo, which is a Dago island. He come to Philadelphia, an' he was dead broke. But Saynt Augustine was a live man, an' he saw Philadelphia was full o' Quakers that dressed plain an' eat humdrum. So he started cookin' Domingo way for 'em, an' they caught right ahold. Terrapin, he gave 'em, an' croakeets, an' he'd use forty chickens to make a broth he called consommay. An' he got rich, and Philadelphia got well known. . . ." (198).

page 33 *". . . Works of Pope, Addison, Fielding and Smollett . . ."*
Alexander Pope, Joseph Addison, Henry Fielding, and Tobias Smollett would be seen as among the foremost writers of the relatively stable culture of eighteenth-century Britain. The first families of Monopolis no doubt considered these writers as more suitable

than either "foreign" ones or those British writers of the nineteenth century who sometimes dealt with the common man and revolutionary political ideas.

Fielding may seem to be odd man out on such a list, given his rather exuberant portrayal of gustatory and other sensual enjoyments, especially in *Tom Jones*. But as Henry Sumner indicates at the end of *Romney*, Chapter x, "Monopolis reminds me of Fielding, somehow"; Sumner, and perhaps Wister, finds Monopolis/Philadelphia "rather convivial" compared to Boston.

page 33 "*. . . the greatest railroad conducted anywhere by mankind.*"

It has been said that there was a time when "good Philadelphia children were taught to pray for the Republican Party, the Girard Trust, and the Pennsylvania Railroad" (Burt, 188). Established in 1846, the PRR eventually became "the most important single enterprise of the city" of Philadelphia and "the single largest corporation in the country" (Weigley, 475). The most visible symbol of this corporate powerhouse and nest egg for Philadelphia investors was the imposing Broad Street Station, designed by Frank Furness. It opened in December 1881 and was abandoned in 1952.

page 34 "*. . . the suburban station Ap Thomas.*"

In the 1870s and 1880s, the Pennsylvania Railroad began to enlarge its facilities for suburban travel and to develop its real estate holdings along the old "Main Line of Public Works" just west of Philadelphia. Large, beautiful, well-landscaped stations were built and given suitably Welsh names, either preserving the original community names (Merion, Haverford) or creating new ones (for example, Humphreysville and

Elm changed to Bryn Mawr and Narberth, respectively). The mnemonic device "Old Maids Never Wed And Have Babies Period" helped riders remember the order of those "Main Line" stations on the "Paoli Local": Overbrook, Merion, Narberth, Wynnewood, Ardmore, Haverford, Bryn Mawr, and—after others— Paoli. The Railroad's directors intended to fashion on the "Main Line" exclusive suburbs for the best families.

Romney's "Ap Thomas" ("ap" is Welsh for "son of") is based on these new "Main Line" communities, which included land purchased from William Penn on 18 March 1682 by John ap Thomas and Wister's ancestor Dr. Edward Jones. The novelist's extended family was thus associated with this "Welsh Tract," now the "Main Line," for six generations. In 1924 Owen Wister himself moved to the area, taking up "Long House" in Bryn Mawr as his principal residence until his death in 1938. Indeed, Bryn Mawr, about ten-and-a-half miles west from Philadelphia's center, seems to be the primary inspiration for "Ap Thomas." The Pennsylvania Railroad built the Bryn Mawr Hotel in 1872 to encourage train travel, and Bryn Mawr at the start was a summer resort for Philadelphia's socially-connected. It then developed into a year-round community. By selling its building lots with restrictive covenants mandating minimum construction costs, the Railroad sought to attract well-placed families who would frequent the railway line and pay thirty cents, the 1883 rate, for each one-way trip to Philadelphia. Bryn Mawr had enough of a reputation for Easterners to discuss it in *The Virginian,* set, like the early episodes of *Romney,* in the 1880s. *Boyd's Blue Book, Season of 1884–85,* lists 183 families in Bryn Mawr, with 55 of them in "summer residence only" at the hotel. Thus Bryn Mawr owed its

FIG 9
Dante Gabriel Rossetti, *Astarte Syriaca*, 1877. Wister may
well have seen this painting, also known as *Venus Astarte*,
during its exhibition in 1883 at London's Royal Academy.
Three decades later, in *Romney*, Wister referred to the
painting in describing women's fashions.

existence and its daily ritual of meeting the trains to and from Philadelphia—about two dozen each way per day in 1884—to the Pennsylvania Railroad. See Barbara Alyce Farrow, *The History of Bryn Mawr, 1683–1900* (Bryn Mawr: Committee of Residents and the Bryn Mawr Civic Association, 1962).

page 36 *". . . Paris had not yet offered Venus Astarte . . ."*
Astarte, goddess of fertility and love, is more ancient than the related Greek Aphrodite and Roman Venus: "Astarte of the Syrians: Venus Queen / Ere Aphrodite was," writes Dante Gabriel Rossetti in a sonnet to accompany his famous and controversial painting *Astarte Syriaca* (1877; originally called *Venus Astarte*). This larger-than-life-size painting erotically portrays a powerful, sensuous and mysterious woman, clad in a diaphanous green gown cut off-the-shoulder and seemingly about to fall off the body. This painting (see page 185 above) is now at the Manchester, England, City Art Gallery; for the sonnet ("Mystery: lo! betwixt the sun and moon"), see *The Works of Dante Gabriel Rossetti* (London: Ellis, 1911), 226.

page 36 *". . . sits well in her basket phaeton."*
Mrs. Delair, a woman who sets her own course in life, appropriately arrives in a phaeton, a low-built and elegant carriage for ladies who prefer to do their own driving.

page 36 *". . . she has called her ponies* Sturm *and* Drang . . ."
"Sturm und Drang" (Storm and Stress) is the name given to the late eighteenth-century German Romantic movement emphasizing idealism, nature, and revolt against established rules; important writers were Johann Wolfgang von Goethe, Johann Gottfried von

Herder, and Johann Christoph Friedrich von Schiller. Sarah Butler Wister, Owen Wister's mother, named a team of horses "Parsifal" and "Siegfried" after title characters of operas by German composer Richard Wagner (1813–1883).

page 37 *". . . demirep . . ."*
"A woman whose character is only half-reputable; a woman of doubtful reputation or suspected chastity" (*Oxford English Dictionary*).

page 38 *". . . leader of the Monopolis bar since the death of a great predecessor . . ."*
"Any man who heads the Philadelphia bar, even in a time of lull, must have qualities that would make him a man of mark at any period in Westminster Hall," observes the Hon. James T. Mitchell, Chief Justice of the Supreme Court of Pennsylvania, in the volume of essays *The Law Association of Philadelphia . . . 1802–1902* (Philadelphia: The Law Association, 1906), 57.

page 38 *". . . the blue seal Johannisberger . . ."*
As might be expected, Evans Gwynedd's taste runs to the elegant and the expensive. One possibility for his wine is the Schloss Johannisberger Kabinett Himmelblau (or sky-blue seal), a Rhine Riesling (see Frank Schoonmaker's *The Wines of Germany* [New York: Hastings House, 1956], 77–78).

page 39 *". . . was just beginning to displace the 'kettle-drum.'"*
"An afternoon tea-party on a large scale" (*Oxford English Dictionary,* citing a passage from 1861: "Then the 5 o'clock tea, the sort of little assembly so happily called 'kettle-drum'"). The *OED* also points out the punning

combination of "drum" (an evening assembly of fashionable people at a private house) and "tea-kettle."

page 40 *"I call any private house as large as that shocking . . .'"*
The "Main Line" communities west of Philadelphia attracted both old and new money, and some of the newly moneyed people spent lavishly to erect palatial estates. In particular, the Pennsylvania Railroad encouraged executives of its own and related enterprises to build there. The house that so shocked the "oldmoney" station party in *Romney* would have several possible sources in the 1880s, including "Bardwold" in Merion (completed 1885). An ostentatious pile looking very like a French château, Bardwold was the home of the widow of Matthew Baird (1817–1877), senior partner of the Baldwin Locomotive Works. One can imagine the reactions of Mrs. Cuthbert and Mrs. Delair to Matthew Baird's progress from Irish bricklayer to recipient of the top annual personal income in Philadelphia (see Baltzell, *Philadelphia Gentlemen,* 108). The two women would also have had choice comments about the miniature steam engine of silver and gold on the balcony overlooking the three-story great hall of "Bardwold."

"Bardwold," though, is just one example of a flurry of Main Line châteaux erected in the last quarter of the nineteenth century. Among those still standing are "Rathalla" (ca. 1889) in Rosemont and "Woodmont" (ca. 1892) in Gladwyne.

In her *Heaven Was Not Enough* (1955), Constance O'Hara describes how Philadelphia society of half a century earlier reacted to the ostentatious display of the *nouveaux riches*: "Philadelphia, in my youth, laughed right heartily at Eva Stotesbury, her diamond dog collar and her Rolls Royce with two men on the box. The Wideners with their mansion at Elkins Park would have been dismissed as utter parvenus. . . . No one ever forgot to mention that the Wideners had been butchers" (109–10, as quoted in Lukacs, 34).

page 40 "... *whether it is a copy of Amboise or Azay-le-Rideau.*"
If the Hythes's newly built château replicated either Amboise or Azay-le-Rideau (both early Renaissance houses in France's Loire River Valley), it was a majestic and vast building indeed. Azay-le-Rideau is set in a loop of the River Indre, thus perhaps giving rise to Gwynedd's comment about a moat; Amboise was occasionally a royal residence. Since the design of the typical Main Line château eclectically echoed several French originals, Gwynedd's confusion about the ultimate source for the Hythes's mansion is understandable and may be a joke on Wister's part.

page 46 "... *the Free Soil Club* ..."
Wister's Philadelphia source for the "Free Soil Club" is probably the Union League at Broad and Sansom Streets, founded by Republicans during the Civil War to support the Union (thus non-slaveholding or "free soil") cause. The 1865 building on Broad Street (called "Great Street" in *Romney*) certainly has magnificent steps for carrying down a drunken Dug. According to Nathaniel Burt, "In old Philadelphia circles it is understood that though the Union League is very honorable and important, it is not really socially flawless" (Burt, 267). The upstart Dug would certainly not have been accepted at Wister's own Philadelphia Club, the oldest in America (established 1834) and without doubt "socially flawless."

page 48 *". . . the horses were admirable English hackneys."*

A hackney is "a horse of middle size and quality, used for ordinary riding" (*Oxford English Dictionary*).

page 50 *". . . our Railroad a relief after the New York and New Haven?"*

Henry Sumner would have come from Boston to New York on the New York and New Haven Railroad, a line far inferior (Evans Gwynedd thinks) to "our Railroad," the Pennsylvania, for which Gwynedd is legal counsel. Perplexingly to Gwynedd, Henry continued his trip to Philadelphia not on the Pennsylvania but on the line of its competitor, the Philadelphia and Reading / Central New Jersey joint route from Jersey City. He would then have continued on to Ap Thomas on the Pennsylvania Railroad, leaving from that railroad's Broad Street Station. The Philadelphia and Reading locomotives were anthracite burners, noted for their low smoke.

Henry's remarks to Evans Gwynedd and his sister become progressively more surprising, culminating in his heretical approval of a railroad commission's forbidding of "excessive dividends." The other railroads Henry mentions all served the Boston area.

page 50 *". . . Slaughter House Cases . . ."*

In 1872 the United States Supreme Court upheld an 1869 Louisiana law granting to a private corporation a monopoly for the building and maintaining of slaughterhouses in New Orleans. Interpreting the Thirteenth, Fourteenth, and Fifteenth Amendments to the United States Constitution for the first time, the Court refused to limit a state's authority to regulate private businesses for the health, safety, and welfare of the public. The dissenting opinion by Mr. Justice Bradley, however, provided arguments the Court would soon use to reverse itself and interpret the due-process clause of the Fourteenth Amendment as the constitutional basis for enforcing the laissez-faire economic system of the late nineteenth and early twentieth centuries. (I am grateful to Joseph Brogan of La Salle University for providing this note.)

page 50 *"Just now I'm interested in sparrows."*
The English or house sparrow (actually a European finch rather than a true sparrow) was introduced to North America in 1853 in an attempt to control the canker worm. Within a few decades sparrows so multiplied that they were considered pests because of their harassment and displacement of native birds, their damaging of crops and defacing of buildings, and their potential for spreading disease.

page 51 *"... surely the welkin would have shouted now."*
Welkin: "Considered as the abode of the Deity, or of the gods of heathen mythology: The celestial regions, heaven" (*Oxford English Dictionary*).

page 61 *"... Eros and Hymen ..."*
Eros and Hymen are, respectively, the Greek gods of love and marriage.

page 66 *"... saw him leap into the dog-cart ..."*
A dog-cart was an all-purpose, two-wheel, horse-drawn, open cart with seats back to back; the rear seat originally could be shut up to form a box for dogs.

page 66 *"She knew by heart the whole of this psalm ..."*
Psalms 19:5.

page 67 *". . . Boston, or in Beverly Farms."*

> Beverly Farms is an exclusive community about two dozen miles north of Boston on the North Shore. Wister knew the area as early as his teens, writing in a schoolboy notebook a poem "At Beverly" (*OWP,* Box 63), and he renewed his acquaintance during his time at Harvard. In 1895 he visited Beverly Farms during a three-week trip to New England; the author wanted to see old friends and to write an Eastern "postscript" to his Western journals (see Payne, 160–61).

page 70 *". . . Patriarch Balls . . ."*

> Wister's Philadelphia source for Monopolis's "Patriarch Balls" is no doubt the "Assembly," dating from 1748 and America's oldest such dancing event. "Admission to the Assembly is, or is supposed to be, strictly hereditary in the male line. That is, sons and daughters of members are eligible, though not automatically, when they reach a proper age." The event is, Burt continues, "probably still the most august of America's social occasions" (278, 95). John Lukacs writes that "membership in the Assembly in Philadelphia was the local equivalent to a European court. . . . It meant an invitation to the social stratosphere" (45). Owen Wister served as one of the six yearly "Managers" of the Assembly in 1898, 1899, and 1900; his wife Mary was one of the six "Patronesses" in 1901 (see *The Philadelphia Assemblies, 1748–1948,* ed. Joseph P. Sims [Philadelphia, 1947], 42–43).

page 70 *". . . Goethe's eternal-feminine drawing us upward."*

> These lines translate the conclusion of Johann Wolfgang von Goethe's *Faust* ("Das Ewig-Weibliche / Zieht uns hinan"). According to Hans Eichner, the Eternal

Feminine here "refers to the ideal of purity that must inspire, though it must not inhibit, even the man of action, and that, to Goethe, always appeared in feminine guise" ("The Eternal Feminine: An Aspect of Goethe's Ethics," in *Faust: A Tragedy,* ed. Cyrus Hamlin [New York: W. W. Norton, 1976], 624).

page 70 *". . . the Buena Vista Hotel."*
The "Buena Vista Hotel" is clearly based on Philadelphia's Bellevue Hotel, opened in 1882 on the northwest corner of Broad and Walnut Streets. The building closed in 1904, when the hotel moved to the newly built structure across Walnut Street (on the site of the old Stratford Hotel) as part of the new Bellevue-Stratford Hotel. Like Monopolis's Buena Vista, the Bellevue had "a homelike brick exterior" and a "quarter century of existence."

page 70 *"The renowned naturalist who declared, that from a single bone he could reconstruct the whole animal . . ."*
Othniel Charles Marsh (1831–1899) and Edward Drinker Cope (1840–1897), the two great (and feuding) American paleontologists of the late nineteenth century, both mentally reconstructed animals from small amounts of fossil remains. Marsh, for example, in 1870 found a single thin, hollow bone and from it postulated a pterodactyl with a twenty-foot wingspan (see Url Lanham, *The Bone Hunters* [New York: Columbia University Press, 1973], 84–85). Marsh was Professor of Paleontology at Yale, the first such appointment in the United States; Cope was born in Philadelphia, and he taught at Haverford College and later at the University of Pennsylvania. For more information on Marsh and Cope, see David Rains Wallace, *The Bonehunters' Revenge:*

Dinosaurs, Greed, and the Greatest Scientific Feud of the Gilded Age (Boston: Houghton Mifflin, 1999), and Mark Jaffe, *The Gilded Dinosaur: The Fossil Wars between E. D. Cope and O. C. Marsh and the Rise of American Science* (New York: Crown, 2000).

page 70   "*. . . Pagliacci . . .*"
I Pagliacci, the opera by Ruggiero Leoncavallo (1857–1919), was first produced in Milan on 21 May 1892. Wister's senior thesis at Harvard was "An Inquiry into the Future of Opera."

page 72   *"Boston had a preacher named Phillips Brooks . . ."*
Ordained an Episcopal priest in 1860, Phillips Brooks (1835–1893) became rector of Holy Trinity on Philadelphia's Rittenhouse Square and knew Wister's mother Sarah. When Brooks moved to Boston in 1869 as rector of Trinity Church, he quickly became a very popular preacher and beloved figure, serving Harvard as an overseer and a counselor of students. Undergraduate Owen Wister occasionally ate the midday meal with Brooks after Sunday services; while at Harvard, Wister was confirmed as an Episcopalian. Brooks is also remembered for having written the lyrics to "O Little Town of Bethlehem."

page 73   "*. . . we'll have that Niersteiner cup.*"
Niersteiner, a Rhine Riesling, is a decent but somewhat bland wine, suitable for making the punch ordered by Joe Gwynedd and Henry Sumner.

page 73   *"But the Dry Monopole's delicious here."*
Heidsieck Monopole Champagne would be a predictable option on the wine list of such a first-class hotel

as the Buena Vista/Bellevue. That brand was a choice of Tsar Nicholas II (see *Newsweek,* 19 July 1999, 12), and it was mid-priced among the seven champagnes on the first-class wine list of the *Titanic.*

page 73   *"'That's Mark Beaver, our political leader, and king bird of prey,' said Joe."*
Matthew Stanley Quay is the source for "Mark Beaver." To make sure that his contemporary readers would make the identification, Wister altered in manuscript the last name of this character from "Davis" to "Beaver"; Beaver, Pennsylvania was, famously, the hometown of Matt Quay. In his near-five-decade career in politics, Quay was Philadelphia city-boss, Pennsylvania state treasurer (1885), United States Senator from Pennsylvania (1887–1904), and Republican national chairman and president-maker in 1888. Whether he controlled Philadelphia politics directly or, after he became a national figure, through his subordinates, Quay was "the new proprietor of Pennsylvania" (Kehl, 67). Quay's statue stands at the head of the grand staircase in the Pennsylvania State Capitol, a building whose construction through graft and corruption Owen Wister excoriated in his essay "The Keystone Crime: Pennsylvania's Graft-Cankered Capitol" (see Appendix 11, below). In that same essay, Wister quotes Quay's philosophy of bossism: "I can sometimes do without a governor, but I always need a treasurer" (437).

Henry Sumner's physical description of Mark Beaver as "thin and sallow, with very plain hair and one drooping eyelid" would also be recognized by Wister's contemporaries as portraying Matt Quay, of whom his biographer writes as follows: "Small in stature . . . Quay was not a handsome man. . . . The right eye was usually dull or fishy. The left eyelid drooped, causing him to squint constantly" (Kehl, xvii).

What Henry Sumner is here beginning to find out about Philadelphia's political corruption will become one of the principal themes of *Romney*. As Lincoln Steffens wrote in his famous article "Philadelphia: Corrupt But Contented," "Other American cities, no matter how bad their own condition may be, all point to Philadelphia as worse—'the worst-governed city in the country'" (*McClure's Magazine,* July 1903, 249). Wister has at least some hope: "Philadelphia may some day cease to be the dirtiest smear on the map of the United States" ("Keystone Crime," 448).

page 74 *". . . on the stage at the Howard Athenaeum."*
Originally a legitimate theater, Boston's now-gone Howard Athenaeum (or "Old Howard") had by Henry Sumner's time become a hall for popular entertainment and burlesque.

page 84 *". . . has been pointed out by an eminent Frenchman."*
Wister's reference is vague, but one French work in which the characters spend much time contemplating, and discussing, the misfortunes of others is Voltaire's *Candide* (1758).

page 84 *". . . the Piedmont Air Line."*
"Air Line" here—and in Wister's later use of the phrase in "Bayside Air Line"—refers to a railroad that approximated or claimed to approximate the shortest distance ("air line") between two points. The phrase was current from the 1850s to about 1900. I am grateful to Christopher T. Baer of the Hagley Museum and Library for providing this information.

page 98 *"'He means Mark Beaver,' said Joe."*

Gwynedd's guests were not the only ones who had trouble deciding whether Mark Beaver/Matt Quay was a "king bird of prey" or a "statesman": by the time of Quay's death in 1904, writes his biographer James Kehl, "All of America had come to know his name, but few spoke of him in neutral tones: he was either revered or despised" (Kehl, xi). Few other than Evans Gwynedd, though, would compare Mark Beaver/Matt Quay to such statesmen-orators as Daniel Webster and Henry Clay; Quay spoke poorly, sometimes mumbling indistinctly (see Kehl, xvi). Gwynedd correctly predicts that Mark Beaver/Matt Quay, second in Pennsylvania in the mid-1880s to the "Cameron Machine" then led by Senator J. Donald Cameron, would in a few years become the Commonwealth's "first statesman"—or, at least, political power. Wister's essay "Keystone Crime" presents a devastating attack on Quay's "forty years of unpunished robbery" (437).

It is not surprising that Johnnie Adair is so struck by Mark Beaver's cigars: Matt Quay was "an inveterate smoker" of Havana cigars, and "he literally and figuratively contributed as much as anyone to the smoke-filled-room image of politics" (Kehl, xvii).

Like Mark Beaver, Matt Quay was a great reader and had a "feeling for the Delaware Indians" that was "deeply touching." A well-educated man, Quay read the Latin classics in the original and was seldom without a book; his favorite writers were Horace, Homer, Virgil, Dante, Shakespeare, John Greenleaf Whittier, and Henry Wadsworth Longfellow (see Kehl, 6). One of the legendary stories (which may have a grain of truth) is that British writer Rudyard Kipling called Quay "America's foremost literary critic" or, in another

version, "the best-read man in America" (Kehl, 283;
Burt, 542). Matt Quay's lifelong devotion to Native
American causes, and especially to the Delaware tribe,
was also well known; an unproven account suggests
that one of his ancestors may have married a Delaware
or Abnaki woman (Kehl, 3; see also 248–50).

page 99 *". . . Gratiano . . ."*
Bassanio says of a character in *The Merchant of Venice:*
"Gratiano speaks an infinite deal of nothing, more
than any man in all Venice. His reasons are as two
grains of wheat hid in two bushels of chaff: you shall
seek all day ere you find them, they are not worth the
search" (1.i.114–19).

page 101 *"Professor Lovejoy used to say in English Five . . ."*
Henry Sumner here remembers his fifth course in
English Literature at Harvard in those days when college courses had titles less descriptive but perhaps
more understandable than at present. In *Philosophy
Four* (1903), Owen Wister told a humorous short story
about one of his Harvard courses. Sumner's "English
Five" in the early 1880s seems to have been commend-
ably up to date in covering then-still-living British
poets Robert Browning and Algernon Swinburne.

page 101 *". . . Australian ballot . . ."*
The so-called "Australian ballot," which provided for
secret voting on an official ballot containing all the
candidates' names, was a favorite cause of reformers
because they hoped a secret ballot would reduce elec-
toral corruption. The "Australian ballot" was introduced in Pennsylvania in 1891 (see Lukacs, 70).

page 103 *"Their new city-hall, not a quarter finished yet, though it's been going on I forget how many years . . ."*

Philadelphia's City Hall indeed took a long time to complete, from the first meeting of the "Commission for the Erection of Public Buildings" in 1871 until the turning over of the building to the city in 1901. Good progress was made during the early years, but construction slowed from the mid-1870s through the early 1880s as the various city councils cut funding (and, for the year of 1877, eliminated it entirely). By 1884, the exterior of City Hall, except for the tower, was completed; the statue of William Penn was lifted to the top of the tower in 1894.

page 104 *". . . chronicle of the Chippendale family, written by my friend Robert Grant."*

Robert Grant's novel *The Chippendales* traces Henry Sumner's sometimes inept fifteen-year courtship of feisty Priscilla Avery, from their meeting at a fancy ball (in the "early eighties," 7) to their marriage in 1898 (see 532, 583–84). Henry stayed true to his reform principles, running for mayor of Boston in December 1897; he lost but finished second: "a moral victory for independence in municipal politics" (532). "Alert he stands, as the angel with the flaming sword at the gate of Paradise, to detect and repel the foes of civic righteousness" (601).

Priscilla Avery's father, at the start of the novel a seemingly impractical tinkerer, develops a process for producing electricity from coke. His fictional company ("Electric Coke") becomes "one of the great industrial corporations of the world" (600), the source of Priscilla's "very large fortune" mentioned by Wister.

At the end of *The Chippendales,* we hear about Henry's and Priscilla's offspring: their first child is a daughter—"with the eyes and dash of her mother"— followed by twin boys (599). Owen Wister calls that daughter, unnamed in Robert Grant's novel, Alix: in Chapter 1 of *Romney,* Aunt Carola refers to Alix as the child of Henry Sumner.

Robert Grant wrote his own account of Henry Sumner's daughter, whom he names Annabel, in *The Dark Horse: A Story of the Younger Chippendales* (Boston: Houghton Mifflin, 1931). Grant's plot has nothing to do with *Romney*.

page 114 *". . . nothing stronger than apollinaris."*
Apollinaris is a brand of imported bottled mineral water.

page 120 *". . . to sit reading his Blackstone . . ."*
Sir William Blackstone's *Commentaries on the Laws of England* (first published between 1765 and 1769) attempted to arrange the whole body of English law into four volumes; Wister refers to the first two volumes, "Rights of Persons" and "Rights of Things," in his phrase "Persons and Things." When asked how to acquire a thorough knowledge of the law, Abraham Lincoln in 1860 recommended starting with Blackstone's *Commentaries,* "reading it carefully through, say twice." Whatever its virtues, the *Commentaries* included some murky byways in listing its many centuries of precedents, such as the Rule in Shelley's Case: "an obscenely obscure point of law on the transfer of property originating in the 1300s." Similarly, "Quia Emptores" (so named from the first two words of this statute of 1290) concerns the buying and selling of land. The study of law by the case-study method replaced

this primary reliance on Blackstone, and Harvard's Law School, whence Wister graduated in 1888, led the way. (See Greg Bailey, "Blackstone in America," *The Early America Review,* 1:4 [Spring 1997], http://earlyamerica.com/review/spring97/blackstone. html, the source of the quotations in this paragraph.)

In 1885, about when his fictional law students were reading their Blackstone, Owen Wister himself was "nibbling at Blackstone" at a Philadelphia law office (see *Roosevelt,* 28).

page 121 *". . . some volumes of Meeson and Welsby . . ."*
Meeson and Welsby's Reports of Cases Argued and Determined in the Courts of Exchequer and Exchequer Chamber covers the years from 1836 to 1847.

page 121 *"Lepidus Senex . . ."*
"Lepidus Senex," which Wister goes on to translate in the next paragraph, is a stock character in Greek New Comedy of the fourth and fifth centuries B.C. and in the adaptations of that work by Roman writers Plautus and Terence.

page 123 *". . . and came out upon the beautiful old square."*
The "beautiful old square" (Independence Square, surrounding Independence Hall) is certainly a spot, as this paragraph goes on to indicate, where "feet historic, feet revolutionary" have walked, and Owen Wister intimately knew the area as it was in the 1880s. His first law office with Francis Rawle's firm was just off Independence Square at 402 Walnut Street. Wister's next law office (which he used for writing fiction rather than practicing law) was at 328 Chestnut Street, also adjacent to Independence Square.

page 124 *". . . the library, quaint with its Greek pilasters and old-time simplicity."*

Those Greek pilasters clearly identify the Library Company of Philadelphia; this building stood (and, despite its demolition in the 1880s, stands again in reconstruction) on Fifth Street across from the eastern side of Independence Square. Founded in 1731 by Benjamin Franklin, the Library Company was the *de facto* Library of Congress when Philadelphia was the nation's capital. The Fifth Street building is today used by the American Philosophical Society; the Library Company, after many years using two locations—the Ridgway Building at Broad and Christian Streets, and a building at Juniper and Locust Streets—is now at 1314 Locust Street.

Mrs. Delair's carrying away of a volume marks her as one of about a thousand Library Company members; they, unlike the general public, were permitted to borrow books as well as to consult them on premises. Owen Wister became president of the Library Company and in 1932 gave its bicentenary address.

page 125 *". . . Jupiter, President of The Railroad . . ."*

The President of the Pennsylvania Railroad during the time in which *Romney* takes place was George Roberts, who held the post from 1880 to 1897. Roberts was preceded by Thomas Scott (1874–80) and succeeded by Alexander Cassatt (1899–1906), brother of painter Mary Cassatt. During the tenures of Roberts and Cassatt, writes Nathaniel Burt, the Pennsylvania Railroad Board of Directors attracted the socially prominent and "became one of Philadelphia's best clubs" (190); hence, Timothy Tingle's desperate desire to be on the Board was for more than simply financial reasons.

Wister was well placed to describe "Jupiters, presidents of railroads" and their associates. For example, among the dozen-and-a-half members of the Mahogany Tree Club at its dinner in November 1902 were Wister, Alexander Cassatt (President of the Pennsylvania Railroad), George Baer (President of the Reading Railroad), author S. Weir Mitchell, Henry du Pont (retired president of the Wilmington Northern Railroad), James Mitchell (Chief Justice of Pennsylvania), and assorted judges, lawyers, and doctors. "My life," writes Wister, "was chiefly passed among the Cassatts, the Baers, and the Mitchells" (*Roosevelt,* 192–93, 201).

At this November 1902 dinner, railroad-president Baer shouted at Wister his opinion about Roosevelt's establishment of a commission to mediate that year's coal strike: "Does your friend ever *think*?" "He certainly seems to act," replied Wister (*Roosevelt,* 193). Wister's portrait of Jupiter draws on George Baer's social outlook. In July 1902, Baer wrote a correspondent: "The rights and interests of the laboring man will be protected and cared for—not by the labor agitators, but the Christian men to whom God in His infinite wisdom has given control of the property interests of the country" (*Roosevelt,* 195). Asked by a member of the Coal Commission whether he might be treating his immigrant workers badly, Baer responded, "They don't suffer; they don't even speak English" (Anthracite Coal Commission, *Report to the President on the Anthracite Coal Strike of May–October, 1902* [Washington, D.C., 1903], 35).

page 125 *"The bird of prey nodded an imperceptible yes."*
The account in the next few paragraphs of Mark Beaver's silences draws on Matt Quay's famous ability to

suggest without saying—and to keep his secrets. James Kehl writes that Quay was particularly adept at obeying "the new commandment of bossism: 'Never write when you can say it; never say it when you can nod your head.'. . . In time this refuge in silence came to be recognized as Quay's social trademark." "One critic who was aware of Quay's linguistic proficiency," continues Kehl, "conceded that he knew how 'to keep silent in sixteen different languages'" (Kehl, xv).

Wister's having Mark Beaver carry a book on Semiramis, a mythical queen of Assyria, nods toward Matt Quay's interests in ancient cultures. Semiramis is also celebrated as the builder of many cities and public works (which would have made her an appealing figure to Mark Beaver); in some versions of the legend, she acquired her husband's throne by contriving his death (which would have made her a suitable figure of corruption to Owen Wister).

Mark Beaver's aphorism about the sheep and wolves was characteristic of Matt Quay's love for such pithy and sardonic definitions. The most famous such remark attributed to him (perhaps inaccurately) is that politics was "the art of taking money from the few and votes from the many under the pretext of protecting the one from the other" (quoted in Kehl, xiii; see also 257 n. 4).

page 126 *"The riparian owners . . ."*

Riparian owners, those owning property bordering a river or other body of water, have rights to access and use of the shore and water. Because such owners have claims to the streambed, as well as to the land between low and high water, they might indeed be able to hold up construction of a railroad line.

page 126 *"I don't want to build a parallel road if I can help it."*
Jupiter wants to expand the Pennsylvania Railroad's routes, using part of the line of another railroad (later identified as Bayside Air Line) if he can obtain enough of its shares to have a controlling interest. Otherwise, the Pennsylvania Railroad will have the expense of acquiring land and building its own tracks along this section, paralleling those of Bayside Air Line. Some other railroad company could then acquire permissions from Bayside Air Line and thus compete with the Pennsylvania Railroad.

page 126 *"Old Cheswold Lawne is getting very shaky."*
Wister probably chose the name "Cheswold Lawne" as a punning reference to "Cheswold," the Haverford mansion (built in the 1870s, razed in 1936) of Alexander Cassatt, president of the Pennsylvania Railroad from 1899 to 1906.

page 127 *". . . the Erie people . . . the New York Central people . . ."*
Both the Erie and the New York Central were railroad companies.

page 127 *". . . Secane . . . Wallingford . . . Chester Chadd . . . Brandywine and the rest . . ."*
These names are drawn from place locations in the Philadelphia suburbs.

page 128 *". . . instead of Pegasus he bestrode locomotives."*
Pegasus, Greek mythology's winged horse associated with poets and creativity, sprang from the blood of the slain Medusa. Mastered by Bellerophon, Pegasus helped him slay the Chimaera. Wister may also have had in mind that Bellerophon's ambition grew to such an extent that he tried to ride Pegasus up to Olympus

to become a god. Pegasus threw his rider, and Bellerophon wandered the earth, an alienated and suffering
man.

page 130 *". . . Baxter Chippendale . . ."*
Wister does not say so in what survives of *Romney,*
but—as is portrayed in the story of this fictional Boston family in Robert Grant's *The Chippendales*—Baxter Chippendale is Henry Sumner's uncle. There is no
mention of "Bayside Air Line" in *The Chippendales,*
but the end of Grant's novel depicts a similar attempt
to gain control by buying (at more than market price)
shares of a company's stock (see 590–98).

page 131 *". . . sowing the wind . . . shall reap this whirlwind."*
"For they have sown the wind, and they shall reap the
whirlwind" (Hosea 8:7).

page 134 *"How are you, Atco?"*
Like many of the names of the Railroad directors,
"Atco" also draws from a Philadelphia-area place—
this time in New Jersey.

page 137 *". . . three superfluous remarks . . ."*
No doubt Wister in his revision of *Romney* would have
added at the beginning of Chapter xi a statement "that
it contains three superfluous remarks" so that his reference here at the beginning of Chapter xii would
make sense.

page 139 *"Reform . . . had seemed to be the coming thing."*
For a time in Philadelphia in the 1880s, it looked as
though reform was at last "the coming thing."
Reformers, supported by the progressive Committee
of One Hundred, proposed a new city charter in 1882.
State boss Matt Quay saw the new charter as a way of

reducing the power of city boss James McManes; Quay and his top aide, Boies Penrose, managed to get the charter through the state legislature in 1885. But the result was not political reform but a transfer of absolute power to a new boss, Matt Quay. For information on Boies Penrose, see Lukacs, 49–82.

page 149 *"'Shrub, I reckon, some kind o' fancy shrub . . .'"*
Ben Staples's after-dinner drink perplexes the platform observers, leading to speculation about a "shrub" (fruit juice, sugar, spice, and usually rum or brandy). Part of the joke may be that the "green stuff from the bottle" is so different from a "raspberry shrub," which, without the spirits, is still a popular drink among Philadelphia Quakers.

page 149 *". . . grease the journals . . ."*
In this mechanical context, a "journal" is "the part of a rotatory axle or shaft that turns in a bearing" (*Webster's New World Dictionary*).

page 153 *". . . Miller coupling . . ."*
The Miller coupler, named for its inventor and incorporating a patented draft gear and buffer, became the first generally successful alternative to the link-and-pin connective for joining passenger cars; the Miller coupler became the passenger car standard for important railways during the 1870s. There is some chance that Wister is mocking Ben Staples here, though. By about 1879–80, the Miller coupler was replaced by the Janney coupler as the Pennsylvania Railroad standard, and the PRR pressured railroads interchanging passenger cars with them to use the Janney. Thus Ben Staples—the not-really-up-to-the-job president of the Chesapeake, Cumberland and Western—may be technologically

out of date in these comments he makes in the mid-1880s. As for Wister, he was particularly interested in such mechanical innovations on the railroad (see *Roosevelt,* 200). I am grateful to Christopher T. Baer of the Hagley Museum and Library for providing the technical information in this note.

page 168 "... *Aransas Pass ... Grand Cascapedia ... Big Horn ... Curry Tuck ... Boeotia Club ...*"

Charles Ronald certainly led a peripatetic existence in his annual travels to Aransas Pass (Texas), Grand Cascapedia (Quebec), the Big Horn Mountains (Wyoming), Curry Tuck (or Currituck, in North Carolina), and elsewhere. Wister's naming of Ronald's Club as "Boeotia" echoes an old slur against Philadelphia, the calling of the city "the Boeotia of America." Nathaniel Burt explains as follows: "Boeotia was a northerly province of Greece which was looked upon by Athenians as the home of boors and numbskulls. Philadelphia is said to be in exactly the same geographical latitude, and to be equally numb to all areas of higher sensibility" (Burt, 321). The name of the Boeotia Club alone would have appealed to Ronald's ironic wit and perhaps would have been reason enough for him to join.

∞∞∞∞ **APPENDIXES** ∞∞∞∞

Wister's Fragments of Texts Related to ROMNEY

"Designs: The Star Gazers"

In 1911, at the J. Y. Ranch at Jackson Hole, Wyoming, Owen Wister wrote "Designs: The Star Gazers" as a sketch for a third novel. "Designs" seems to be part of a prospectus prepared for Macmillan, his publisher, because its text repeats facts Wister and his editors already knew: for example, that his character Augustus was the narrator of his previous novel, *Lady Baltimore*. Even though there is no evidence that Wister ever wrote anything of "The Star Gazers," some of his ideas for the book (such as Augustus as narrator and a large Eastern city as setting) did become elements of *Romney* when Wister, back home in Philadelphia, began that novel late in 1912.

Wister wrote "Designs" in ink on three sheets of 8½ by 11-inch paper. These sheets are preserved in the Owen Wister Papers (Box 83) at the Library of Congress in a folder entitled "Ideas for Novels." Despite the plural form of "Ideas," the prospectus for "The Star Gazers" is the only item in that folder. The text below is an exact transcription of the manuscript, preserving its underlinings and its idiosyncratic use of dashes as a major feature of punctuation.

Designs

The Star Gazers.

A short novel with 4 principal characters, scene laid in that sort of society which in any large place like New York, Boston, or

Philadelphia, sets up some kind of club to meet once a month
and be "intellectual"— The scene is to open at one of these
meetings— I think the story will be told by "Augustus"—the
same person who narrated Lady Baltimore. The Club is all
excitement to see & hear the great new female astrologer. Two
cousins of Augustus are amid the throng—a young fellow & a
girl just engaged to be married—both very rich & of the best
society. The astrologer & her beautiful husband, who is a poet or
painter, arrive— She is also young & strangely attractive— Her
lecture makes a great hit— Society takes both her & her husband up— Augustus very curious— He has her cast his 'horoscope'— This leads to his finding she has also cast the horoscope
of his two engaged cousins. Augustus gradually makes sure that
the astrologer doesn't believe in herself, & that her poor husband
does believe in her. He also begins to suspect that his young cousin
who is engaged is becoming interested in the astrologer—who is
unquestionably a charmer— He next gradually discovers that
the fiancée, piqued & unhappy, is getting solace by visits from
the astrologer's beautiful poet husband— The astrologer's very
brilliant social success and her remarkable accuracy in horoscopes gradually transform her into believing there is something
in the influence of the stars. This psychological change (or rather
growth, for it is shadowed from the first) culminates in her
becoming completely sincere and self-deceived—and then she
begins to fail in her horoscopes—and her husband correspond-
ingly grows aware she was a fraud— But the engaged cousin
doesn't care what she was astrologically, & she leaves her husband & goes off with the engaged cousin, which is promptly followed by the fiancée going off with the poet husband—
Ultimate marriage consecrates these two new unions—

　　Note. The chief thing to be "done" here is the development of
the astrologer's mental state—the conquest of her cynicism by
her vanity. The study of the next importance is the fiancée. She
of course is an instance of something very prevalent. The badly

brought up child of parents who in their day were strictly brought up, but who have failed in parental duty— The bad conduct proposed for this girl has its original suggestion in two incidents which occurred in my own "circle"— Nevertheless, such a picture of a young maiden in American fiction will be so unusual & so displeasing, that I hesitate. My far weaker alternative is to take Hortense Rieppe & her millionaire broker husband from <u>Lady Baltimore</u>, & substitute them for the engaged couple. It would be "easy," because such an outcome of Hortense's marriage is practically latent in <u>Lady Baltimore</u>. But to make this substitution would be a concession to that part of the public which would wish all books to end well, & which positively forbids the American girl to be anything but an angel of purity in the novelist's hands.

J. Y. Ranch. Jackson Hole.
September 19. 1911

Draft for a Possible Preface

Romney begins abruptly in all three incomplete manuscripts, implying that the reader would already know about Augustus and his Aunt Carola. Many readers in fact would have met the two characters in *Lady Baltimore*. Still, it seems an artistic flaw to depend on such prior knowledge in all readers of *Romney,* and it is easy to imagine either editor George Brett asking Wister to work on the opening or Wister himself deciding to do so. This draft for a possible Preface, and the two revisions of Chapter 1 following, would have more explicitly established the central characters and their social class.

This draft for a possible Preface appears on an 8½ by 11-inch typewritten sheet in front of the 8½ by 14-inch typewritten, and much hand-revised, sheets of *Romney* MS. 2 (see page LIII above). Since the draft is on paper of a size different from the main manuscript, it is difficult to determine the precise relationship between the two. The draft could have been written at any time and simply inserted in this folder; it could even have been misfiled with MS. 2 and actually belong with one of the other two manuscript versions of *Romney*. Because Wister introduces both *The Virginian* and *Lady Baltimore* with remarks about their social landscapes, this *Romney* draft is most likely intended for a similar purpose. In the *Romney* text, however, it is unclear whether the speaker in the fragment is the fictional Augustus or the author himself meditating upon the world of Augustus, Aunt Carola, and Uncle Andrew. Another possibility is that Wister may have thought of the *Romney* draft as something he would someday use as part of an intended revision of the opening of Chapter 1. Given these uncertainties, as well as the absence of the material from *Romney* MS. 3, I have not included this fragment in *Romney*.

The house described in the following passage owes much to Wister's own childhood home of Butler Place, where he again lived with his family after his mother's death in 1908. Like Aunt Carola and Uncle Andrew's home, "Butler Place" was "a house that has grown slowly." Wister's ancestral Philadelphia home contained a framed letter from George Washington to his ancestor Pierce Butler, as well as portraits of his Kemble forebears by Thomas Sully (1783–1872; English born, but moved to Philadelphia) and by English painters Sir Joshua Reynolds (1723–92) and Sir Thomas Lawrence (1769–1830). Sully painted many portraits of Fanny Kemble, Owen Wister's grandmother; Wister and his bride Mary had one of these portraits in the parlor of their first house at 913 Pine Street in Philadelphia and moved it with them to Butler Place (see *OWW,* 14). Painter Gilbert Stuart (1755–1828), also mentioned in the text below, produced many portraits of Philadelphia's first families, especially while he was in the city from 1794 to 1802. Wister's town home at 1112 Spruce Street, Philadelphia, contained a portrait of his aunt Nancy Pennington by Gilbert Stuart. On the various locations of these paintings, see Fanny Kemble Wister [Stokes], *That I May Tell You: Journals and Letters of the Wister Family* (Wayne, Pennsylvania: Haverford House, 1979), 158, 224–25.

[Draft for a Possible Preface]

I often like to tell the truth; but when New Yorkers ask me why I do not live in New York, I am forced to tergiversate. They mean well, they mean kindly, they mean a compliment. How then without lacking in good manners, as we understand these in our town, could I be direct? The answer I should like to make these friendly New Yorkers, and it would be gentle, and it would contain the whole truth, would be to take them to call upon Aunt Carola and Uncle Andrew. If they were not at home, to see their house would be enough. Such a house is possible in New York no longer. You are scarce across the threshold before you feel glad that you have come. Family portraits, going back to Sully and Gilbert Stuart, hang in the hall. Serenity goes with you as you ascend the staircase to the drawing-room. You pass beautiful things brought from Italy long ago. Ample fire-places are in all the rooms, and in Winter the smell of their wood-fires mixes delicately with that of the flowers from Uncle Andrew's greenhouse in the country. Books are everywhere, books inherited, books bought to-day; and in the cellar is a whole dynasty of good wine. This is a house that has grown slowly. It is a shock-absorber. Human automobiles do not rush shrieking through it. Our deafening present is muffled. You can hear yourself think.

Two Revisions of Chapter 1

Like the draft of a possible preface printed above, the following two pieces would have revised the opening of the novel, both leading more gradually into the story than does the abrupt first sentence in *Romney* MS. 3: "Augustus, I desire to speak to you in the library for a few moments." Wister wrote the two passages in ink on a single sheet of 5 by 8-inch paper, now to be found in the same folder as *Romney* MS. 1 (see page LIII above). The first piece, much corrected, must have been written first. The second fragment has few changes and begins mid-page, immediately below the conclusion of the first passage.

These two texts may well be the final work Wister did on *Romney.* They probably date from late 1915, as is suggested by an unrelated draft on the same sheet. In that draft for a letter, Wister recommends his friend John Jay Chapman for something unnamed, and he refers to Sainte-Beuve's comment about Balzac from Chapman's "latest book" (also unspecified). In fact the book Wister refers to is Chapman's *Greek Genius and Other Essays* (see the section on Balzac on 255–56), which was published by Moffat, Yard, and Company about October 1915. Wister's letter of recommendation nominated Chapman for the National Institute of Arts and Letters, as Chapman tells a friend in a letter of 11 November 1915, explaining why he turned it down (see *John Jay Chapman and His Letters* [Boston: Houghton Mifflin, 1937], 318).

The text of the following two revisions of Chapter 1 records the final version of each.

[First Revision of Chapter 1]

It was just on a usual Tuesday or Wednesday or Monday or some kind of day that I, suspecting nothing, had dropped in to lunch with Aunt Carola and Uncle Andrew—which was quite usual too; a standing welcome there was mine; but we hadn't been sitting a minute, the second man was handing the first dish while the butler had the sherry decanter tilted decorously above Uncle Andrew's glass, when I found myself to be sorry that I had come. It set me to fingering nervously for my napkin before

I remembered that Aunt Carola didn't have napkins at lunch; and straight through the meal she cut short whatever I began, no matter how bright and intelligent it was, by saying nothing. What interruption is worse? Long before the early afternoon paper was brought in to Uncle Andrew, I had been driven to a mere whistling flippancy. "How's the good old market?" I asked him, for he always opened the paper there first; "Eternal Vigilance keeping her eye on Liberty or Steel Common to-day?" It is a joke I have made before, but I was in no state for new ones. From her end of the table Aunt Carola presently vouchsafed: "There'll probably be some account of those vulgar people's ball in their Fifth Avenue house." "Which reminds me," said I, still attempting cheerfulness, "who are the old New York families this year?" Uncle Andrew had evidently begun to feel that somebody should stand by me, for he smiled and ran off a string of glittering millionaires. "Nothing hereditary there," said I, "except divorce." Uncle Andrew chuckled kindly; but Aunt Carola now addressed me:

"Augustus, if you have quite finished, I wish to speak to you in the library for a few minutes."

She rose; I rose; there was silence; as I passed Uncle Andrew, he gave me his God-speed:

"What's left of you had better come back for a cigar."

[Second Revision of Chapter 1]

I was welcome as usual, of course; my place was laid, my chair pushed up, the second man brought me the first dish, the butler brought the decanter, the wood fire burned generously, Uncle Andrew was affable and jocular—but Aunt Carola can have a manner which puts me at my worst. I don't know how she does it. I wish I could do it. It would be of great use at times— when a hotel clerk is going to pat my shoulder, for instance; but I think you have to date from 1840 or so to know the trick. Even then it's not everybody— Well, Aunt Carola sat eating her lunch with this manner; so that I soon found myself to be sorry that I had come in to-day; plainly something hung over me. I did not cut a creditable figure, as you will see; but as nobody is spared throughout the following pages, not even my hero, why should I spare myself?

Owen Wister wrote the three works printed here between 1907 and 1914. During the time he was greatly concerned with the civic problems and possibilities of Philadelphia, and in 1908 he ran—unsuccessfully—as a reform candidate for what was then called the city's Select Council. Each essay also illuminates the backgrounds and themes of *Romney* (written 1912–14), such as the analysis of Germans (the Pennyslvania "Dutch") and Quakers in "The Keystone Crime," and the blend of civic responsibility and cultural awareness in such famous Philadelphians as Horace Howard Furness and James Logan. Those two biographical essays, interesting and important Philadelphia pieces in themselves, are here published for the first time.

Although Wister wrote about Philadelphia before 1907, his focus then was chiefly on social problems. In "Where Charity Begins" (*Harper's New Monthly Magazine,* July 1895, 269–72), for example, he extols The Evening Home, an organization for homeless boys—and the Home's unusual but apparently successful attempts to build self-esteem and self-reliance through encouraging these boys to perform in *H.M.S. Pinafore, The Pirates of Penzance,* and *Iolanthe.* Gradually, though, Wister started to dissect political practices that exacerbate social problems and—as in *Romney*—to consider the nature of democracy itself. In the year in which he began *Romney,* Wister portrayed Philadelphia's struggles for political reform as emblematic of the nation's, employing in his account the old personification of the United States as "Columbia":

The case of the Quaker City is the case of Columbia's whole system, cities, States, and Nation. To democracy are we committed. Does this mean that we are forever to live loosely, scandalously, until nature rebels and we have to fly to a violent cure, a political Carlsbad, a civil war, to be cleansed only to begin over again each time? Does the theory of democracy exact more from human nature than human nature has to give? Upon the virtue of ourselves and our children it depends whether Columbia has hitched her wagon to a fixed or falling star. ("The Case of the Quaker City," *Outlook*, 25 May 1912, 162–73)

A few months later in 1912 he outlined to Theodore Roosevelt a novel then to be called *Dividends in Democracy*, and Wister hitched his own wagon to that fixed star. His inability to finish *Romney*, however, as well as his lifelong failure to resolve the problems inherent in a government composed of and elected by disparate peoples, raise the specter of democracy's falling star.

From "The Keystone Crime: Pennsylvania's Graft-Cankered Capitol" (Originally published in Everybody's Magazine, *October 1907, 435–48)*

As its title implies, this is Wister's angriest political essay. It documents to the penny the outrageous graft involved in erecting the State's new Capitol Building in Harrisburg and flays the individuals responsible. The state got putty instead of the paid-for mahogany, plaster instead of marble, fireplaces with no chimneys; the public treasury was raided to pay political cronies ten times the going rate for nearly everything. What made graft on such a scale possible, Wister charges, was "forty years of unpunished robbery" by Pennsylvania's "den of thieves" led by political bosses J. Donald Cameron and Matt Quay. Nor was the wreckage simply monetary, as various political figures (faced with exposure of their corruption) committed suicide. The entire essay, lengthy and detailed, is still worth reading, but its concluding section (which is all I reprint below) shows Wister analyzing his fellow citizens' tolerance for corruption, thoughts about English Quakers and "Pennsylvania Dutch" (or Germans) that he later developed more fully in *Romney*.

After reading "The Keystone Crime," President Theodore Roosevelt wrote to Wister of his being "immensely amused over the fluttering in the dovecotes over your remarks on non-resistance whether of German or English stock" (*Roosevelt,* 268–69).

[From "The Keystone Crime," by Owen Wister]

That the political case of Pennsylvania is a very sick one, both acute and chronic, can scarce have escaped the notice of the reader who has followed this narrative down, from Cameron through Quay and the suicides, to this point. And how, it will naturally be asked, and why, has any community of self-respecting people tolerated such a state of things for forty years? The briefest answer is—*the people of Pennsylvania are not self-respecting. In the place of self-respect they substitute an impregnable complacency.* Yet this explanation is inadequate. Mere complacency would hardly sit down and be robbed for forty years, getting leaky reservoirs and putty mahogany for its money; and we find upon analysis that with complacency must be joined also stupidity and cowardice. It is a sweeping indictment, and of course it applies to by no means every voter in the State; but it does apply to the majority, since it is the majority that elects. Yet still the question remains, How does all this come about? How is it that Pennsylvania is not only dishonest—all states are that at times—but ridiculous as well?

The reader has heard of monopolies and trusts. *The Government of Pennsylvania has been, since the Civil War, a monopoly, an enormous trust, almost without competition, like Standard Oil, but greatly inferior, because Standard Oil gives good oil, while the Pennsylvania machine gives bad government.* It shields and fosters child labor; we have seen how it steals; it has given Philadelphia sewage to drink, smoke to breathe, extravagant gas, a vile street-car system, and a police well-nigh contemptible. This monopoly rests upon two special causes—a special soil and a special people; coal and iron and the tariff could not by themselves have brought a community so low. It required a people ready and willing to be brought low, and the people were there—the Pennsylvania "Dutch," and the Quakers. The former, to their good qualities of thrift and a certain stolid horse-sense, unite a servile acquiescence in things as they are; no "Dutch" country has ever turned its boss out. The Quaker to his well-known good qualities adds a timidity that also acquiesces in things as they are. This *racial acquiescence* is at the bottom of Pennsylvania's plight, and has drugged every standard, save money. *Lethargically prosperous, Pennsylvania is all belly and no members, and its ideals do not rise higher than the belly. Of the traditional Philadelphian this is as true as of the rustic, only it is more shameful. Well-to-do, at ease, with no wish but to be left undisturbed, the traditional Philadelphian shrinks from revolt. When wrongs so outrageous as the Gas Lease are thrust at him, he may rouse for a while, but it is grudgingly in his heart of hearts; and when the party of reform makes mistakes, he jumps at these to cover his retreat back into the ranks of acquiescence.*

After electing a reform party in November, 1905, he immediately began to notice all that the party failed to reform and to ignore all that it accomplished. He jeered at every piece of mismanagement of the City party; it made him happy; it was another pretext for him to return to the party that had been managing the Treasury for forty years. One year of independence was too much for him. Long before its close he was tired and frightened of it. The next November, 1906, he began to run back; the following February he ran the whole way, glad to forget he owed the Capitol exposure to the independent party, pretending hard to believe that it was exaggerated. He elected, instead of the independent candidate for mayor, a machine mayor, who in the words of a machine leader "has been taking orders for thirty years," and whose latest act of obedience has been the signing—against strong protest—of a street-railroad bill that gives about as much to the interested few and about as little to the citizens as the Capitol job itself—all this quite in the face of the mayor's paraded promises of independent watchfulness of the city's welfare. Were this mayor wholly harmless, he would be wholly ridiculous. For this mayor neither the "Dutch" nor the "Quaker" is to blame. The Irish, moved presumably by the gifts to their church of the notorious leader of the "contractors' combine," voted for a despotism far worse than that they had crossed the seas to escape—this to the disgust of the better Catholic element. Thus has Philadelphia, like the dog in Scripture, returned to its own vomit.

The people of Pennsylvania walked last autumn by thousands and thousands through their new Capitol, and to most of them it was superb and beautiful. Its total lack of individuality and distinction, its great aimless bulk, its bilious, overeaten decoration, its swollen bronzes, its varicose chandeliers, expressed their notion of the grand and the desirable. Now that they have learned that it was all another robbery, and that their carved mahogany is mostly putty, they are not much disturbed. **Do not pity them. They deserve everything they get, for Pennsylvania is to-day a government by knaves at the expense of fools.**

Black is the retrospect; the outlook somewhat brightens. Governor Stuart is so much better than his party that his candidacy saved it. The State is fairly restless. Harrisburg has shaken off its den of thieves. Pittsburg is trying to. Philadelphia may bring up the rear; its spark of liberty is not quite trampled out; it may some day cease to be the dirtiest smear on the map of the United States.

"Address Read at the Memorial Meeting of Horace Howard Furness" (College of Physicians of Philadelphia: January 1913)

"There is something absurd in being asked so constantly to speak in public, a thing which I do with great difficulty and not at all well," confided Wister to his diary (OWP, Box 101; entry of 25 November 1914). But he must have been honored to be asked to give the memorial address for his kinsman, Horace Howard Furness (1833–1912), the great Shakespeare scholar. Furness, a generation older than Wister, was his young relative's friend and mentor, and their personal contacts and correspondence were both extensive (see OWP, Box 21). When Wister heard of Furness's death, he wrote John Jay Chapman that he felt "as if I could not go on" (Payne, 281). Family connections with Furness also extended to Wister's wife, Mary, who as a girl read German texts to the scholar. In speaking on the state of American education at Harvard College in 1907, Wister listed half a dozen Americans of "education, enlightenment, and character" and included both Furness and S. Weir Mitchell, Philadelphia's foremost cultural leaders at the beginning of the twentieth century (see Payne, 253–54). To Furness, Wister had dedicated his *Members of the Family* in 1911 (physician and novelist S. Weir Mitchell, another Wister relative, is the dedicatee of *Lady Baltimore*). In addition to his Memorial Address, Wister wrote two other pieces about Furness, the first in *The Harvard Graduates Magazine* (December 1912, 201–12) and the second as "A Message from Philadelphia" to the American Academy of Arts and Letters on the occasion of the Shakespeare Tercentenary in 1916 (see OWP, Box 56).

In his address Wister, the principal literary figure in early twentieth-century Philadelphia, memorializes the man who was the city's great nineteenth-century cultural powerhouse. Wister begins by setting Furness's work in the context of a group to which both men belonged: the Shakspere Society of Philadel-

FIG 10
Horace Howard Furness in his study at "Lindenshade" in Wallingford,
Pennsylvania. Owen Wister wrote part of his memorial essay on
Furness in this room.

phia (as the group—but, curiously, not Wister—spells the play-
wright's name). The main focus is, as it must be, on Furness's
monumental achievement, his sixteen volumes of the New Variorum Shakespeare, which provided detailed interpretation and
commentary on the plays. Wister, however, also introduces
themes that occupied his thoughts in 1913 while he was at work
on *Romney,* including a comparison between Boston and Philadelphia, and a meditation on what it means to be an informed
and cultured citizen in an age of materialist excess. A few pet
peeves also surface, such as the flaws in the elective system at
Harvard compared to the requirement to take specific courses.

The Shakspere Society of Philadelphia still exists, functioning in the same way that Wister described in 1913—or, for that matter, as the Society did at its foundation in 1851. Furness has found an enduring legacy in his native city in the Horace Howard Furness Memorial Library at the University of Pennsylvania. The books of Furness and of his son were acquired by Penn in 1931, and have been augmented ever since for the study of Shakespeare and his contemporary Tudor and Stuart dramatists.[1]

The text below is taken from what appears to be the typewritten copy used by Wister to deliver his address (see OWP, Box 50, Folder "Horace Howard Furness").

"Address Read at the Memorial Meeting
of Horace Howard Furness" [by Owen Wister]

Mr. Chairman; Ladies and Gentlemen:

It is in the name of the Shakespeare Society of Philadelphia that I have the great honor to address you. A few of you undoubtedly know something of this Society, but probably more of you do not—which is most natural. The Society has published nothing, privacy has been its tradition, this is its first public appearance. From its beginning, citizens of eminence have belonged to it, literature being generally their recreation, and law their profession in many instances. It is an accident—if anything in human affairs can be called accident—that Dr. Furness himself did not become a Philadelphia lawyer. Such was his intention, such his education; he was admitted to the bar, some of his legal writing stands upon the shelves of the Law Library. And since his extraordinary wits were filled with nimbleness

---

1. For more information on Furness, see James M. Gibson, "Horace Howard Furness: Book Collector and Library Builder," *Shakespeare Study Today: The Horace Howard Furness Memorial Lectures* (New York: AMS Press, 1986), 169–89.

and resource, and since his memory was apparently without limits, and since to these gifts were added a strong constitution, an unflagging power of work, and a decidedly combative nature, it is not unreasonable to believe that his legal career would have been brilliant. But we all know that deafness put an early end to this, and in its stead we have the New Variorum.

Of our Society it is the proud boast that we are—to borrow a phrase from the books—the First Cause of the New Variorum; and you will presently see that the boast is not an empty one, that we are indeed the acorn whence grew this oak. The Proximate Cause—again to borrow a phrase from the books—was the discovery and the predicament that our meeting brought forth fifty years ago. The story of our Society is a pleasant one, and soon told.

On March 14th, 1903, Sidney Lee dined with us. You know that nothing of any importance happens in Philadelphia without a dinner; in this admirable and mellow custom we resemble the English, and prolong the Eighteenth Century; and I will here disclose to you that every year from November till mid-April, on the night of every second Wednesday, we also, we Shakespeareans, congenially dine together. Then, our bodies being nourished, the table-cloth is removed, the big and little books are brought out, and we proceed to take up the chosen play of the year from the point reached at the previous meeting; line upon line we read it aloud, discuss it and explain wherever explanation is needful— and possible! On March 14th, 1903, Dr. Furness, in honor of the occasion, made a speech which he began in these words: "I want our distinguished guest to know that he is dining with the oldest Shakespeare Society in the world."

Now at such a proud statement as this, uninformed fancy flies back at random through the Coleridges, the Lambs, the Dyces, the Johnsons, the Goethes, the Grimms. It wanders among the Stendahls, the Ducis, the le Tourneurs, whose brave battles for Shakespeare in France have been written so absorbingly by our

distinguished visitor the ambassador—through all these does
fancy roam to bring up possibly at Benjamin Franklin. Did he,
by any chance, originate us? No, we are among the few good
institutions in Philadelphia that he didn't originate, and Shakespeare Societies are nowhere of venerable age. Until the middle
of the last century there was none in any country, and the earliest, founded in London in 1840, lived only fourteen years. Ourselves, the next, founded in 1851, are thus strictly the second, but
equally strictly the oldest, this being our sixty-second year.

What occasioned our existence was perhaps chiefly the read-
ings of Fanny Kemble. Some are living today who can remember these, though scarcely their beginning, which was in 1849.
They induced a lively interest in the plays of Shakespeare, and
within two years our Society came into being, dedicated to a
thorough and critical study of the poet. As the grandson of
Fanny Kemble, I will recall to you the old story of a certain strict
Quaker, who summoned his boy and said: "Son John, I hear
thee has been to the reading of this actress woman.— Yes,
father.— Has thee been more than once?—Yes, father.— Has
thee been more than twice?— Yes, father.—How many times
has thee been?— Every time, father.— Has thee a ticket in thy
pocket for tonight?— Yes, father.— Son, John, thee may give
me thy ticket and go to bed."

It does not appear that Son John became a member of the
Shakespeare Society of Philadelphia. As enrolled upon its honorable roster, however, let the name of Editor Fish, of the *American Law Review* be mentioned. The law knows him better than
the laity, he was an able annotator of several important technical
books; he was the Dean of our Society and Dr. Furness called
him its moving spirit; but the laity, even today, does know the
name of Judge Sharswood, who was one of us in 1860, when
Horace Howard Furness, then twenty-seven years old, became
a member. You will see, therefore, without the longer list which

I could easily give, that the future editor of the New Variorum joined no common company of minds, but found a highly trained set of intelligences expanding themselves in the still better company of Shakespeare. Together with the company he found something else that was unusual—a collection of books, an equipment for study, gathered by Dean Fish judiciously and judiciously amplified from time to time. A few years later, after a season dedicated to *The Tempest,* the Society printed privately the notes resulting from its study. Very significant is this act on the part of these students. In it we discover as plainly as if they had made themselves explicit, their dissatisfaction with existing texts and notes, with all the tools of study and criticism which they had been able to procure. After fourteen or fifteen years of bending their informed and sharply trained minds together over Shakespeare's obscurities and the explanations of these offered by editors and commentators, they were dissatisfied. They had found their predecessors out. Blessed is the man who is never found out! Blessed the scholar who finds some other scholar out! The mere act makes him happy. From the beginning of erudition to this present moment, down the whole ladder of time, scholars perch on every rung, each prying into some scholar on the rung preceding him, finding him out. Thus is knowledge whittled and whittled, and polished and polished, until its final shape. One day I exclaimed to Dr. Furness at his work: "And that single word has cost you four months"— "Almost five— with other things of course, too. I have to be mighty careful"; here he threw into his face a delightful, comic expression of slyness: "Mighty careful. The other fellows are all crouching for a spring. But they've never fairly caught me yet!" Then he sat back and flourished his ear trumpet, and we had a good time laughing.

Here, then, in the late sixties, had the Shakespeare Society of Philadelphia reached its discovery and its predicament; here was the Proximate Cause, full-fledged. The annotators and commentators were inadequate. This fact the study of *Romeo and Juliet* in 1866–67 merely emphasized the more. Early in 1871, appeared a volume dedicated thus:

To the Shakespeare Society of Philadelphia

This Volume

Is Affectionately Inscribed.

It was *Romeo and Juliet,* the first volume of the New Variorum Shakespeare, the first block of the intellectual monument by which Philadelphia is honored and Dr. Furness remembered.

Much discussion at our meetings had gone into its preparation; what print should be used, what shape the book should have. Specimen pages had been submitted to the members for their opinions—and their opinions were worth listening to. To some of them, the editing of books was a part of their own experience, and to the eyes of all, the appearance of other editions of Shakespeare was a matter of familiar and critical knowledge. But Time has signally ratified the judgment of the Shakespeare Society of Philadelphia as to another aspect of the New Variorum. Very soon after the appearance of the *Romeo and Juliet,* at a meeting held February 7th, 1871, in a resolution then adopted, and following a sentence of congratulation to Messrs. J. B. Lippincott and Company, the Publishers, it is said that: "In the opinion of the Society no single volume yet published in America is at all equal to this in value as a contribution to Shakespeare literature." Time, with the fifteen volumes that have followed *Romeo and Juliet* during the forty years since 1871, has indeed ratified on both sides of the Ocean this home opinion so early given, so unreserved, and so odd. Would you know why it is odd, this home opinion? Have you ever observed how Philadelphia differs from—Boston, let us say? When a Bostonian hears that a fellow Bostonian has distinguished himself, he exclaims: "Quite natural!" When a Philadelphian hears that a fellow Philadelphian has distinguished himself, he exclaims: "Quite impossible!" Whether or no this may be set down to brotherly love, the Shakespeare Society of Philadelphia on February 7th, 1871, in its prompt appreciation of the first Volume of the New Variorum, and long before England and Europe had taught us what to say about it, was one of the exceptions which prove the rule.

You have heard, now, the story of our Society; you will have seen that when we style ourselves the First Cause of Dr. Furness's great book, we do not make an empty boast. Once thus set editing—as there is no need to tell you—volume after volume marks his way to the very end. With us he came to sit less often as the years went on; his work possessed him, and deafness more and more isolated him; but our annual dinner, held to commemorate Shakespeare's birthday, always brought him back to us for that evening. Only last April, he dined with us and read to us the "Winter's Tale."

And now a brief word about the man himself—or rather, not quite that; I cannot talk much about him here—a brief word about the three-fold public significance of his life and work.

Many of us think of him as a solitary, as a recluse. He was by no means so. His early years were full of action, associated with men and public events. Then deafness came, but around his heart deafness could build no wall. The warmth that radiated from his affection reached out and enveloped many and many, both near at hand and far away, translating itself into daily deeds of kindness. He would drop his work and travel to Boston to read aloud to a friend who was ill. When another ill friend had to have absolute quiet, he sent for his children and kept them two months at his own house. To the very latest years he journeyed about, reading to many audiences, talking with innumerable people. Visitors were constant beneath his roof. By his morning paper he tied himself close to daily events. He was alert to all happenings of moment in politics and science.

Deafness indeed drew a circle around him—a circle not wholly unblessed: for thus a great gift of inward continuity was bestowed upon Dr. Furness, and he used it. Such work as his cannot be done by those who live the interrupted life that prevails in our Democracy. This is significance the first.

Significance the second. Harvard College bestowed a great gift upon him too, as she did upon his scholar friends, Lane, Child, Goodwin, and Norton. She does not bestow this gift today. We believe that she will again some day. Horace Furness escaped the Elective System. He was compelled to study the Classics and the Past. Discipline was given his mind. To quote the dearest Dean that Harvard has ever had: "I still doubt whether we can do better for our children than, first to drill them in a few subjects, mostly old ones." Such work as Dr. Furness's cannot be done by a mind too early specialized and ignorant of everything but its own specialty.

Significance the last. Quite lately a man distinguished in his profession, in speaking of Dr. Furness, remarked that he was not a citizen but a scholar, that he did not deserve civic honors but academic honors. Being challenged, he stuck to his opinion. Angels and ministers of grace defend us, if such idea prevail in our Democracy! If the man who builds a great fortune is a citizen, but not the man who has brought the supreme poet of the world closer to the world! Such an idea was not Martin Luther's. He said:

> The prosperity of a country depends not on the abundance of its revenues, not on the strength of its fortifications, not on the beauty of its public buildings; but it consists in the number of its cultivated citizens, in its men of education, enlightenment and character; here are to be found its true interest, its chief strength, its real power.

To Luther's opinion let one nearer home be added. On December 11th, 1909, the Pennsylvania Society of New York, at its annual dinner, began a new custom. This custom was the presenting of a gold medal to some citizen of Pennsylvania in recognition of distinguished achievement. Their first choice was Dr. Furness. Here is part of the letter they wrote him, announcing this intention:—

> The Gold Medal of the Pennsylvania Society . . . is a symbol and evidence of appreciation and regard from busy men of the world, men of finance, of commerce, of industry. . . .
>
> The achievements of Pennsylvanians have been many and notable, and have covered well nigh every department of thought and science and human interest. It might well have seemed that a Society of the world, as ours is, might properly have begun its company of Medallists with a name closely identified with the commercial, manufacturing or inventive interests with which our members are most nearly associated. I am sure I violate no secret of the Council chamber when I say that when the award of our first Medal came to be made it was felt that we might better with greater honour to ourselves, select a name distinguished in the intellectual life of our State, rather than concerned with its material aspect.

So we, the Shakespeare Society of Philadelphia, perceive and commemorate the three-fold lesson of Dr. Furness's life: he turned his infirmity into a strength; his non-elective education, classic and historic, nourished his intellect, made him a rounded scholar where specialization might have starved him into a pedant; and his work, received and valued wherever Shakespeare is known, increases our city's store of that intellectual distinction without which no city in all history has ever yet achieved and retained greatness. If this is not being a citizen, where shall a citizen be found?

"Address Delivered before the Logan Improvement League"
(12 February 1914)

The two titans of eighteenth-century Philadelphia life were
Benjamin Franklin (1706–1790) and James Logan (1674–1751).
After accompanying William Penn on his second journey to
Pennsylvania and staying on as his agent in the colony, Logan
held such offices as Mayor of Philadelphia, Secretary of the
Province, President of the Council, and Chief Justice of the
Pennsylvania Supreme Court. Like Franklin, Logan was a poly-
math: in addition to discharging his considerable civic responsi-
bilities, Logan ran a very successful fur business, assembled one
of the largest libraries in the New World, wrote and had published in Leyden an account of his scientific experiments with
Indian corn, produced the first translation of a Latin classic to be
published in the Americas, and also studied Greek, Hebrew,
French, Italian, Spanish, and Arabic. Of him it has been said
that "he became perhaps the only person in America in his time
who could read and understand Newton's *Principia Mathemat-
ica*" (Weigley, 41). Like Horace Howard Furness, James Logan
represented for Wister a most excellent example of the Philadelphia "citizen," a type that the novelist portrayed in *Romney* as
endangered in a world of burgeoning capitalistic greed.[2]

Wister's address to the Logan Improvement League on Lincoln's Birthday, 1914, was his first major public appearance after
the death of his wife, Mary Channing Wister, on 24 August
1913. By such speeches, he was trying to warm himself back to
life—as he was trying to resume writing *Romney* by beginning
a process of revision (see OWP, Box 101, journal entry of 3 Jan-

---

2. For further information on Logan, see Frederick Barnes Tolles, *James
Logan and the Culture of Provincial America* (Boston: Little, Brown, 1957), and
Edwin Wolf, 2nd, *The Library of James Logan of Philadelphia, 1674–1751* (Philadel-
phia: Library Company, 1974).

uary 1914). Wister's acceptance of the invitation from the Logan Improvement League pays homage to his wife, as he noted in his journal on the day of the speech: "M. C. W. would have liked me to address this League" (OWP, Box 101, entry of 12 February 1914). As a tireless advocate for civic improvement herself, Mary would certainly have felt at home at the Logan Improvement League, and she was a direct descendant of its namesake, James Logan. She and her husband lived from 1907 to her death at Butler Place in the Logan area of Philadelphia, and Owen Wister's speech begins with his childhood memories of what later came to be known as the Logan section.

In his speech Wister presents a short popular biography of James Logan in the style of the author's well-received biographies *Ulysses S. Grant* (1900) and *The Seven Ages of Washington* (1907). The "lesson" drawn from Logan's life, the way "he should be a pattern for us all," highlights Logan's true patriotism and his civic responsibility as opposed to the Philadelphia of 1914 in which so many people focus only on "feathering their own nests." That lesson imparted in his address to the Logan Improvement League is also a theme of *Romney,* in process at the same time. "I think," Wister wrote hopefully in his journal after his speech, "they were interested" (OWP, Box 101, entry of 12 February 1914).

Wister's journal entries show that he discussed the Logan speech with friends on 28 January 1914, began writing it on 30 January, and finished it on 5 February (OWP, Box 101). His main source was John Fanning Watson's *Annals of Philadelphia,* first published in 1830 and reprinted many times thereafter. The one surviving typescript of Wister's speech is headed "2nd Copy," but fold marks suggest that it is probably the one from which he delivered his talk. The typewritten copy (see OWP, Box 49, Folder "Feb. 12, 1914") is extensively revised in ink, mainly to shorten the address.

A section of Philadelphia, a railroad station, a post office, a school, a building on the University of Pennsylvania's campus, a

library branch, and a fountain-splattered square on the Benjamin
Franklin Parkway preserve James Logan's name. His mansion,
the first in the Georgian style to be erected in Philadelphia, also
remains; it is owned by the city and has been meticulously cared
for since 1900 by the National Society of the Colonial Dames of
America in the Commonwealth of Pennsylvania. Logan's precious library is now at the Library Company of Philadelphia,
founded in 1731 by that other famous Philadelphian of the eighteenth century, Benjamin Franklin.

"Address Delivered before the Logan
Improvement League" [by Owen Wister]

It is altogether fitting, my neighbors, on this day which com-
memorates a great patriot, that you and I should talk of public
spirit. We are all living in a neighborhood whose growth will be
more and more rapid. It is right that we should know each other
and exchange views for the sake of the welfare of this neighborhood that we are all helping to make. We want to make it as good
a place as we can. A good place for the young people who are
growing up in it and who will be influenced by the surroundings
which we give them, and we want to make it a good place for
ourselves also. First and foremost, we want to make it a place
that is wholesome both for the body and for the mind. We want
to have physical conditions that are wholesome, and we want to
have mental conditions that are wholesome.

It is not so very long ago that there was no such place as
Logan. It is not so very long ago that there was no railroad
between Wayne Junction and what used to be called the North
Pennsylvania Railroad. Nothing but fields and country was
here. Few houses, no pavements, no light, no streets. Country
roads everywhere. Now the City, reaching out in this direction,
has laid her hand upon all this country and changed it into a

suburb. Thus we have the place, Logan, and the Society named the Logan Improvement League.

I feel like the oldest inhabitant. I don't know that I am the oldest inhabitant, but I certainly feel as if I were. I cannot remember when I first came here, because that must have been in 1860 or 1861, when I was a child in arms, but by 1867 I begin to remember this place very well. And after 1873 I lived here altogether. That is a pretty good long while ago, and you will not quarrel with me for speaking as if I were the oldest inhabitant.

In those days the York Road was a country road, deep in summer dust or winter mud, according to the season, and it was little travelled except by farmers' wagons and those few dwellers in the neighborhood who drove in and out of Philadelphia. At the corner where now stands that magnificent and humane institution built by Dr. Widener for crippled children, there was a country place surrounded by trees. South of that nothing but fields, with an occasional farm, could be met for a very long distance. Broad Street did not come to this corner then, nor was Olney Avenue in existence. Broad Street did not come within a couple of miles of this point, and it was an almost impassable highway where it did exist. I used to drive or rather, used to try to drive, along it to the station which is now called North Philadelphia but which was then called Germantown Junction. The railroad that connects Wayne Junction with Tabor and Olney was built in 1876, and that marks the time when Logan came into being as a station.

I am going this evening to remind yourselves and myself of the man from whom this place is named. The Logan Improvement League would be a very welcome institution to this man and no improvement league in our city bears a name that can compare with this one. James Logan might almost be called an Improvement League himself, because he was connected with so much improvement that went on in his day. I want to tell you something about him. I want, if possible, to bring before you that man, that colonial ancestor of our neighborhood, that distant colonist who stands so large a figure in the history of our town that time has not been able to veil him from our sight. It is a good thing for us to know something about the past. In fact, I am beginning to lay emphasis upon the value of knowing the past. You may say that this is because I am the oldest inhabitant. But that is not the reason. The reason is because I notice a growing tendency in this present day to wipe out the past altogether. To forget it. Not to teach it in the proper way to young people. To imagine that it has nothing to do with us. To suppose that it contains no lessons which can guide us. My friends, I wish to tell you that the country which does not respect and value its past, is not likely to have much future.

And now, for James Logan! His father, Patrick Logan of Scotch-Irish blood, was a Quaker, and so was he. He had a good education, and was of a practical turn of mind as well as a scholarly one. He had a good business sense and was a hard worker. He had also the highest integrity of character. All these things were noticed by William Penn, and in the year 1699, when young James Logan was twenty-four years old, and just beginning a profitable business as a linen draper, Penn invited him to go across the ocean to the new country as his secretary. He wanted just such a man as this young James Logan was—trust-worthy, competent and well educated. James Logan took a little time to consider the invitation, and accepted it. He sailed, with Penn, on the Ship *Canterbury,* on September 9th, 1699. Something that happened on the way over tells you at once something about James Logan and the sort of character that he was. The *Canterbury* was attacked by pirates, which was a very common thing to happen to ships in that day. Now Penn, being a Quaker by conversion, and not by birth, and therefore, probably, with what we might call a double dose of Quaker in him, because when a man is converted to any religion, he takes it hard, like his first vaccination, William Penn, I say, felt that he must obey the Quaker principles of non-resistance so faithfully that when the pirates attacked the Ship he went below and took no part in the fight. Don't misunderstand me. William Penn was a perfectly brave man, but his religion compelled him to abstain from resistance. But James Logan did not go below. He stayed on deck and fought the pirates. The fight was successful, the pirates were driven off, and when it was all over what did William Penn do but come on deck and severely reprimand James Logan for disobeying the rule of his religion and fighting the pirates. But James Logan told Penn that if he did not wish him to fight the pirates, it would have been better if he had come on deck and told him so. Now you see by that what sort of a fellow James Logan was at the age of twenty-four.

There is another Quaker story about pirates which happened about this time and which I cannot help telling you because it is so very amusing. Another ship was attacked in a similar way by pirates and there was on deck an old Quaker, who, like Penn, felt that he must obey the principle of non-resistance. But this is the way in which he did it: Observing that a pirate was climbing up a rope from the water and had got rather near the deck, the Quaker whipped out his knife and saying in a very kind voice to the pirate, "Friend, thee may have that," cut the rope.

The *Canterbury,* bringing Penn with his young secretary, James Logan, landed at Philadelphia early in December 1699. Please notice one great difference between that time and our time. The ship took from the 9th of September until early in December to cross the ocean. You know that we consider eight days rather a long time now. Almost everything else in life today is full of the same increased rapidity over the pace that was kept then. A month after his arrival, Logan went with Penn to live in the "Slate Roof House," Second Street and Norris Alley, a house of numerous other historic associations. Thence in 1704 he removed, renting with Governor Evans and others the Clarke

Mansion. This was in the country, with gardens and fruit trees, at Third and Chestnut Streets. I need not tell you all the events of Logan's life; I merely wish to touch upon enough to sketch for you the character of this ancestor of our neighborhood. The ability which he showed, both in public and private business, justified Penn's good opinion of him from the very first, and when Penn returned to England he left James Logan behind him as his representative and his land agent. At this time James Logan was twenty-five years old. Here is part of a letter addressed to him by William Penn: "I have left thee in an uncommon trust, with a singular dependence on thy justice and care, which I expect thou wilt faithfully employ in advancing my honest interest." The letter then proceeds to enumerate various matters to which Logan is to devote his watchfulness and care, and then concludes thus: "For thy own services I shall allow thee what is just and reasonable, either by commission or a salary. But my dependence is on thy care and honesty. Serve me faithfully, as thou expects a blessing from God, or my favour, and I shall support thee to the utmost, as thy true friend, William Penn."

This was written on the ship in which he sailed on the 3rd of October 1701. As I have said, Logan was then twenty-five. It may be as well to tell you here that his duties to Penn became extremely important, that he fulfilled them not only faithfully, but successfully in the face of a great deal of opposition and difficulty for many years, and that the salary which he was willing to charge and accept was only one hundred pounds a year, a little less than $500.

Before he was thirty he had been made a member of what was called the Provincial Council in the year 1703. I may roughly describe the Council as a body of an advisory kind which acted, or was supposed to act, in connection with the governor.

Very soon young Logan became involved in political disputes that not only rose, but raged, in Philadelphia. You and I have had opportunity in our own lives to observe that party politics are not always harmonious. Perhaps some of us have seen daily papers in which prominent citizens have been abused somewhat as if they were pickpockets. We know what abuse they heaped upon some of our very most honorable public officials. If this be the case, it may be of some comfort to us to reflect that this experience of ours is not by any means a new one, and that it was by no means a new one in the days of James Logan either. In fact, I think we may conclude that party politics is something which is generally apt to be discordant, unsatisfactory, muddy, imperfect at best and something which we must simply make the best we can out of. At any rate, my point just now is that you and I should never be discouraged because they are not what we wish they were, and because we see the powers of selfishness and greed often hindering the best interests of the community.

James Logan got into what is called hot water. He was apt to express himself in language not minced. He had decidedly the gift of words and those upon whom he chose to make his words fall felt their sting pretty thoroughly. Moreover, when he had an opinion he did not back down from it, but stuck to it.

There is no doubt that when a young man of ardent temperament and decided force is unlucky in love, his disappointment may disclose itself in various ways. James Logan set his heart upon Miss Anne Shippen, not long after he had gone to live in Clarke Hall, with Governor Evans, William Penn, Jr., and Judge Mompesson. We may suppose that the gaieties of two of his fellow bachelors had already grated upon the nerves of the young Quaker of staid habits, and that he looked to a domestic life not only as an escape from his present associations, but an entrance into a safe haven of happiness. Edward Shippen, first Mayor of Philadelphia, was the father of the young lady whom he desired. Unfortunately she preferred somebody else, Thomas Story whom she married. This disappointment evidently caused the powers of irascibility of young Logan to manifest themselves somewhat at large. And so his troubles of the heart did not assist

him in his public relations. He seems to have shown temper on
various occasions, and thus to have caused considerable antago-
nism and begun all sorts of troubles for himself which lasted a
long while. In 1705 William Penn writes to him thus: "I am anx-
iously grieved for thy unhappy love . . . and thy discord has been
of no service here, any more than there; and some say that come
thence that thy amours have so altered or influenced thee that
thou art grown touchy and apt to give rough and short answers,
which many call haughty. I make no judgment, but caution
thee, as in former letters, to let truth preside and bear imperti-
nencies as patiently as thou canst." Young James Logan does not
seem to have relished these objections from his counsellor, and
he answers: "I cannot understand that paragraph in thy letter
relating to T. S. and myself; thou says our discord has done no
more good there than here, and know not who carried the
account of it. . . ."

We may be entertained at these tribulations of the heart; but
from the above letters we may be tolerably sure that the young
man was very cross to a good many people at this time, little
aware as he appears himself to have been in his reply to William
Penn. Nevertheless, he writes to William Penn, Jr., later in the
same year, about his successful rival: "Thomas Story carries very
well since his marriage. He and I are very great friends, for I
think the whole business is not now worth a quarrel, and I
believe he will be serviceable to thy father's interests here. I
therefore request thee to abate all thy former resentment. . . ."
Does not this reveal pretty conclusively that the young man in
love with Anne Shippen and crossed in love was the same young
man who had fought the pirates and retorted somewhat decidedly to William Penn on being reproved for this? Somehow, to
my thinking, these glimpses of James Logan incline us to like
him; possibly to like him better than if no such turbulence and
hot blood were revealed to us through all these many years since
he lived in our Colony. Almost immediately after the affair of

Miss Anne Shippen, Governor Evans, the gay bachelor with whom James Logan had resided, not being very judicious and feeling some ridicule for the Quaker principle of non-resistance, played a very bad practical joke upon the city. He found the Quakers averse to military requisitions, and he planned to give them a little fright. He caused a rumor to spread that ships of an enemy were sailing up the River. This rumor was spread only too well and the staid Quakers were immediately thrown, in consequence, into a most discreditable panic. With their broad brimmed hats, and their buff suits and their knee breeches, they scurried all about the streets, burying their silver in their back-yards, putting money into their stockings, and leaving the city like a herd of frightened rabbits, to get under cover in the creeks and upper parts of the Delaware River. This they did while young Governor Evans rode bellowing about the town, pretending to assemble a force to resist the imaginary fleet.

Other disturbances over a tax that was much resented fol-lowed quickly upon this, so that we find James Logan writing to William Penn: "These are very cloudy times indeed, and, to us, a day of severe trial . . . and Pennsylvania, thy former darling, is now become thy heavy affliction; and I can but lament my own fortune, that I should be concerned in it, at such a time when it is made so. But I have the comfort to think that, designedly or accidentally, I have contributed to no part of it."

James Logan was accused of being in the plot with Governor Evans regarding the false alarm about the enemy's fleet. This seems to have been an entirely ungrounded accusation, but it was by no means the last. In 1709, when he was Secretary of the Province, and a member of the Provincial Council, the Assem-bly endeavoured to impeach him. He instantly and indignantly demanded an investigation of the various charges brought against him, and his political enemies, quite aware of the flimsi-ness of such charges, dodged the investigation, in order that Logan's character might continue under a cloud, and this was the climax of a discord that had begun three years earlier and had been increasing in bitterness. He petitioned the Assembly that steps be taken for his immediate trial, in order that he might carry out a plan which he had to go to England. Taking advantage of this, the Assembly issued a warrant to put him in prison. But Governor Gookin indignantly stepped in here and, to use an informal expression, sat heavily upon the Assembly. He commanded the sheriff that he suffer James Logan to be molested in no wise by virtue of any order, or pretended order, of any Assembly whatever; and in case any of the said Assembly or others, under pretence of any authority derived from them, "shall attempt to attach or molest the said James Logan in his person, I do hereby command you to oppose such attachment, and that you by all means in your power take effectual care that the peace of our Sovereign Lady the Queen be kept, and all offenders against the same be opposed or committed as rioters; for which this shall be sufficient authority." This was in October 1709.

James Logan went to England and there spent a year engaged upon the affairs of the Colony, and also somewhat upon his own private affairs. After this he returned, and public and private business were still carried on. In 1714, it is quite evident that he had recovered from his disappointment regarding Miss Shippen, for he consoled himself with marrying Sarah Reed. The marriage was happy and he had several children.

Being now established, with a wife and home, and with many private enterprises which demanded his attention, he might have retired from private life, as many situated like himself have done. But James Logan was no man to sit back and look on. His inborn public spirit and his sense of duty to the community in which he lived were the sort that would compel him to take a hand as long as his strength allowed him to do this. The following years saw him much engaged with the public affairs of the Colony and the City, and in 1723, he was Mayor of Philadelphia. A still greater honor came to him in 1731, when he was made

Chief Justice, a position which he held for eight years. Between 1736 and 1738 he was also President of the Council. It is worthy of remark that in those days a legal education was not deemed necessary to qualify a man to be Chief Justice. Common sense, good education and integrity of character were sometimes sufficient for this position, and James Logan was one of the examples of this. It is also worthy of note that when unable to get to the City and attend to the duties of his Court, the duties came from the city, so to speak, to him in the country, and he held his court at Stenton. All in all, he was completely deserving of the honors that came to him, and throughout his life he was a hard worker. During his active years, he was clerk, merchant, real estate agent, law maker, farmer, and judge. About how many of us of the present generation could so much be said? But somewhat in our excuse it may be said that life now is much more exacting and the demands upon a man's strength much greater than they were in the days of James Logan.

This is the proper place to mention an important fact concerning James Logan. Although his uncompromising rectitude, as well as his strong temper, made him frequent enemies among the white people, it was very different among the red men, the Indians with which the Colony was then filled, and with whom constant troubles arose. These difficulties had to be met and arranged with skill and patience. Not seldom the white men were the wrong doers and it was the Indians who had suffered injustice. Upon these matters James Logan was employed and so conducted himself as to win the permanent confidence and friendship of the Indians. And we may quote the words of Canassatego, chief of the Ononadagoes, who thus, in 1742, expressed himself:—

> Brethren, we called at our old friend, James Logan's, in our way to this city, and, in our grief, we found him hid in the bushes and retired through infirmities from public business. . . . He is a wise man, and a fast friend to the Indians; and

we desire, when his soul goes to God, you may choose in his room just such another person, of the same prudence and ability in counselling, and of the same tender disposition and affection for the Indians. In testimony of our gratitude for all his services, and because he was so good as to leave his country-house and follow us to town, and be at the trouble, in this his advanced age, to attend the Council, we present him with this bundle of skins.

You will notice that the Indians speak of finding James Logan at his country-place hiding in the bushes. This is their fanciful phrase to express that he was surrounded by his garden. It was here that they saw him, and it was here that the conversation took place which makes an interesting anecdote. Another Indian Chief once manifested his friendliness by proposing that they exchange names. The Chief should call himself James Logan, and James Logan should call himself Wingohocking. It is possible that you and I might have felt ourselves to be in quite a predicament upon receiving such an invitation from a personage so august as an Indian Chief. But James Logan's tact escaped from this dilemma, and yet did so without in the least wounding his friend. Said he: "If you give your name to me, I shall die presently and your name will be no more known, but if you let me give it to this beautiful stream which winds through my place, then it will remain remembered forever upon the earth." This idea appealed to the Indian and so those of us who are old enough to remember it can recall a clear stream called the Wingohocking winding among the adjacent fields and woods. Alas! That stream is no longer clear and charming as it was in those days. Nothing is gained in this world, apparently, without something being lost. The City of Philadelphia has gained in fame, in size and in population, in consequence of which the Wingohocking has disappeared from the face of the earth and is now little more than a sewer.

It was about the year 1728 that Stenton, the country seat which James Logan called his plantation, was completed. The whole property was a grant of about five hundred acres, situated then partly in Bristol and partly in Germantown Townships, and after that in the 22nd and 23rd Wards. This large tract was partly bounded on the West side by what is known as the Main Street above Nicetown, and it ran over in an easterly direction to what was then and is still called the York Road. Through it, as has been said, the Wingohocking ran, finally meeting the Tacony. This historic house is one that I trust most of you, if not all, are familiar with. It is not far away from where we are gathered this evening. Most fortunately it is destined to be preserved. The care and the solicitude of Mayor Reyburn and a society of patriotic ladies insures this. So that the home of the ancestor of this neighborhood will always remain here, reminding us of him. It is pleasant to think of that home as it was in those days, and a very charming picture of it has been given by a lady who once lived in this neighborhood and who wrote an account of Deborah Logan,[3] in which the following passage occurs.

> Round the house there was the quiet stir and movement of a country place, with its large gardens full of old-fashioned flowers and fruits, its poultry-yard and stables. The latter were connected with the house by an underground passage which led to a concealed staircase and a door under the roof, like the "priest's escape" in some old English country-seats. . . . The offices surrounded the main building, connected with it by brick courts and covered ways. They were all at the back, and so disposed as to enhance the picturesque and

---

3. The "lady who once lived in this neighborhood" is Owen Wister's mother, Sarah Butler [Mrs. Owen Jones] Wister. The quotation is from her essay "Deborah Logan: The Quaker Lady," in *Worthy Women of Our First Century,* ed. Mrs. O. J. Wister and Miss Agnes Irwin (Philadelphia: J. B. Lippincott, 1877), 293.

dignified air of the old mansion, the interior of which is as curious to modern eyes as it is imposing. One enters by a brick hall, opposite to which is the magnificent double stair-case, while right and left are lofty rooms covered with fine old-fashioned woodwork, in some of them the wainscot being carried up to the ceiling above the chimney-place, which in all the apartments was a vast opening set round with blue and white sculptured tiles of the most grotesque devices. There are corner cupboards in arched niches over the mantelpieces, capital showcases for the rare china and magnificent old silver which adorned the dinner-table on state occasions. Half of the front of the house in the second story was taken up by one large finely-lighted room, the library of the book-loving masters of the place.

Many trees both old and rare ornamented the grounds; the old trees belonged to the original forest and the others had been imported by the master of the place who, besides caring much for plants and flowers, had a scientific knowledge of botany, on which subject he later wrote certain articles.

An unlucky accident about this time brought considerable suffering to James Logan and also put an end to much of his activity. The head of one of his thigh bones was broken near the socket by a fall and it was a long time before he was able even to go about on crutches. This did not occur in the country, but in the city, where he remained until his movements became freer. Of his condition at this time he speaks as follows:

For these twelve months past it is certain I am much weaker, yet should be very easy in my mind could I be freed from other people's business, and left to amuse myself with no other care on me than what my family requires. Having a true helpmate, children not undutiful, and a plantation within five miles of this town, to which I am retiring this summer, I believe that if I were troubled with nothing but what truly concerns me, notwithstanding I have had much greater losses since I received this hurt than in all my life before, I should be able to have my family tolerably supported and be helpful to my children in their education. . . . And for a variety I would amuse myself with some small entertainments from science, for in Dryden's words, which have always affected me, I take it to be true that "Knowledge and innocence is perfect joy."

After this time, as has been seen, he was both Chief Justice and President of the Council, but his accident led him from business gradually into intellectual pursuits. He devoted himself to the classic languages, to science and to the entertainment of distinguished people. In earlier years he had befriended Benjamin Franklin, and it is to be regretted that political differences later separated them. But to the translation of a famous work by Cicero which was made by James Logan, Franklin wrote a preface, of which the concluding words are as follows: "I shall add to these few lines my hearty wish that this first translation of a classic in this western world may be followed with many others, and be a happy omen, that Philadelphia shall become the seat of the American muses."

A few words of Logan's written to his old rival, Thomas Story, shows his attitude toward education:—

I have four children now all with me, who, I think, generally take more after their mother than me, which, I am sure, thou wilt not dislike in them; yet, if they had more of a mixture, it might be of some use to them, to bring them through the world. And it sometimes gives me an uneasy thought, that my considerable collection of Greek and Roman authors, with others in various languages, will not find an heir in my family to use them as I have done; but, after my decease, must be sold or squandered away.

This fear that his books might be squandered away was possibly the germ of the thought which later culminated in his bequeathing to the City of Philadelphia his library of three thousand volumes. That library, which bears his name, is now merged with the old Philadelphia Library founded by his personal friend and political enemy, Benjamin Franklin, and thus also is the name of James Logan perpetuated.

It is very remarkable to think that a man so active in practical affairs, a man who was clerk, farmer, mayor and Chief Justice, and who was able to amass a handsome fortune by his ability and industry, should also have been the author of the first translation of a Latin classic ever made in this country. Surely, unless I have spoken in vain, he must appear to you an honorable figure, this James Logan, who was the ancestor of our neighborhood. He was sixty-four when he retired from public service which he declined to enter again although he was requested to do so. He died in 1751, in the 77th year of his age. And before we leave him, let us recall his personal appearance as described by Watson:—

James Logan was tall and well-proportioned, with a graceful, yet grave demeanour. He had a good complexion, and was quite florid, even in old age; nor did his hair, which was brown, turn gray in the decline of life, nor his eyes require spectacles. According to the custom of the times, he wore a powdered wig. His whole manner was dignified, so as to abash impertinence; yet he was kind, and strictly just in all the minor duties of acquaintance and society.

I have omitted some somewhat distinguished scientific business connected with James Logan and his wide intelligence and interest in many matters because it would take us too long to go into these. My wish now is to draw a brief lesson for ourselves and for all citizens active in Philadelphia at the present time and anxious that our city's fame should not only be maintained but increased and that the affairs of her household should be more and more well managed for the benefit of us all and as an example to other places. Let us carefully note that James Logan died a rich man. Not inordinately rich, but well provided with many of the goods of this world. But while we remember this, let us also note with equal care that for forty years, through prosperity and adversity, through thick and thin, he also served his city. That he gave her his strength and his brains. That he filled many public offices with honor. That it was only when his bodily strength had left him that he declined to enter her service any more, and this was very near the end of his life.

Today, in Philadelphia, there are hundreds and thousands of men who work only to the first end to which James Logan gave his strength and his brains. They work only to feather their own nests. They accept from the city all the improvements and all the facilities which have come to Philadelphia since the time of James Logan and which in his day did not exist. In his day there were no public schools, no hospitals, no libraries, no police, no organized fire department and no public conveyances. If a man wanted to go from Philadelphia to Germantown, he must walk, or else he must ride on his own or a borrowed horse or in his own or a borrowed carriage. It is in consequence of the labors of such men as James Logan that we have now the libraries, the schools, the police, the fire system and all the facilities which render modern life in some ways much more comfortable than the life of the old days. Of these things we are the beneficiaries. That we pay our taxes is not a sufficient return for what our city gives us.

I will ask you what you think true patriotism really is? Do you think it is a complacent sitting down and looking on and being proud of your city's name, without doing anything to cause that name to be a source of pride? Is it a childish jealousy of other places and an ignorant belief that no place can be as good as your own? That the buildings of Philadelphia schools are preferable to the buildings of the schools of any other city of the United States? Do you think that true patriotism consists either in staying at home and never learning anything outside of your own town or, if you travel, keeping your eyes shut so that you cannot see in what things other places are superior to your own town? This has been considered true patriotism in Philadelphia. We are a very provincial community. It has been our habit so to ignore what other cities were doing in the way of progress that we earned that terrible epithet "Corrupt and Contented." Do you think that to be corrupt and content is true patriotism; or do you think that a life like James Logan's makes the patriot?

I cannot help thinking that James Logan should be a pattern to us all, and that he has not been a sufficient pattern to many thousands of Philadelphians. But I could not say these things did I not believe that we had really entered upon a new era—that the mere existence of such a thing as the Logan Improvement League and of many other similar associations is a proof that we are waking up to the interests of our city, that we look upon her with affection but also with critical eyes:—Not in order that we may idly find fault with her, but that we may discover those things in which we may make her better. Let us go on in this path; let us see that we have more fresh air spaces. Let us see that our children have every facility of education, both of healthy minds and healthy bodies. Let us see, as far as we can, that our government is honest and that for every penny we spend in taxes we get a just return. Let us quarrel politically as little as we can. Let us rather unite and, no matter what our national politics be, let every shoulder be put to the civic wheel.